Mathematics for Dyslexics

A Teaching Handbook

Second Edition

D0544455

Mathematics for Dyslexics

A Teaching Handbook
Second Edition

STEPHEN J. CHINN and J. RICHARD ASHCROFT

Mark College, Somerset

Consulting Editor in Dyslexia: Professor Margaret Snowling,
University of York

Whurr Publishers Ltd
London

© 1998 Whurr Publishers Ltd
Second edition first published 1998
First edition published 1993 by
Whurr Publishers Ltd
19b Compton Terrace, London N1 2UN, England

Reprinted 1999 and 2001

British Library Cataloguing in Publication Data
A catalogue record for this book is available from the British Library.

ISBN 1 86156 043 5

Printed and bound in the UK by Athenaeum Press Ltd,
Gateshead, Tyne & Wear

Dedications

For Emily, Jamie, Simon and Sarah (SJC), for Steve Marr and George Adie (JRA) and for all the dyslexic mathematicians who have taught us so much.

Steve Chinn
Richard Ashcroft

Contents

Foreword

The first edition of *Mathematics for Dyslexics: A Teaching Handbook* by Steve Chinn and Richard Ashcroft put a previously neglected area of education on the map for those concerned with dyslexia. Teachers have found much support and inspiration from the guidelines set out by the authors. This second edition, updated and expanded, will again be welcomed by both teachers and learners.

The mysteries of mathematics have always posed some problems for me and therefore I add my personal welcome to this edition and would like to wish both authors and users achievement and success.

Marion Welchman, MBE
1915–1997

Preface to the Second Edition

Our combined experience of thirty years of teaching in specialist schools for dyslexics has led us to the conclusion that all our pupils have difficulties in at least some areas of mathematics. The first edition of the book was written as an attempt to provide some guidance in teaching mathematics to dyslexic pupils.

This second edition has been updated and expanded as new research and ideas have emerged. We have continued to learn from our pupils.

We have learnt that there is no single answer to teaching and learning problems. Each class we meet is a reminder that every child has individual needs, even if these needs are grouped around a basic common core. To address this individuality, we have developed a flexible approach, based on an awareness of dyslexia, an understanding of how our pupils learn and fail to learn, combined with an appreciation of the structure and nature of mathematics.

We have collected, tested and organised the most effective ideas from many sources, including material for pupils of the highest potential. The subjects covered go back to first principles to act at the root of the problem.

The focus of the book is on numeracy. This is the first experience of mathematics for children and it is here that initial attitudes and concepts are formed. The methods described are developmental and acknowledge the sequential nature of mathematics, so, for example, the methods for learning times table facts will contribute to an understanding of estimation and the use of the algorithm for long multiplication.

The contents and structure of this book can be applied to dyslexic children throughout the school age range, to class or individual teaching and to other, non-dyslexic children who experience difficulties with mathematics.

We have used the pronoun 'he' to avoid the rather clumsy 'he/she'.

Steve Chinn
Richard Ashcroft
1997

Preface to the First Edition

Although there is a wide range of material available to help in teaching language to dyslexic children, there is very little available for teaching mathematics. This book offers practical advice gleaned from 20 years of classroom experience of teaching mathematics to dyslexic children.

We have learnt that there is no single answer for problems with teaching and learning. Each class we meet is a reminder that every child has individual needs, even if grouped around a basic common core of needs. To address these needs, we have developed a flexible approach, based on a knowledge of dyslexia and an understanding of the nature of mathematics.

We have collected, tested and organised the most effective ideas from many sources, including material for pupils ranging from low attainers through to those who will reach the highest levels. Subjects covered go back to first principles to act at the root of the problem.

The contents and structure of this book are such that they can be applied to class or individual teaching, for children from year 1 to year 13, and to dyslexic children or other children who are having difficulties with mathematics.

We would like to point out that we have tended to use the pronoun 'he' more often than 'she' in the text; this is because the ratio of dyslexic boys to dyslexic girls is 4:1, and so it seems more appropriate to use 'he'.

Steve Chinn
Richard Ashcroft
April 1993

Chapter 1
Dyslexia and
Mathematics

Introduction

When we moved from working in mainstream schools and began teaching in schools for dyslexic pupils, our initial expectation was that teaching mathematics would be much the same as before. At that time (1981) we could not find any source of guidance to confirm or contradict this expectation. We thought dyslexia meant difficulties with language, not mathematics. Experience would change this impression!

Over the last 16 years we have accumulated experience, tried out new (and old) ideas, researched, read what little appropriate material was available (far less is published on learning difficulties in mathematics than language), learned from our pupils, and have become convinced that although difficulties in mathematics go hand in hand with difficulties in language, a different teaching attitude and approach is needed.

The first four chapters of this book look at the background that influenced the evolution of these teaching methods. This necessitates a look at the learner, the subject (mathematics) and the teacher. The main mathematical focus of the book is numeracy. This is the first area studied by children and thus provides the first opportunity to fail. Evaluations of a child's mathematical potential are often based on performance in early numeracy. The remaining chapters describe the methods we use to teach our dyslexic pupils.

Definitions of Dyslexia

The year 1996 marked the 100th anniversary of the publication of the first paper describing a dyslexic pupil (Pringle–Morgan, 1896, reproduced in Crisfield [ed], *The Dyslexia Handbook*, 1996), yet it is only relatively recently that definitions of dyslexia have included difficulties in mathematics (often as numeracy) alongside difficulties in language. Our hypothesis is that a profile similar to the one created by the factors which can cause difficulties in mathematics (p. 6) could affect language.

1

A brief survey of definitions of dyslexia (and learning disabilities—an American term) shows how difficulties with mathematics have been introduced alongside difficulties with language.

In 1968 the World Federation of Neurology (cited in Pumfrey and Reason, 1991) defined dyslexia as

> A disorder manifested by a difficulty in learning to read, despite conventional instruction, adequate intelligence and socio–cultural opportunity. It is dependent upon fundamental cognitive difficulties which are frequently of a constitutional character.

In 1972 the Department of Education and Science for England and Wales did include number abilities in its definition of specific reading (*sic*) difficulties. In the USA, the Interagency Conference's (Kavanagh and Truss, 1988) definition of learning disabilities included 'significant difficulties in the acquisition of mathematical abilities' and, in the UK, Chasty (1989) defined specific learning difficulties as

> organising or learning difficulties, which restrict the student's competence in information processing, in fine motor skills and working memory, so causing limitations in some or all of the skills of speech, reading, spelling, writing, essay writing, numeracy and behaviour.

By 1992 Miles and Miles, in their book *Dyslexia and Mathematics*, wrote:

> The central theme of this book is that the difficulties experienced by dyslexics in mathematics are manifestations of the same limitations which also affect their reading and spelling.

Perhaps the most exciting recent publication is from Light and Defries (1995) on the comorbidity of language and mathematical difficulties in dyslexic twins.

Resources and research

There is a paucity of research in this field, as noted by Austin (1982), Sharma (1986) and Miles and Miles (1992). There are many examples of minimal mathematical content in dyslexia publications, including the *Annals of the Orton Dyslexia Society,* which had not one paper on mathematics in the five years from 1986 to 1991. In the UK, *Specific Learning Difficulties (Dyslexia): Challenges and Responses* (Pumfrey and Reason, 1991) makes only passing reference to numeracy and mathematics. At the past two International Conferences of the British Dyslexia Association less than 5% of the submitted papers concerned mathematics.

There is, however, some reference material. Magne (1996) has compiled what must be the most extensive bibliography of publications on mathematical low achievement, but has cast his net wide. Sharma (1986) and Miles and Miles (1992) have also produced thorough lists of references of relevant research.

One of the earliest papers to suggest a multisensory approach to the teaching of mathematics to dyslexics was written by Steeves (1979). Steeves advocated the same teaching principles for mathematics as Orton had suggested for language. Joffe (1983) provided an excellent overview of the relationship between dyslexia and mathematics. Within this relatively short paper, Joffe provides many observations which add to a clearer understanding of difficulties in mathematics, most notably that there is a deficit in the essential skill of generalising.

Sometimes the advice given is contradictory. Ashlock et al. (1983), in an otherwise very useful book, state that all children learn and come to understand an idea in basically the same way, whereas Bley and Thornton (1989) start their book with the sentence, 'Learning disabled children are unable to learn the way most children do'. (We consider Bley and Thornton's statement to be the correct one, hence this book!)

Dyslexia and Mathematics (Miles and Miles, 1992) collects together a wealth of material, including a thorough review of the history of dyslexia and mathematics and a range of practical ideas for teachers. The journal, *Focus on Learning Problems in Mathematics* and the associated *Math Notebook* provide ongoing support.

Dyscalculia

The problem of the specific mathematics difficulty, dyscalculia, needs to be mentioned. The term suggests learning difficulties which are solely related to mathematics. The little research that exists suggests that the proportion of children with this problem is small. In a study by G Hitch (1991, private communication) of 1200 children aged 9 to 12 years, only 18 were identified as having specific mathematics difficulties. Hitch did not find any one pattern or reason why. Sutherland (1988) states that on the basis of his study, few children have specific problems with number alone. Rather, Miles (in Miles and Miles, 1992) suggests that mathematical difficulties and language difficulties are likely to occur concurrently and we come to the same conclusion in the last part of this chapter. We have to consider the impact of the learning environment which may specifically affect mathematics. The work of Kosc, a pioneer in the field of dyscalculia, and a review of the literature on dyscalculia can be found in *Focus on Learning Difficulties in Mathematics* (Sharma, 1986).

The Nature of Mathematics

In order to teach successfully, you need a knowledge of the pupil and a knowledge of the subject. To teach mathematics effectively you must have some understanding of the nature of mathematics and its progression beyond the immediate topics being taught. Mathematics is a subject which builds on previous knowledge as it extends knowledge.

This is the situation in numeracy which is the first experience of mathematics for most children (and the mathematics most people use in later life). Early experience of success or failure at this stage sets the scene for later. Some pupils learn competence in limited areas of numeracy—for example, they are comfortable with addition, but cannot carry out subtraction. What can create significant problems are programmes which require mastery before progression (for example, Kumon mathematics) because mastery, especially of rote learning tasks, is a transient stage for many dyslexics. Consolidation and sustained mastery without frequent reviews and revision is a difficult task for most dyslexics. Finding the right balance between mastery and progress will be a consequence of knowing the child well and of the structure and adaptation of the teaching programme.

Numbers can be exciting and challenging (McLeish, 1991) or the cause of great anxiety (Buxton, 1981; Cope, 1988). Mathematics is a sequential subject, building on early skills and knowledge to take the student on to new skills and knowledge. It is a subject of organisation and patterns (Ashcroft and Chinn, 1992), of abstract ideas and concepts. Gaps in the early stages of understanding can only handicap the learner in later stages, in the speed of processing number problems if nothing else.

Mathematics has an interrelating/sequential/reflective structure. It is a subject where one learns the parts; the parts build on each other to make a whole; knowing the whole enables one to reflect with more understanding on the parts, which in turn strengthens the whole. Knowing the whole also enables an understanding of the sequences and interactions of the parts and the way they support each other so that the getting there clarifies the stages of the journey. Teachers are (usually) in the fortunate position of being conversant with the subject and can bring to the work knowledge and experience beyond the topic they are teaching. The pupil is rarely in this position and thus is vulnerable to assumptions about his levels of knowledge and experience, often made unconsciously by the teacher.

It is important that the pupil develops a clear, broad and flexible understanding of number at each stage, that he begins to see the interrelationships, patterns, generalisations and concepts clearly and without anxiety. To teach a child to attain this understanding of mathematics requires that the teacher also understands mathematics and numbers. This is not to say that every teacher who teaches arithmetic needs a degree in mathematics, but it is to say that there is a need to understand where mathematics is going beyond the level at which it is taught, so that what is taught is of benefit to the child at the time and helps, not hinders, him later on as his mathematics develops. Teachers need to be mindful of what is coming after what has been taught, because the development of a concept starts long before it is addressed directly.

To illustrate this point, consider the strategy advocated in this book for teaching the nine times table (see Chapter 6). The method uses previous information (the 10 times table), estimation, refinement of estimation and patterns. Although a child may not need to realise that he is doing all these things when he learns how to work out 6×9, the processes are being used, concepts are being introduced and foundations are being laid. We agree with Madsen et al. (1995) that instruction should be conceptually orientated.

A second illustration of the influence of early ideas involves a subtraction such as

$$
\begin{array}{r}
93 \\
- \ 47 \\
\hline
\end{array}
$$

A likely error is the answer 54, which occurs when the child subtracts 3 from 7. This is an easier process than the correct one, but can also be the consequence of earlier subtraction work where the child is told to 'take the smaller number from the larger number'. Dyslexics have a tendency to take instructions literally and feel safer in the consistency of procedures.

Margaret Rawson said of teaching English to dyslexics, 'Teach the language as it is to the child as he is'. Harry Chasty says, 'If the child does not learn the way you teach, then you must teach the way he learns'. This advice is apposite for teaching mathematics. One of the attributes of an effective teacher is clear communication. This is usually a consequence of knowing the child and presenting work in a way that pre–empts as many of the potential difficulties as possible. Thus, the teacher needs to understand the way each child learns and fails to learn, although individual learning can be frustrating in that a lesson which works superbly with one child may not work at all with another (see Chapter 2). This combined understanding of the child and all his strengths, weaknesses and potential plus a knowledge of the nature, structure and skills of mathematics will help to pre–empt many potential learning problems.

Finally, it should be remembered that an insecure learner values consistency. This characteristic must be linked to automaticity, in that consistency, like automaticity, allows the brain to devote more capacity to what is different or to invent an extension of a known procedure.

Factors which may contribute to learning difficulties in mathematics

Different children bring different combinations of strengths and weaknesses to mathematics. These will interact with each other, the mathematical topic, and the learning situation to create different levels of success and failure. Homan (1970) and Chinn (1991) have looked at deficits which may affect performance in mathematics. Recently Chinn

(1995b, 1996) has conducted studies on error patterns, speed of working, basic fact knowledge, auditory sequential memory and IQ.

The deficits and difficulties interrelate and combine to form a large part of the picture of what the child brings to the problem. Each deficit may make a different contribution to the overall problem and the contribution may affect the situation at different times, so, for example, reading will not be a major problem until the child reaches word problems. Interactions between factors are also varied and influential. As a consequence there is an enormous variation among dyslexic children, a fact which most specialist teachers readily recognise. A knowledge of the deficits and difficulties provides a general background which you, the teacher, must have firmly fixed in your mind as you individualise your approach to each child or as you work with a group.

Factors which are Potential Contributors to Difficulties in Mathematics

Directional confusion

Children may write numbers backwards, Ɛ for 3, or may be confused by the inconsistent 'starting points' of algorithms, e.g. addition, where the child starts at the right and works left, versus division, where the child starts at the left and works right. Dyslexic pupils often rely on the consistency of work. Changes which are seemingly irrational will confuse.

This situation is illustrated in the four operations below. In addition it does not affect the answer whether the top number is added to the bottom number or vice versa. Although it is normal practice to add from right to left, if the sum does not involve 'carrying' and the child adds from left to right the answer will still be correct as in example A. (Indeed some children scan the sum to see if this is the situation and then add left to right.)

A   362
      + 431

This will not work as well, although I have seen pupils do this successfully, with 'carry' examples, such as B.

B   578
      + 266

Subtractions are less open to flexibility. It now matters which number is taken from which, but the normal practice of starting from the right (units) column is not needed if there is no renaming required as in example C.

```
C      875
     - 562
```

This work is also susceptible to early experience where it is tempting to describe subtraction as 'taking the little number from the big number' creating problems with examples such as D.

```
D      643
     - 276
```

Long division makes another assault on consistency when, traditionally, the procedure starts at the left and moves right to the smaller place values. The pupil also has to remember to write some numbers at the top and some underneath, making this a very demanding algorithm.

An example of the interactions of factors was provided by a pupil who found difficulty with decimals. From his perception it seemed illogical that, using the decimal point as a focus, the place values to the left are units, tens, hundreds, thousands, and so on, increasing by a factor of 10 each time, whereas to the right of the decimal point the place values are tenths, hundredths, thousandths and so on, decreasing by a factor of 10 each time. There are implications here for concept, direction and language.

Sequencing problems

There are many sequences in mathematics. Being able to recognise and remember sequences is a useful skill. Children often manage safe, familiar sequences such as 10, 20, 30, 40, but fail to recognise a variation such as 12, 22, 32, 42. Such transfer of knowledge cannot be assumed.

Some children find one–to–one correspondence difficult and have to rely on strategies such as touching the nose with one finger while touching the objects to be counted with the other hand.

Many of the sequences are not automatised as demonstrated in an interesting exercise (Fawcett and Nicholson, 1992) where dyslexics could balance successfully on one foot, but lost their balance when asked to count backwards from 100 at the same time. It is not uncommon to find children for whom counting backwards is difficult.

Children may write 18 as 81 (which has some logic) or 26 as 62 (which does not) (Sharma, 1987). There may also be a difficulty in remembering the sequence of steps to follow in algorithms, for example for long division.

Visual–perceptual difficulties

The pupil may confuse +, ÷ and × (especially if written carelessly) or 6 and 9 or 3 and 5. The presentation of a worksheet or exercise can be confusing, especially if items are written too closely together. Some form of separation, for example lining off, will help reduce visual confusion. Sometimes a coloured overlay can help.

Spatial awareness

Spatial awareness is needed for work such as geometry, place value, algebra (distinguishing between $2x$, x and x, for example). In the classroom the pupil may lose his place on the page (or board) from which he is copying. He may use the wrong question number. He may not be able to relate two–dimensional drawings to the three–dimensional shape they represent.

Spatial awareness also affects organisation of work on paper so that what seems straightforward may in fact be a very demanding task. For example, the sum

$$\begin{array}{r} {}^16{}^138 \\ + \ 794 \\ \hline 1432 \end{array}$$

needs to have the place values lined up correctly, the 'carry' numbers in the right place (and remembered) and the relevant numbers have to be added together.

Questions such as $2(x + 2x)^2$ can be a real challenge!

Short–term and working memory

Poor short–term and working memory can create several areas of difficulty and have a strong influence on how a pupil processes numbers. Deficits in short–term memory combine with long–term memory deficits to give a working memory problem. For example, a child trying to add 47 to 78 mentally has to hold the sum in his memory, probably work out $7 + 8$ (poor memory for basic facts), remember 5, carry 1, remember that he has to add 4 and 7 (and the carried 1), work out $7 + 4 + 1$, recall the 5 and put them all together in the right sequence, 125.

Short–term memory difficulties may even prevent a pupil from starting a problem (see also the section on anxiety, stress and self–image on p. 12). He may simply forget some or most of the teacher's instructions, especially if distracted in some way. If his short–term memory is overloaded, he may be so confused as to have no clues as to where to start. The pupil may not be able to 'hold' the visual image of the sum he is trying to solve. He may not be able to hold the sum in visual or auditory memory while he searches for a necessary number fact. (Indeed the working out of that fact, say $9 + 6$, by counting on, may overload the memory and leave him not remembering any of the initial sum.)

Short–term memory is obviously a problem with mental addition, but it also impacts on written work, causing the pupil to use extra notations which may lead to confusion and will certainly lead to slower work. Ackerman et al. (1986) make an interesting speculation on differential achievement in reading and arithmetic, observing that the child's acquisition of reading is monitored more closely than the acquisition of number facts. The child reads aloud and the teacher corrects him on the spot when he falters compared to more independent practice in arithmetic. (See also Buswell and Judd's comments in the section on conceptual ability, on p. 11).

Long–term memory

Rote learning as a means of loading information such as spellings or times–table facts into long–term memory is rarely effective with dyslexics (Pritchard et al., 1989), although teachers still persist in trying, often under pressure from a 'back to basics' approach (Hackett, 1996), and parents are often encouraged to use ingenious methods (McDougal, 1990) with varying degrees of success. Dyslexics have significant difficulties learning basic facts such as times tables (Pritchard et al., 1989, Chinn, 1995, Turner Ellis et al., 1996). This is particularly frustrating for parents who encourage the child to practise until he achieves mastery one day only to find that he has forgotten again soon after. Poor long–term memory may also handicap other areas of mathematics, such as recall of algorithms (methods) or formulae.

In his 1995 pilot study, Chinn presented basic addition facts (e.g. 4 + 7, 6 + 5) at 4 second and 12 second intervals using a tape recorder and working with 11 to 13–year–old pupils in mainstream and specialist dyslexia schools. Dyslexic pupils scored much lower on average than their mainstream counterparts on the 4 second (instant recall) task. Given 12 seconds, the dyslexic pupils could use strategies (even the most basic of strategies, finger counting, is effective in 12 seconds for addition) to score almost on a par with the mainstream pupils. However, this was not the case for the times–table facts, where there seemed to be less availability of appropriate strategies (for example, finger counting for 8×7 is not efficient). This deficit will affect accuracy and speed.

Ackerman et al. (1986) draw attention to a contrary effect of speed of working, '... standardised arithmetic tests may fail to reveal automatisation failure in younger schoolchildren because of over–generous time limits'.

Speed of working

Many of the factors described in this section, plus other factors such as speed of writing, affect the speed of work in mathematics, and speed of working is often an issue in mathematics. For example, the Kumon mathematics scheme looks for 'demanding but realistic standards for speed and accuracy' and Ladybird Books publish a times–table practice book which evaluates success on the basis of completing an exercise in 30 seconds.

Chinn (1995b) compared the average time to stop work on 21 basic numeracy questions for a mainstream school population and a specialist dyslexia school population. The results of this pilot study showed that, on average, dyslexic pupils took 50% longer to do the task.

Ackerman and Dykman (1996) suggest that slowness impedes automisation in reading, spelling and arithmetic.

The language of mathematics

Mathematics has its own language and symbols and this brings further problems for the dyslexic whose language skills may be weak. To complicate the issue further, the same symbol often has different names, e.g. + means add, more, plus, and, positive (Henderson, 1989).

It is interesting to note that this confusing choice of vocabulary is most apparent in early numeracy, the area of mathematics the child meets first. Other examples include the variety of names for 2, the inverted presentation of the teen numbers (*eigh*teen as against twenty *eight*). The need for consistency is again threatened, 'language is the key to learning' (Rothman and Cohen, 1989). Later, the language becomes more mathematically specific, for example, exponential x.

Word skills (Kibel, 1992; Miles, 1992)

A child needs to be able to read a problem with accuracy, speed and comprehension. He also needs to be sufficiently sophisticated in his skills to be able to adjust his style of reading to the task in hand. The wording for mathematics problems tends to be precise (and sometimes deliberately confusing) and so needs accurate reading and interpretation. A child who misses key words or perhaps small words such as 'not' will be disadvantaged.

In an interesting study by Smith (1996), the dyslexic pupils' error rate compared to controls was much greater for the question, 'How many is 6 less than 28?' than for 'What is 4 more than 32?' A possible reason for this is the greater importance of the sequence of numbers in the subtraction question than in the addition question. Even a subtle language difference such as this can have an enormous impact on success.

Siegel and Fonzi (1995) looked at the diversity of reading tasks in a secondary setting, emphasising reading's contribution to the learning environment. A child who has difficulties with reading will be disad-vantaged, perhaps more than we might think in a subject which is usually considered to be less intensive in its use of words. Rothman and Cohen (1989) discuss the importance of teaching the vocabulary and language of mathematics.

Sharma (1985) advocates the use of a reverse 'translation', that is the pupil translates a number problem into a word problem as well as vice versa. We have found this a very effective technique.

Cognitive style (see also Chapter 2)

The child's cognitive style, the way he works out a problem, is significantly influenced by the factors above. To be a successful mathematician a child needs to be flexible in his cognitive style (Krutetskii, 1976), but this goal may not be achieved because of the child's learning experiences. If a pupil's cognitive style is inflexibly set at one extreme he is at risk of failure. There is an additional problem if the teacher's style is also inflexible and unresponsive to the pupil's style. For example, marks awarded for different problem–solving styles may vary from teacher to teacher (Chinn, 1995a).

This particular facet of mathematics learning and teaching was highlighted by Cockcroft (1982) who stated (p. 242):

> We are aware that there are some teachers who would wish us to indicate a definitive style for the teaching of mathematics, but we do not believe this is either desirable or possible.

and, later (p. 256)

> ...the now well established fact that those who are mathematically effective in daily life seldom make use in their heads of the standard written methods which are taught in the classroom.

Conceptual ability

In a recent study, Chinn (1996) looked at the WISC (Wechsler Intelligence Scale for Children) scores and the GCSE mathematics grades for 26 dyslexic boys. The (expected) relationship between full IQ and grades was found with grade C and above achieved by all pupils with an IQ above 115. However, for pupils with IQ's in the average range, the controlling factor seemed to be motivation and confidence (all 26 subjects were pupils at Mark College and so we could estimate these somewhat unquantifiable factors). Interestingly, verbal IQ gave better correlation than performance IQ and, although showing a low average score (8.65), the arithmetic subtest showed high correlation (also consider that this subtest focuses on mental arithmetic). The study also showed that it would be very unwise to make predictions for individuals on the basis of any full or subtest score, an observation echoed by Ackerman et al. (1986).

> We likely will never find one–to–one associations between hypothesised cognitive weaknesses and achievement outcomes. In part, this is because we can never be certain people are giving their best effort, especially children and adolescents. But, even more there is the problem of devising tasks that measure only one aspect of cognitive processing.

(Chinn would call this a 'clean' task). Ginsburg (1997) is more mathematically specific;

> Mathematics presents many faces, for example, arithmetic is vastly different from topology, which in turn has little in common with probability. Each of these topics may require different mental processes. Mathematical thinking is not unitary.

and

> This complexity makes it likely that there is no *single* cognitive defect that causes failure in mathematics.

A child's ability to form concepts will be aided by the range and extent of the experiences he receives. 'Drill and practice' is often used to reinforce a new topic. A dyslexic student is typically slower and will often manage less practice for this reason alone. A child who continually fails in mathematics will also have a smaller variety of experiences and consequently will be less likely to be able to see patterns and to generalise and thus to form concepts. This has the effect of compounding his difficulties and retarding his progress.

Dyslexic children are also at risk from a phenomenon described by Buswell and Judd (1925). They point out a potential consequence of practice. Say a child misunderstands a new idea and then uses the wrong procedure or method in his first practice at this new topic, then subsequent remediation and even mastery will not be sustained. The child will return to the first method he used. It is advisable to check the first few examples a pupil tries before an incorrect procedure becomes embedded in his brain. This obviously links to the observation of Ackerman et al. (1986) (see the section on short–term and working memory, p. 8).

Anxiety, stress and self–image

Overlying all the above areas of difficulty is the child's poor self–image and his anxiety about mathematics (Buxton, 1981).

An ex–student of the authors (now studying mathematics at degree level) told us that one of the biggest causes of stress for him was to be told, on failing at some task, 'Never mind, you did your best'. He would anticipate potential failure and not do his best so that when he did fail he could say, 'Well, I didn't try'. This situation was further illustrated in a study of the mathematics errors made by dyslexics (Chinn, 1995b). The most notable difference between dyslexic and mainstream pupils was the percentage of no attempts (a characteristic error of most general mathematics students). We have always tried to develop understanding as a way of reducing this problem, a procedure endorsed by Madsen et al. (1995) who investigated the effect of conceptually orientated teaching on mathematical competence. One of their observations of the effects was the decrease in 'no attempts'. This 'no attempt' situation is somewhat compounded by society's attitude to mathematics and its acceptance of being unable to 'do' mathematics.

There are beliefs associated with these attitudes (Mtetwa and Garofalo, 1989) such as 'Mathematics problems have only one answer'. and 'Only geniuses are capable of creating mathematics'. These exacerbate anxiety in that they imply inflexibility and restricted access to success in mathematics.

Anxiety is a cumulative and cyclic problem—more failure, more anxiety, poorer self–image, more failure, more anxiety, etc.

General Principles of Remediation (see also Chapter 15)

Looking at the factors which may lead to difficulties in mathematics sets up a background awareness of the characteristics of the pupils. This has to be matched to the subject being taught, mathematics, and the present level of knowledge of the pupil.

Certain parts of our programme are built very much on typical knowledge levels of dyslexics. For example, with times tables the usual knowledge base is 1x, 2x, 10x and 5x. Other times tables are addressed by using these facts, for example, the 4x table can be computed from twice the 2x table.

Our remediation is aimed to help the pupil to 'catch up' with his peers. There are some cautionary notes to this ideal. Some areas of mathematics will remain a considerable challenge, for example, instant recall of times–table facts. The teacher has to look at the target and the investment required (by teacher and pupil), and make a decision as to how much time (and frustration) can be expended on the target and whether the target can be bypassed without undue impact on general development. The teaching has to be efficient and effective.

In addition, the remediation needs to be developmental. This helps concepts by ensuring reinforcement of ideas and strategies. Our programme spirals through content, but concepts often occur obliquely as well. We try to capitalise on this. For example, breaking down a times–table fact such as 7×8 into 5×8 plus 2×8 is the same principle we will use for 23×47 (breaking it down into 20×47 plus 3×47). Generally, we try to check a teaching idea by asking ourselves if it is leading anywhere.

The principles are, in summary, awareness and acknowledgement of what the child brings, the use of methods that are developmental for the pupil and for his mathematics learning, empathetic and responsive teaching, and effective communication.

Summary

The understanding of dyslexia has been expanded from a consideration of just language difficulties to an inclusion of numeracy/arithmetic difficulties. There is now a greater awareness that difficulties in at least some areas of mathematics frequently occur concurrently with language difficulties.

We have focused on areas which may create difficulties in learning mathematics. Chinn (1995b, 1996) has tried to investigate the influence of individual factors and is now convinced that any prediction, either of success or failure, is not a simple matter. There are not only the interactions between areas of difficulty, but also the learning environment, the learner's ability to adapt to his problems and circumvent them (often a learner is unaware of his differences and abilities) and, of course, motivation. These influences are effectively impossible to quantify. Thus, it is possible to say that a particular factor, for example, auditory sequential memory (Chinn, 1997), will impact on learning, but it is not possible to predict levels of success or failure based on even a quantified deficit.

Mathematics is a sequential subject, so if early difficulties are not addressed effectively then 'classroom–acquired' difficulties will be added to inherent difficulties and will compound the child's failure. If the remediation is started at the right time but is too slow, or continues for too short a time, the extent of the child's problems will still be increasing for, while his peers progress, the dyslexic child will be marking time (or even regressing).

Thus it is recognised that many dyslexics have difficulty in at least some aspects of mathematics, but this is not necessarily in all areas of mathematics. Indeed some dyslexics are gifted problem solvers, despite persisting difficulties in, for example, rote learning of basic facts. An inappropriate education may leave such a child floundering in early numeracy when he has the ability to leapfrog over these difficulties into more advanced aspects of mathematics. If the problem is not appropriately (and continuously) addressed, these learning difficulties may reduce the extent of the child's mathematical experiences, making it harder for him to develop concepts and to progress past the very basic levels of knowledge. The difficulty may create a cumulative effect beyond its original potential if it is not addressed at an early stage (and thereafter).

Teachers require both an understanding of the strengths and weaknesses which the child brings to each lesson (our experience is that a child often knows more than he realises he knows, but has not gener-alised or organised his knowledge, a situation also observed by Askew and William, 1995, p.6) and a knowledge of the structure and interre-lating nature of mathematics. It is the successful interaction of these areas of knowledge which helps to make an effective teacher.

Chapter 2
Cognitive Style in Mathematics

Introduction

We use cognitive style in mathematics to refer to the way a person thinks through a problem. Allport (1937, quoted in Riding and Cheema, 1991) describes cognitive style as a person's typical or habitual mode of problem solving, thinking, perceiving and remembering. Mathematically, its history can be dated back as far as Descartes (1638, cited in Krutetskii, 1976), who described two types of problem–solver. The first solves problems by a succession of logical deductions, whilst the second uses intuition and immediate perceptions of connections and relationships. These two contrasting styles are described again in later literature. Boltevskii (1908, cited in Krutetskii, 1976) and Harvey (1982) labelled learners with the two styles algebraists and geometers, where the algebraist links most closely to the logical, sequential style and the geometer to the intuitive style. Kovalev and Myshishchev (Krutetskii, 1976) used the term 'intuitive' to describe a person who is not conscious of every step in his thought processes but who perceives essential connections more clearly and quickly than his complementary stylist, the 'discursive' thinker. Skemp (1971, 1986; also Choat, 1982) describes relational and instrumental understanding.

Although Polya (1962) identified four styles of problem–solving, the four can readily be combined in pairs, reducing them to two distinct styles. Polya called the four styles groping, bright idea, algebra and generalisation. The first two describe intuitive thinkers and the last two sequential thinkers.

Riding and Cheema (1991) provide a good overview of cognitive styles as applied to all areas of learning.

Qualitative and Quantitative Style

More recently, Sharma (1986, 1989) identified and labelled two extreme styles (personalities) as quantitative and qualitative. The characteristics of the quantitative style are essentially sequential/logical and those of the qualitative are intuitive and holistic. Sharma also suggested that most personalities lie on a continuum between these two extremes. He uses the order in which the Rey Osterrieth Complex Figure is copied as one of the instruments to diagnose the preferred learning personality. This figure (Figure 2.1) is detailed and Sharma looks to see if the detail takes precedence over the outline when the figure is reproduced.

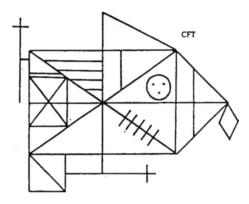

Figure 2.1 The Rey Osterrieth Complex Design Test

Sharma's qualitative learner approaches problems holistically and is good at spotting patterns. He uses an intuitive approach, tends not to show his working and does not like practice exercises. This contrasts with the quantitative learner who processes information sequentially, looking for formulae, methods and 'recipes'. This learner attempts to classify problems into types and to identify a suitable process to use in solving the problem.

It is worth noting that the intuitive style is not always viewed favourably. For example, Skemp (1971) considered it a hit–and–miss method, which is not always reproducible. Most people have experience of the teacher who says, 'I am not marking that mathematics until I can see some method written down'. (Whilst there are some very valid reasons for this to be a reasonable comment, it often indicates a lack of understanding of learning style.)

The brain

Some writers have linked cognitive style to hemispheric specialisation. Kane and Kane (1979) suggested the roles played by each hemisphere in a variety of different modes. For thinking, the right brain is described as deductive, divergent, intuitive, holistic, relating to concepts, simultaneity and geometry, whilst the left brain is described as inductive, convergent, segmented, logical and algebraic. Wheatley (1977) and Wheatley et al. (1978) linked problem–solving styles with left and right brain specialisations. He described the right brain as all–at–once and gestalt and the left as one–at–a–time and serial. Wheatley also concluded that a good problem–solver achieves a smooth integration of the two modes of thinking.

The interpretation (or speculation) as to what the brain is doing is of some interest, in that it gives more credit to intuitive thinking. It is somewhat dismissive to describe the 'global' thinker as intuitive, a term which infers little conscious thought, when the intuitive process is probably based on rapid consideration of possibilities, using experiences and knowledge rather than being a type of inspired, unconsidered guess.

Springer and Deutsch (1993) add some caution to those who claim that schools fail to educate the right side of the brain.

> But are these right–hemisphere functions? We do not think it is as simple as that and there is certainly no conclusive evidence to that effect. Our educational system may miss training or developing half of the brain, but it probably does so by missing out on the talents of both hemispheres.

They go on to agree with Sagan about the need to educate broadly,

> He concluded that the most significant creative activities of a culture—legal and ethical systems, art and music, science and technology—are the result of collaborative work by the left and right hemispheres. We completely agree. Sagan also suggested, 'We might say that human culture is the function of the corpus callosum'. This may be true, not so much because the corpus callosum interconnects 'analytic' and 'intuitive' thinking, but because every structure in the brain plays a role in human behaviour, and human culture is a function of human behaviour.

Cognitive Style in the Classroom

Grasshoppers (intuitive/answer) and inchworms (consecutive/formula)

The work of Bath and Knox (1984) and Bath et al. (1986) on cognitive style arose from work and observations in the classroom, more specifically from teaching dyslexic children of secondary school age. It therefore has its roots in the observation of children with specific learning difficulties as they studied mathematics. Bath et al. labelled the two extremes of the continuum of cognitive styles as grasshoppers and inchworms. The characteristics of the two styles are summarised in Table 2.1 (Chinn, 1997) by looking at the three stages of solving a problem: identification, solution and verification.

The teacher's role

Bath et al. (1986) investigated cognitive style by classifying answers to a series of selected mathematics questions, thus taking directly into account how a child actually does mathematics. One of the main recommendations of this book is the necessity for teacher and child to be flexible in their approach to mathematics—Krutetskii (1976) uses the wonderful word 'harmonious' to describe the blending of styles—yet to be aware that pupils (and teachers) may not always achieve this goal. Sharma (1989) commented on the need for teachers to be aware of cognitive style:

All of us show and use different and unique mixtures of the two (personalities) but one approach is more dominant than the other in different individuals. And that is what the teacher should be aware of almost constantly.

Since the teacher is usually in the controlling role, then the source and sanction for this flexibility must come predominately from him or her. This situation is well expressed by Cobb (1991):

We do not mean to imply that the teacher's beliefs are simply transferred to the student. Rather, the teacher has the authority to legitimize what is acceptable and to sanction what is not acceptable.

Table 2.1 Cognitive styles of the inchworm and grasshopper

	Inchworm	Grasshopper
I. Analysing and identifying the problem	1. Focuses on the parts and details. Separates	1. Tends to overview, holistic, puts together
	2. Looks at the numbers and facts to select a relevant formula or procedure	2. Looks at the numbers and facts to estimate an answer or restrict range of answer. Controlled exploration
II Solving the problem	3. Formula, procedure orientated	3. Answer orientated
	4. Constrained focus. Uses a single method	4. Flexible focusing. Methods change
	5. Works in serially ordered steps, usually forward. (Rifle)	5. Often works back from a trial answer. Multi–method. (Shot gun)
	6. Uses numbers exactly as given	6. Adjusts, breaks down/builds up numbers to make an easier calculation
	7. More comfortable with paper and pen. Documents method	7. Rarely documents method. Performs calculation mentally
III Checking and evaluating	8. Unlikely to check or evaluate answer. If check is done, uses same procedure or method	8. Likely to appraise and evaluate answer against original estimate. Checks by alternate method
	9. Often does not understand procedure or values of numbers. Works mechanically	9. Good understanding of the numbers, methods and relationships

Source: Chinn (1997)

The structure of mathematical abilities

Krutetskii (1976), in presenting a broad outline of the structure of mathematical abilities during school age, specifies a need for flexible thinking (and some skills which dyslexics may find hard). He specifies:

- The ability for logical thought in the sphere of quantitative and spatial relationships, number and letter symbols; the ability to think in mathematical symbols.
- The ability for rapid and broad generalization of mathematical objects, relations and operations.
- Flexibility of mental processes in mathematical activity.
- Striving for clarity, simplicity, economy and rationality of solutions.
- The ability for rapid and free reconstruction of the direction of a mental process, switching from a direct to a reverse train of thought.
- Mathematical memory (generalised memory for mathematical relationships), and for methods of problem solving and principles of approach.

These components are closely interrelated, influencing one another and forming in their aggregate a single integral syndrome of mathematical giftedness.

Although Krutetskii makes these observations concerning giftedness in mathematics, they are equally appropriate for competence. The reader can see where dyslexics typically may be at a disadvantage and where learning difficulties may create problems.

There are other sources of support for different learning styles (for example, and in more general terms, de Bono, 1970), but the emphasis of the remainder of this chapter is to paint a clearer picture of the background reasons for and consequences of different cognitive styles in mathematics.

Learning styles

To expand and clarify the picture of the two extremes of the cognitive style continuum, consider some mathematics problems and the solutions which an inchworm and a grasshopper might use. There is no implied value judgement on the two (extremes) of style. Indeed Kubrik and Rudnick (1980) suggested that teachers should encourage a wide variety of approaches, ideas and solutions. As has already been quoted, Krutetskii looks for a 'harmonious' approach.

Examples

Some of the questions below are taken from the *Test of Cognitive Style in Mathematics* (Bath et al., 1986).

$2 \times 4 \times 3 \times 5$ (to be done mentally; no writing)

An inchworm will see first the 2 and the times sign. He tends not to overview the problem. Also he tends to take the problem 'literally', that is, if it says $2 \times 4 \times 3 \times 5$, then that is the order and it is not to be changed, and since 2 is an easy times table, he will begin $2 \times 4 = 8$. The next stage may be a little more challenging for times–table facts, but $8 \times 3 = 24$. The last stage (24×5) may be too much of a challenge because of the load on short–term memory in multiplying 4×5, remembering that the unit digit is 0, carrying the 2, holding it in memory while multiplying 2 by 5, remembering the 2, knowing where to incorporate it, remembering the unit digit 0 and putting it all together to give 120. Some children will just say, 'That's as far as I can get'.

A grasshopper, especially if he knows he has limited times–table knowledge, will overview the problem, reading through to the end to see if there are any short cuts or easy strategies or rearrangements. He may also be trying to get an estimate of the value of the answer. He is likely to rearrange the problem to $(3 \times 4) \times (2 \times 5)$, i.e. $12 \times 10 = 120$. Thus he has taken a more global and flexible view of the question. In doing so he has reduced the demand on his times–table knowledge and the load on his short–term memory.

Find three consecutive numbers which add up to make 60

An inchworm with some algebra skills will develop an equation;

Let the first number be n;
then the second number is $n + 1$
and the third number is $n + 2$.

So $n + (n + 1) + (n + 2) = 60$ which is then solved:

$3n + 3 = 60$
$3n = 60 - 3 = 57$
$n = 57/3$
$n = 19, n + 1 = 20, n + 2 = 21$

The three numbers are 19, 20 and 21. The process is logical and sequential and is (effectively) independent of the value of the numbers involved; it will work for any similar problem. It takes the solution almost directly from the way the question is presented.

An inchworm without algebra skills will find it difficult to make a reasonable guess at a starting number. His subsequent adjustments to his guess will most probably be step by step, one at a time. So if his first guess is 10, his next guess is likely to be 11, irrespective of the answer generated with 10.

A grasshopper will start with a controlled exploration, leading to an estimate. He will see that the three numbers are approximately equal and that a good estimate of their value is given by $60 \div 3 = 20$. It is only a short and easy step to 19, 20, 21. Again the strategy is holistic/global and peculiar to these numbers. It is an answer–orientated strategy.

How many squares in Figure 2.2 are black?

Figure 2.2

The pattern of 7×7 squares in Figure 2.2 is not equally divisible into black and white squares, which makes the problem less straightforward.

The inchworm will probably resort to counting each square, thus focusing on the parts of the square. In a formula mode, an inchworm may see a square, count the number of black squares on each side as 4, multiply 4×4 and say '16'. Sometimes if the tester says, '49 squares and 16 are black?' hinting that 16 does not match the almost half relationship. The inchworm will feel secure in the use of the formula ($4 \times 4 = 16$) for a square and not see the obvious inaccuracy of the solution.

The grasshopper is holistic in his initial overview. The 7×7 squares make 49 and 'half' will be seen to be 25 since observation (of the corners or numbers of black rows) shows the larger number of squares are black.

This problem illustrates the 'whole to parts' against the 'part to whole' contrast in the two styles.

$$37 + 85 + 36 + 19 + 43$$

The inchworm will rewrite the sum in vertical form:

```
    37
    85
    36
    19
+   43
  _____
```

The addition may be carried out with tallies to mark progress and help the child to keep count as he moves down the numbers. The child is unlikely to use a pre–estimate or a check.

The inchworm will work in the order in which the numbers are given.

The grasshopper is likely to look for pairs and clusters of numbers which add up to 10 or 20, e.g. in the unit column there is $7 + 3 = 10$ and $9 + 6 + 5 = 20$. In the tens column there is $3 + 3 + 4 = 10$ and from $8 + 1 + 3$ (carried from the units) he can extract $8 + 2$, leaving 2. Answer 220. The grasshopper will probably have already grouped 85 and 19 as a little over 100 and 36, 37 and 43 as a bigger bit over 100—estimate 200 and a bit. He uses numbers as parts of a whole, where the whole is 10 or 100 or 1000. He takes the numbers out of the order in which they are presented.

Deductions from the examples

These examples are used to show how pupils with the two styles approach problems. Our experience of teaching dyslexic students leads us to some observations:

- There are some pupils at the extremes of the continuum.
- An individual pupil may use both styles.
- The style an individual pupil uses can depend on the type of question or even on the level of difficulty of the same type of question.
- The type of compensatory strategy (e.g. finger counting or interrelating facts) that is used relates to cognitive style.
- There are more inchworms than grasshoppers.
- Inchworms with poor memory for basic facts are at risk in mathematics.
- Grasshoppers in the school system need to learn how to document their work.
- Inaccurate grasshoppers are at risk in mathematics.
- Some questions favour grasshoppers, others favour inchworms.
- Having a dominant style does not necessarily mean the child is successful in using that style.

The teacher has to be aware of these different styles and the fact that the child may not use the style he has been taught (Hart, 1978) or may, as Duffin (1991) observed, use his own method first and then diligently reproduce for the teacher the standard method he has been taught.

We could speculate which of the subskill deficits listed in Chapter 1 affect the way a child would solve such problems. For example, poor long–term memory for basic facts could contribute to a grasshopper style, in that a child may have to overview and combine data in order to avoid facts that he cannot recall. What is clear is that the way a child (or adult) solves a question depends on the blend of deficits and strengths he brings to the problem. You can usually go a long way to finding out how a child solves a problem by asking the simple question,

'How did you do that?' This interest (based on awareness), rather than a judgement, will be a major source of help for many pupils, especially when combined with an awareness of what the child brings to the question.

Teachers and cognitive style

A pupil may not have the same cognitive style as his teacher. If neither party is aware of this there are likely to be consequences. For example, the marks awarded for an answer could be affected. Chinn (1995a) has carried out a survey of teachers' marks for three very different, yet correctly answered methods used to solve a word problem. The range of marks for each answer varied from 0 to 10 (out of 10), so a child could be with one teacher and receive an encouraging 10 or be with another teacher and score 0 out of 10. The awarding of a particular mark can usually be rationalised by the teachers concerned. This is a very good reason for a mathematics department to meet and discuss marking policies. Mackay (1994) noted the restricted range of methods accepted for mathematics test at Key Stage 2 (National Curriculum).

Sharma (1989) has noted that quantitative and qualitative personalities prefer different learning materials, distinguishing between discrete or quantitative materials (e.g. number lines) and continuous or qualitative materials (e.g. base–ten blocks).

Summary

If you are to teach effectively and diagnostically then you must be aware of and respond to the nature, variety and consequences of the child's strengths, weaknesses and cognitive style. An awareness that there is a range of cognitive styles in any teaching group can help the teacher present a lesson more effectively and to a broader spectrum of learners.

Chapter 3
Testing and Diagnosis

If you are working with an individual student, you should use a diagnostic approach to teaching. You need to appraise the student's skills and deficits in mathematics. It is the authors' experience that children often know more than tests reveal, for example, an algorithm may be almost mastered, but a small misunderstanding causes failure. Remediation is not always from square one, and testing should bear this in mind.

After some background considerations, this chapter suggests a testing procedure. There could be many other equally valid procedures, and any procedure should be adapted to respond to the child's answers. Ginsburg (1997) states that the clinical interview method—that is, the researcher's deliberately nonstandardised and flexible questioning of the child—has emerged as a major research tool in the investigation of mathematical thinking.

Chinn (1992, p. 23) has discussed the use of testing, in particular the benefits and disadvantages of norm–referenced and criterion–referenced tests. However, before returning to this discussion, we should step back and ask the obvious and fundamental question, 'Why test?'. Some of the answers to this question include:

- Parents may wish to know how their child's achievements compare with those of his peers.
- A teacher may wish to monitor the progress of his or her group and/or identify those who need extra help and/or collect data with which to stream groups.
- There may be a need to measure rates of progress.
- There may be some mandatory requirement to test.
- The test may be used to assess the ability of the child to progress to higher levels of study or to a new school.
- The test may be used to provide information for an educational statement of special needs (which may be the same as the previous item).

- The test may be used to award a certificate recording a level of achievement (for example, GCSE or National Curriculum Key Stage 4).
- It may be used for diagnostic reasons (for example, to find the child's strengths, weaknesses, knowledge base and learning style).

It is understandable for a parent, or indeed a concerned educator, to wish to have an idea of the depth of a child's problems, measured in terms of a direct comparison with his peers. Tests which are 'normed' against a large population of children are used for these comparisons, for example the Vernon Miller Test, the Mathematics Competency Test, the NFER 8–12 Tests, the Profile of Mathematical Skills, the Basic Number Screening Test or the Wide Range Achievement Test (see the References and Appendix 1 for details). It is not the function of these tests to provide a diagnosis of 'dyslexic' problems. If the examiner wishes to derive a diagnostic profile of the child's strengths, weaknesses and learning style, additional testing will have to be done. Standardised tests set the baseline for diagnosis.

Criterion–referenced tests are more diagnostic (by design) than norm–based tests. Interpretation of a criterion–based test can identify particular tasks that the child can and cannot do, but not necessarily his error patterns (Ashlock, 1982) or why he can or cannot do a particular task. Such tests can be lengthy if they are designed to be thorough and/or cover much ground (see Wilson and Sadowski, 1976). Ashcroft (see Appendix 1) has designed a test based on items which tend to generate the errors typically made by dyslexics.

If these tests are used with groups, say as a class test, then the accurate interpretation of an individual child's errors can be uncertain and relies heavily on how much of his method the child has documented. Of course, if the test is administered on an individual basis, then diagnostic questioning can be used to supplement the written evidence. As with the *Test of Cognitive Style in Mathematics* (Bath et al., 1986), the key question is 'How did you do that?'. Careful, knowledgeable, well–timed and informed questioning is usually non–threatening.

A Diagnostic Test Protocol

This diagnostic procedure, structured for a dyslexic child, links back, as does all the work in this book, to a knowledge of the child and what he brings to the subject. The procedure is designed to be appropriate to the child and to the mathematics he is likely to encounter. It also relates to the teaching strategies described in this book, indicating which are likely to be more effective for the child. Although the test items suggested here have been carefully selected, they may be modified to suit the individual. The structure and rationale of the test should, however, be followed.

The diagnostic procedure will examine the child's knowledge of basic facts, his level of understanding of fundamental concepts (such as place value), his use of strategies (if any) and his learning style, and it should provide the examiner with enough information to construct a teaching programme appropriate to the child's needs.

The basic structure of the test protocol suggested below is designed to measure the child's present level of achievement and to ascertain why and in what ways the child is having difficulty. Although the basic premise must be that each child is a unique individual, there are certain common areas that are likely to create difficulty for the dyslexic (see Chapter 1). The protocol is designed to investigate these areas and to provide the examiner with a profile of the child's mathematical abilities. The test is aimed at early mathematics and therefore concentrates on numeracy. It is primarily designed for an age range from around 9 to about 13 years, depending on the extent of the deficit. The test need not be given in one session, but may be spread over whatever time the examiner considers manageable for the child. Some items will be easier than others. The examiner should unobtrusively encourage the child to try his best.

Structure of the Diagnostic Protocol

The test structure includes the following components:

- A norm–based test (see Appendix 1).
- Counting/adding on tasks and number bonds.
- Times–table facts.
- Place–value tasks.
- Mathematics language.
- The four operations.
- Money.
- Word problems.
- Attitude/anxiety.
- A cognitive style test.

A norm–based (standardised) test

There are several to chose from (see the References and Appendix 1 for suggestions). The individual requirements of each examiner will probably reduce the choice. It is worth having several tests at the ready as many dyslexic children have a long history of being tested and may well have already recently done your first choice.

Counting and adding on tasks

A good starting point is to scatter about 60 matchsticks or counters on a table top and ask the child to count them. The test is looking at one–to–one correspondence, speed of counting, accuracy and whether or not the child groups the counters/matchsticks and in what size of group.

The examiner can also ask the child to count the number of dots on a card, a task where he cannot handle and move the items he is counting. The dots can be presented in a regularly spaced line and then at random.

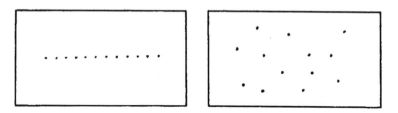

A series of fact cards may be made (on index cards) and used to check basic addition and subtraction skills. When testing for basic addition and subtraction fact knowledge and strategies, the examiner should also be aware of the Einstellung effect (Luchins, 1942), which is the lack of flexible interchange between operations (add, subtract, multiply and divide) and which is observed when a child stays with the original operation even after the operation sign has changed (a behaviour different to misreading signs).

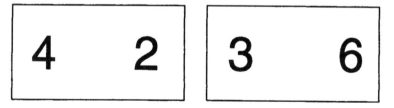

- 4 + 2 checks a basic, low number addition fact and whether the child counts on to 4, counts from 1 to 4 and then on to 6 or just knows the answer.
- 3 + 6 checks as above and to see if the child changes the order to the easier counting on task 6 + 3.
- 4 + 3 = [ ] introduces the child to the 'box' for an answer, a number to make the question right. The examiner says, 'What number goes in the box to make the right answer?'.
- 5 + [ ] = 9 checks if the child is flexible enough in his knowledge of addition (and subtraction) to understand what is required, that is, does he count on or subtract 5 from 9 to obtain 4. The examiner asks 'What number goes in the box to make this sum right?'.
- 6 + 4 = [ ]. The number bonds for 10 are an important set of data to learn, so the child's level of knowledge of these facts needs to be checked.

- 'Can you write three more pairs of numbers that add up to 10, like 6 and 4?' Does the child immediately give you 4 + 6, or does he have a strategy such as 9 + 1, 8 + 2, 7 + 3?
- Give the child two 5p, six 2p and ten 1p coins and ask him to show you some ways of making 10p. Here the test is examining how many ways he produces 10p and whether he works to a system, e.g. 5 + 5 to 5 + 2 + 2 + 1 to 5 + 2 + 1 + 1+ 1, etc.
- 10 = 7 + [ ]. Can the child use his number bonds for 10 in a different (subtraction) format?
- 8 + 7 = [ ]. Many children, even if they say they 'just know' the answer, can be gently persuaded to tell you exactly how they worked it out. Some children will simply count on, using their fingers or objects in the room. The finger movements may be very slight, so the examiner will have to be observant. Some children extend their limited lexicon of facts by interrelating number facts. So 8 + 7 becomes 1 less than 2 × 8, i.e. 15.
- 9 + 8 = [ ], 9 + 6 = [ ], 9 + 4 = [ ]. In asking this sequence (one at a time) the examiner is trying to see if the child has a consistent strategy for adding onto 9. Has the child started to see patterns?
- 17 - 8 = [ ]. Checks a problem similar to those above, but presented as a subtraction.
- 60 - 6 = [ ]. Can the child extend his number bonds for 10 to other '10' situations?

Times–table facts

Pritchard et al. (1989) found that dyslexics often knew the 2 times, 5 times and 10 times tables, so the protocol can acknowledge this. The examiner can resort to straightforward questions, especially if he has established a good rapport with the child. He can simply ask 'Which of your times tables do you know?' and maybe prompt, 'The twos?'.

If the child says he does know the 2 times table the examiner should ask, 'What are seven twos, what is seven times two?' The examiner must observe whether the child has instant recall or if he counts up 2, 4, 6, 8, 10, 12, 14 or if he uses a strategy, such as 5 × 2 and 2 × 2, added to make 7 × 2. Similar, careful diagnostic questioning can be used to establish a broad picture of the child's times–table knowledge.

The examiner may also wish to determine how many (if any) strategies the child uses to work out times–table facts. For example, if he knows that 2 × 8 = 16 does he add on a third 8 for 3 × 8, or if he knows 5 × 8 = 40, does he add another 8 to obtain 6 × 8? Another common strategy is to halve 10 times–table facts to obtain 5 times–table facts. (A child who has developed his own strategies is more likely to be aware of the interrelationships between numbers.)

The commutative property is expressed as $a \times b = b \times a$, or in numbers, $7 \times 8 = 8 \times 7$, that is, it does not matter whether a rectangle is 9 $\times 4$ or 4×9, the area is the same (36). The commutative property is useful knowledge and worth including in a test procedure. So a child may be asked to give the answer to 4×8 if he is told $8 \times 4 = 32$.

Place value

The child is asked a series of questions. The numbers should be written on cards and shown to the child.

- If this number is fifty–six (56), what is this number—243?
- What is this number—8572?
- What is this number—4016?
- Write the number (as digits) four thousand, two hundred and thirty three.
- Write the number sixteen thousand and seventeen.
- What is the value of each digit in this number—5656?
- Work out 14×2, 14×20, 14×200.

The language of mathematics

- The child is asked to match the sign to the name. He can be told that there may be more than one name per sign. (The examiner needs two sets of cards, one set with four each of $\times + \div - = /$, the other set with add, divide, subtract, times, multiply, share, minus, plus, equals, same as, take away, more, less.)

- Make up an addition sum. The examiner may need to talk the child into this (e.g. $5 + 6 = 11$).

Concepts/understanding

- 'Explain what you understand by the word divide (or multiply). Tell me how you would explain to someone what divide is.' The examiner will have different levels of expectation for this and may find that discussion can lead to a clearer picture of the child's understanding of these deceptively simple concepts.

- 'Give me an estimate, an easier number to use, for 87.' The child may be bold enough to go to 100, but many will go only as far as 85 or 90. The examiner is looking to see if the child has understood the need to take an estimate to a number which is easy to use in calculations.
- Make up a word problem using, in a mathematical way, the word 'share'.

The four operations ($+ - \times \div$)

Ashlock's (1982) book *Error Patterns in Computation* introduces the idea of analysing a child's errors and then providing appropriate remedial instruction. Careful selection of computation items should give useful diagnostic information. This stage of the protocol also allows the examiner to introduce some criterion–referenced items. Chinn (1995a) has recently studied the errors made by 11–13–year–old dyslexic students. Smith (1996) also makes some interesting observations on errors.

Addition

These questions can be presented on a worksheet. The questions must be well spaced out and preferably ruled off from each other. The child can be asked to make an estimate for each question first. The use of a worksheet format does not preclude the continued use of the question, 'How did you do that?'.

$$\begin{array}{r} 36 \\ + \ 21 \\ \hline \end{array}$$ checks two digit plus two digit with no 'carrying'.

$$\begin{array}{r} 20 \\ + \ 47 \\ \hline \end{array}$$ checks adding to a zero.

$$\begin{array}{r} 357 \\ + 469 \\ \hline \end{array}$$ checks three digit plus three digit with two 'carries'.

$8 + 5 + 7 + 5 + 1 + 9 + 2$ checks if the child uses number bonds for 10, rewrites the problem vertically, finger counts, tries to use memory, uses tallies, either to count each unit or as 'carries for 10s'.

Subtraction

A further question sheet can be prepared, as the examiner is also looking at methods and errors instead of just whether the answers are right or wrong. Indeed both sets of questions investigate the typical errors a dyslexic may make.

$$\begin{array}{r} 46 \\ -\ 23 \\ \hline \end{array}$$ checks two digit minus two digit with no renaming.

$$\begin{array}{r} 73 \\ -\ 44 \\ \hline \end{array}$$ checks two digit minus two digit with renaming. renaming refers to changing 73 to 60 and 13, written $\overset{6}{\cancel{7}}\overset{1}{3}$

$$\begin{array}{r} 840 \\ -\ 427 \\ \hline \end{array}$$ checks three digit minus three digit with subtraction from zero.

$$\begin{array}{r} 1000 \\ -\ 699 \\ \hline \end{array}$$ checks use of renaming algorithm as opposed to rounding up the 669 to 700.

The questions are designed to investigate the typical errors dyslexics may make.

Multiplication

$$\begin{array}{r} 23 \\ \times\ \ 2 \\ \hline \end{array}$$ checks two digits times one digit with no carrying (with easy number facts)

$$\begin{array}{r} 37 \\ \times\ \ 2 \\ \hline \end{array}$$ checks two digit times one digit with carrying

$$\begin{array}{r} 23 \\ \times\ 20 \\ \hline \end{array}$$ relates to the first example to see if child can extend times two to times twenty.

$$\begin{array}{r} 42 \\ \times\ 22 \\ \hline \end{array}$$ checks two digit times two digit.

$$\begin{array}{r} 514 \\ \times\ 203 \\ \hline \end{array}$$ checks three digit times three digit; also if the middle line is written as 000, i.e. 'blind' use of an algorithm.

Note that although these examples are 'easy' they allow the child to demonstrate his ability to solve the problem without failing because he does not know times–table facts beyond 2, 5 and 10. They also provide the examiner with information about the way the child solves basic multiplication problems and his error patterns.

Division

$2\,\overline{)\,46}$ checks two digits divided by one digit with no carrying.

$2\,\overline{)\,74}$ Checks two digit divided by one digit with one carry.

$5\,\overline{)\,56}$ Checks two digit divided by one digit with remainder (or decimal).

$2\,\overline{)\,4008}$ checks dividing into zeros.

Again the information required centres on methods and number concepts rather than basic fact knowledge.

Word problems

Word problems should not be solely a test of reading ability, although the examiner needs to know if this is another barrier to success in mathematics. Again a clear worksheet should be written.

The child is asked to read and solve the problems.

1. What is 7 add 3?
2. What is 49 minus 7?
3. Take 12 from 25.
4. If six boxes contain 2 pens each, how many pens altogether?
5. Mike has ten red pens, three paper clips and seven pencils. How many things can Mike use for writing?
6. Pat goes to the shop and buys two sweets at 5p each and ten sweets at 3p each. How much does he pay?
7. Sally and Kath have twenty two model cars to share equally between them. How many do they each get?

- Questions 1 and 2 are the simplest and most straightforward.
- Question 3 reverses the order in which the numbers are to be subtracted.
- Question 4 mixes numbers as digits and numbers as words.
- Question 5 contains extraneous information.
- Question 6 has more than one stage.
- Question 7 is asking the child to divide and does not include any digits.

Thus each question probes a different aspect of the child's knowledge and abilities. His answers should give the examiner a good picture of the child's expertise with basic word problems. Although the questions are presented as a written exercise, once again the examiner can ask 'How did you do that?'.

Money

Knowledge of money is a survival skill. It is also interesting to see how a child's ability to solve money problems compares with his ability to solve equivalent number problems. Later, the child's knowledge of money problems can be used, for example, to work with decimal fractions (see Chapter 10).

1. How many pence in one pound?
2. How much is half of a pound?
3. Show the child a card with £1.00 – 24p and ask him, 'How much change is there from a pound if a bar of chocolate costs 24p?'.

4. Show the child a card with £100 and £19 written on it and ask, 'If you have £100, how many computer games can you buy if each game costs £19? Do you have any change?'.

5. You have £5 and you want to buy four things which cost (show the child a card with £1.50, £2.50, 75p, 75p). Have you enough money to buy all four things?

- Question 1 checks basic knowledge (essential to complete the other questions).
- Question 2 is asking if the child has absorbed what 50p is.
- Question 3 is 'real' life mathematics and looks at division.
- Question 4 is asking if the child has a concept of the value of money. Does he know that £100 is an identifiable amount of money?
- Question 5 is looking at another typical 'shopping' exercise.

Attitude and anxiety

It may also help and encourage the child if he is asked questions such as the following:

- 'How do you like mathematics?'
- 'Do you think you are any good at mathematics?'
- 'Which bits of maths do you like best?'
- 'Are there any areas where you think you could do with a little help?'

Cognitive style

See Chapter 2 and Chinn's *Diagnostic Inventory of Basic Skills and Learning Styles in Mathematics* (Chinn, 1998).

Summary of the Test Protocol

The answers to the questions, combined with a knowledge of the way the child solves each question, should provide the examiner with a comprehensive picture of what the child can do and how he does it, i.e. the examiner has a measure of the child's basic knowledge and his use of numeracy skills. The child's cognitive style can also be deduced from behaviours such as whether or not he finger counts to solve $8 + 7$ or if he uses $(2 \times 8) - 1$, his estimate for 87, or how he solves $1000 - 699$. As well as providing a picture of the child's strengths and weaknesses, the protocol helps the teacher to obtain a clearer idea as to what strategies the child is likely to find easy and which he will find harder to absorb.

The protocol described here is a guide to a structure for diagnosis. As the tester gains experience he will adapt these ideas and introduce new questions which enable him to follow where the child's responses lead.

Chapter 4
Concept of Number

Introduction

When a child has problems learning the basic facts of number, then his problems may be compounded by his consequent failure to develop an understanding of the values and interrelationships of numbers (of course, it does not automatically follow that a child who successfully rote learns the basic facts will develop an understanding of numbers). It is important that any child should develop a 'feel' or 'facility' for number, i.e. he needs to learn:

- A sense of the size or value of a number.
- Recognition of the other numbers which are near to it.
- How near it is to other numbers, particularly 'key/anchor' numbers such as 10s, 100s, etc.
- Whether it is larger or smaller, and by roughly how much.
- Its relationship to other numbers (twice as big, etc.).

For children with dyslexia/learning difficulties in mathematics, the development of this facility is a likely alternative route to coping with early numeracy. Their early failure to learn basic number facts can keep them from the extent and quality of experiences needed to develop number concept. Of course, learning the basic facts does not guarantee the development of concept of number for anyone, so the ideas advocated here may have benefit for a wider population than just dyslexics.

This chapter looks at the very early stages of number work. These are the stages where a dyslexic child may have started to fail. Thus, even an older child may need work to recover the experiences he has not taken on board earlier. As with much of the material in this book, the work described may not be age–specific. The tutor/teacher needs to adjust the style and approaches of presentation of the work to avoid patronising the child.

Early Recognition of Numbers and Their Values

A *small* number of objects can usually be recognised instantaneously by using a visual sense of number, so that a child seeing two different clusters of, say, four spots will recognise them as the same quantity. This ability disappears with larger numbers (although some children are able to extend this skill to remarkably large numbers).

Slightly larger numbers may be more quickly recognised if:

1. The objects are arranged in a recognisable pattern, or
2. The number can be seen as a combination of other numbers. Thus, even at this early stage of development, the child can be introduced to the use of patterns and interrelationships.

So, for example, nine can be shown as

or   (domino pattern).

Teachers (or parents) can also introduce certain special numbers that can be used as landmarks, reference points or stepping stones towards understanding other numbers. For example, nine can be seen as one less than 10, and 12 can be seen as two more then 10. Thus 10 is introduced as a key number.

The Language of Mathematics

In this chapter, we use the word 'number' to mean one of the following:

- The mathematical symbol for the number, e.g. 8.
- The written form of the number word, e.g. eight.
- The sound of a number word, e.g. ate (phonetic: āt).

So already we have three interpretations of even such a basic word as 'number'.

For most of the dyslexics we teach, the problem of mathematics as a 'foreign' language becomes particularly acute when there is a necessity to write numbers down. The situation is exacerbated by the conventions of place value (base ten). As an example, we have seen 11–year–old boys write 'six hundred and five thousand and twenty' as 600500020, and as a less obvious error, 5620.

Early Number Work

Sorting/classifying

An important mathematical pre–skill is the ability to differentiate objects and group together those with common attributes, such as colour, size or function. This activity is the first stage towards counting the objects in a set.

The number zero is an important concept to introduce, even at this early stage. It can be introduced here to represent the complete absence of any objects in the set (or group). This early exposure is important and quite easy to introduce in a clear way to a child.

Correspondence between sets of objects

Understanding that two sets contain the same number of objects can be achieved by matching each object from the first set with each object from the second. If there are any objects left after such a matching process, then one set contains more objects and the other contains fewer objects.

This level of understanding allows sets of objects to be compared, even though the actual number in either set is not established. This acts as an early introduction to the concept of 'more than' and 'less than'. The same approach can be extended to compare more than two sets and thus the idea of rank orders.

The idea of comparing two sets can be extended to record the number of objects in the first set by using 'tallies' in the second set. The tallies should be a familiar, standard set of objects such as fingers or marks recorded on paper, one tally for each object,

e.g. 1, 11, 111, 1111, 11111, 111111, 1111111, 11111111
      1, 11, 111, 1111, ⊥⊢⊤, ⊥⊢⊤1, ⊥⊢⊤11, ⊥⊢⊤111

Correspondence between objects and numbers: counting

Stage 1

Introducing the number words and number symbols gives, in effect, abstract sets, which can be matched with sets of actual objects. For example, when the set of three objects is seen to correspond with the symbol '3', we begin to call the number of objects three.

It can then be seen that if the objects are counted in any different order, the correspondence shows that there are still three. Furthermore, if other sets of different objects are also seen to correspond with 3, then the relationship of a constant 'three–ness' for the 'different' sets can be developed. Another important move forward comes if the child can be encouraged to explore the arrangements of objects within a set to discover that the number is conserved even though the arrangement is different. In this way the child learns the interrelationship of numbers, e.g. $3 = 2 + 1$ or $1 + 2$ and $3 = 5 - 2$ so that the interrelationships between key numbers, 1, 2, 5, and 10 is an early experience.

Stage 2

At this stage the child is starting to link together the objects, the symbol for the number of objects, and the word (sight and sound) for the number, and the 'break down' of the number (Table 4.1).

Table 4.1

Objects	1	11	111	1111	11111	111111	1111111	11111111	111111111
Number symbols	1	2	3	4	5	6	7	8	9
Words/ sounds	One	Two	Three	Four	Five	Six	Seven	Eight	Nine

It is necessary for the number symbols and sounds in Table 4.1 to be known by heart. The exact spelling of the number words is of less importance (and less achievable) for children with this type of learning difficulty. The ARROW strategy (Lane, 1992) may well be of use in helping to achieve this target. ARROW is a multisensory learning and teaching approach developed in schools and researched under the auspices of Somerset County Council and the University of Exeter. ARROW uses a child's own voice, the self–voice, to develop skills central to reading, spelling, speaking and listening. ARROW is an acronym for Aural–Read–Respond–Oral–Written in which the self–voice, replayed on tape, is linked to writing, listening and speech skills in a series of processes involving spelling, comprehension and reading books.

Stage 3

Counting can be used to associate the movement from object to object with a movement to the next number. In the early stages, while counting aloud, a child cannot always synchronise these movements and it may help if he counts against a regular rhythm or beat (e.g. a metronome). This can also be used to develop speed of counting.

Stage 4

The extension of the skill of counting forwards to the skill of counting backwards is not easy for the dyslexic child. More practice in the reverse operation of removing one object at a time while counting the numbers backwards will almost certainly be needed.

Stage 5

The Number Line (Figure 4.1) is useful at all levels of mathematics. Here it associates each extra mark with the next number and confers an evenness and proportionality on the counting process. It also establishes the order of the numbers, as well as the convention of increasing to the right and decreasing to the left. Furthermore, the regular spacing of the numbers begins the connection between numbers and length. This is reinforced by using apparatus of the Dienes and Cuisenaire types. Counting in both directions along the number line is beneficial.

Figure 4.1 The Number Line

Some link between the symbols and the values of low numbers can be (somewhat artificially) drawn by stylisation of the number symbols. This may be a useful mnemonic for some children, e.g.

$$1\ Z\ 3\#\ 5\ 6$$

For this stylisation the number of bold strokes suggests the number of objects.

Visual Sense of Number

Experiments can show that the visual sense of numbers is limited to about five or six. That is to say, most children will immediately recognise the number of objects in sets of one, two, three, four, five or six (without time for counting). This seems to imply that children have an in–built 'feel' for the sizes and values of these numbers.

From about six objects onwards, the visual sense of number is exhausted and the objects have to be counted, unless there are other clues in the arrangement of the objects. In other words, the child has to use a one–to–one correspondence, treating each number as a separate identity; he begins to relate numbers, build them up and see constituent parts.

Visual Clues to Number Concept

Numbers can more easily be 'assessed' if they form a recognisable pattern or if they can be seen as a combination of simpler numbers (this can be done in the early stages without a formal understanding of addition or multiplication). At this stage such an exercise adds further reinforcement to the idea of breaking down and building up numbers. The work can be extended to bigger numbers, as shown in Figure 4.2. Many of the numbers are instantly recognisable through their patterns, familiar from dice and dominoes.

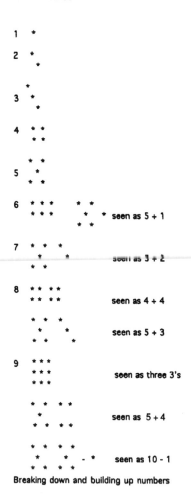

Figure 4.2 Breaking down and building up numbers

Any attempt to 'standardise' on a particular version is likely to be counterproductive, because each child will feel happiest with the version that suits him individually. Our experience is that children start to build up their own idiosyncratic lexicons of facts and links. The best version is the one that works for a particular child, although sometimes a little intrusion helps to rationalise and organise the child's ideas.

Number Bonds

The number bonds (for sums below 10) are fundamental in aiding number concept. The preceding work has built up to this formal presentation of number facts. Knowledge of the number bonds is also important when addition is tackled formally. There are therefore two important reasons why they should be understood and learned at this early stage. The following are likely to be the most useful:

	A	B	C	D
2 as	1 and 1			
3 as	2 and 1			
4 as	3 and 1	2 and 2		
5 as	4 and 1	3 and 2		
6 as	5 and 1	4 and 2	3 and 3	
7 as	6 and 1	5 and 2	4 and 3	
8 as	7 and 1	6 and 2	5 and 3	4 and 4
9 as	8 and 1	7 and 2	6 and 3	4 and 5

Column A gives practice at adding 1, column B at adding 2, column C at adding 3 and column D at adding 4.

Practice can, for example, be scheduled in the following ways:

- Add 1 to each number from 1 to 8.
- Add every number from to 2 to 7 to the number 2.
- Add the numbers randomly.
- Add numbers in every possible way to make a given sum, such as 7.

The practice can be supported by using 'concrete' materials.

- Any form of counters that remain separate, so that the child sees the 'ones' in each part and the resultant whole.
- Blocks, like centicubes, which can be joined together and separated, so that the child starts to see the numbers holistically.
- Cuisenaire–type rods, each number represented by a different length and colour, so that the child visualises the 'sizes' of the numbers.
- A number line, which links the numbers to a sense of proportionality.
- The child can use two spinners which can take any value from 1 to 8, or an eight–sided dice (used in conjunction with the above items if necessary).

An important consequence of this work should be the establishment of the commutative law, which states that the order in which the numbers are added does not affect the answer, i.e. $5 + 2 = 2 + 5 (= 7)$.

The teacher will need to establish the law by reminding and organising the child to see the logic of the demonstrations he has just undertaken.

This latter concept, plus that of number bonds and the results of the practice described above are summarised as:

+	1	2	3	4	5	6	7	8
1	2	3	4	5	6	7	8	9
2	3	4	5	6	7	8	9	
3	4	5	6	7	8	9		
4	5	6	7	8	9			
5	6	7	8	9				
6	7	8	9					
7	8	9						
8	9							

This table can be used for reference by the child and as a compact source from which to memorise the data.

Place Value

The use of base 10 and the consequent place value of numbers are conventions. The most frequent (and predictable) difficulty that occurs is that the child does not understand that the value of a number depends on its place in a group of numbers. This difficulty is not to be confused with the transposition of numbers (e.g. 34 for 43). There are also some problems with misunderstanding the language of these conventions. Many subsequent problems can be traced back to a lack of under-standing of place value. This therefore needs careful attention. (See Appendix 1 for details of Sharma's video on place value.)

Grouping in tens

The number 10 owes its significance to the number of our fingers and their use in counting. Ten retains its significance as a collective unit in the written symbols we use for numbers, so we have 10 fingers and 10 different number symbols. When we ran out of fingers, we had to use something else (a second person's fingers, for example), so when we ran out of number symbols we had to use a second, additional symbol (in another column or place).

The following approach attempts to show a logical connection between a number of objects and the symbols used to write the numbers. The approach moves from the concrete to the abstract, 'foreign language', written form in progressively more abstract/representative forms.

Step 1. Using physical grouping

Objects do not naturally form themselves into groups of 10. Practice in doing this can be the first step towards understanding. The type of exercise here is simply to provide a group of items and let the child group them in 10s. What the child sees are groups of 10s which are numerically proportional to their value (Figure 4.3).

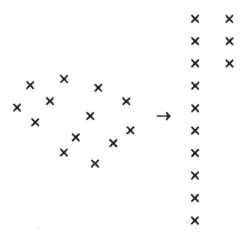

Figure 4.3 Physically grouping

Step 2. Using counting blocks

Certain types of counting blocks (especially Dienes/base–10 blocks) have a different block for 10, which is in direct proportion to the length of 10 unit blocks (Figure 4.4).

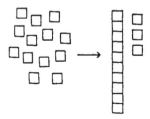

Figure 4.4 Counting blocks

Step 3. Using money

Although a 10p coin is physically larger than a 1p coin, it is not proportionally 10 times bigger. It is a different colour. The use of money therefore brings further progress towards abstraction (Figure 4.5a).

Step 4. Using written tally symbols

The use of different tally symbols for 10 and 1, such as the ancient Egyptian ∧ and 1, gives a written symbol parallel for the money activity above (Figure 4.5b).

Figure 4.5a Using money

Figure 4.5b Using tally symbols

Another suitable manipulative type of object here is bundles of 10 cocktail sticks and single cocktail sticks. The material retains proportionality, but emphasises the 'collecting together' of units into 10s.

Step 5. Recording in words

Writing numbers down can be achieved using the words 'Tens' and 'Ones' as labels (Figure 4.6).

Figure 4.6 Recording in words

Step 6. Using headings instead of labels

Writing word labels for each number is inefficient and time consuming, but using them as headings (Figure 4.7) saves some of this effort while leaving a clear reminder of the existence and value of the number places. Later we will use place value cards to help maintain the concept during addition and subtraction.

Step 7. Omission of the headings

Eventually, the headings can be dropped when they are 'understood' to be there, defining the place value of the digit (Figure 4.8).

			Tens	Ones
2 Tens	4 Ones	→	2	4
6 Tens	9 Ones	→	6	9
5 Tens	2 Ones	→	5	2
8 Tens	3 Ones	→	8	3

Figure 4.7 Using headings

2	4
6	9
5	2
8	3

Figure 4.8 Omission of headings

Tens alone

When we write 10, we mean 1 ten and 0 ones. In some number systems, it would be redundant to mention the 0 ones, because zero means there are no objects there. Place value uses fixed relative positions (reinforced by column headings where place value is less well understood). So an understanding of the role of 0 as marking that a particular 'place' is empty is essential, as is its role of maintaining the 'place' of the other digits. One good way of demonstrating this with children is to make each child a place value and his fingers the digits, so that 30 looks like Figure 4.9. The teacher can discuss with the children why the second (unit) child is needed to demonstrate 30.

Figure 4.9 Hands showing place value

Figure 4.10 shows three ways of depicting four tens. They must be identified as tens, classified, counted and recorded together. The 0 in the written version 40 makes it quite clear that:

- the 4 objects are tens, and
- there are no ones.

In the spoken form, ten became abbreviated to –ty. Hence six tens became sixty, etc. Although it is obviously incorrect and contrived there is some good teaching value in the use of 'tenty' for one hundred. For example, it is a logical extension of the pattern of the other '–ty numbers and helps the child realise something new is happening if we change the rule/pattern to a new word—hundred. It is also useful in subtraction if renaming from the hundred column is used.

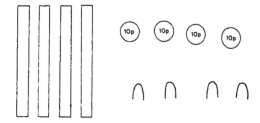

Figure 4.10 Three ways of depicting four tens

Grouping in hundreds

After 10, 20, 30, 40, 50, 60, 70, 80, 90, it is impossible to record any more tens in the tens column (we have run out of number symbols again). If the example used 10p pieces, there would also be an argument against having too many coins. The solutions to the two situations are parallel; we use another collective unit, hundred (in another column), or we use another coin, £1. In each case, the hundred can be seen as 10 tens. Cocktail sticks may again be used here, especially if available in boxes of 100. In Figure 4.11 the number 237 is represented in various ways.

Grouping in thousands

Thousand is the next collective unit, constituted from 10 hundreds. The next collective units are ten thousand and hundred thousand. The analogues of the counting blocks, money, tally symbols and labels are less effective in contributing to an understanding of numbers above a thousand, although discussions about how many base–ten thousand blocks would be needed to construct these higher value numbers are helpful. Fortunately, if place value has been properly understood up to this point, further extension of the system offers no further fundamental problems.

Certain large numbers with thousands can cause problems because of language, the word hundred being repeated in hundred thousand and/or the large number of digits, many of which can be zeros. For example, the number two hundred and six thousand and fifty can be incorrectly written as 200600050, 2006050, 20600050, 2060050, 6250, etc. It can be helpful to consider the number in two parts: the thousands separate from the rest, which must fill three places (for hundreds, tens and ones) set aside in advance, e.g. for the above number the first step would be 206---, then 206*50, then 206050.

Figure 4.11 Representations of the number 237

Millions and billions

The collective unit million virtually completes the picture. The first new word after thousand, it is probably best considered as 1000 thousand. Again consideration of the space occupied by a thousand 'thousand' blocks can help the concept. This space is, of course, the space occupied by a metre cube.

Some children can cope with exercises such as finding how high a pile of a million pound coins would be. Ideas like this make useful investigations which can be used to develop concepts of large numbers.

It is worth noting that base ten blocks follow a repeating pattern in thousands. Unit cube, long ten, flat hundred, thousand cube, (decimetre cube), long ten thousand, flat hundred thousand, million cube, (one metre cube). This continues on again to one billion and makes a good discussion topic. "How big is the billion cube? What object do you know that is about this size?"

Reminders

At this stage any doubt about a number will usually be clarified by the reintroduction of column headings.

Reinforcement

A useful game for place value uses the place value cards and asks the learner to collect a target number of coins, for example 56p. Dice are used to collect 1p coins which are placed in the units column. When the units column contains more than nine 1p coins then trading ten 1p coins for a 10p coin is used until the target is reached. The game then continues taking away 1p coins back to zero, using trading again, but now trading down from a 10p coin to ten 1p coins.

Diagnostic ideas

Questions of the following kinds can be used for practice, and for diagnosing difficulties:

- What is the value of the 7 in the number 4725?
- Write in figures thirty thousand and five.
- Write in words 12065.
- Write down the largest and smallest three–digit numbers you can make with the three digits 2, 6 and 9.

Number Bonds for 10

Because of its universal importance, it is essential for a child to have a good concept of 10. It is worth making a special study of the number bonds for 10 and, if at all possible, helping the child to learn these facts. This is said with the clear understanding that rote learning is extraordinarily difficult for most dyslexics, but then, if the child does have to learn facts, let those facts be the ones with the most value. There are several illustrations and exercises which can be used to help the child understand and visualise these facts.

$10 + 0$
$9 + 1$ Especially useful for estimation/mental arithmetic purposes
$8 + 2$
$7 + 3$
$6 + 4$
$5 + 5$ Some children readily understand and remember
                'doubles'—5 is exactly half of 10

4 + 6
3 + 7
2 + 8
1 + 9
0 + 10

All the different ways of making 10 can be found, for example, by:

- Joining together 10 centicubes, then breaking them up in various ways.
- Laying down a Cuisenaire rod for 10, then laying down beside it combinations of other rods to give the same length.
- Using an abacus.
- Using coins or poker chips.

Diagrams such as Figures 4.12 and 4.13 can help the memory.

Figure 4.12

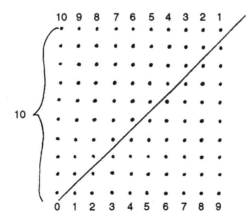

Figure 4.13

Numbers near to 10, 100 or 1000

Ten, hundred and thousand are major 'landmarks' and reference points in the base–10 system.

- From them, steps outwards can give meaning to numbers nearby, above or below. For example, the number 8 is just less than 10, and the number 1100 is just over 1000.
- Later, a question such as 4×98 can be seen as just below 4×100. This can give the approximate answer 'just below 400', or can form the starting point for estimation work and (mental) calculations of the (grasshopper) form

$$
\begin{aligned}
4 \times 98 &= 4 \times 100 - 4 \times 2 \\
&= 400 - 8 \\
&= 392
\end{aligned}
$$

- Figures 4.14, 4.15 and 4.16 give a picture of the relative sizes/positions of the numbers 10, 100, 1000 and of the numbers near to them.

The pseudo–logarithmic scale in Figure 4.14 shows all the numbers 10, 100, 1000, on the same line, but the unequal gaps between the numbers would confuse some children, and it is in parts difficult to read.

The number lines with periodic curves in Figure 4.15 show the relative positions clearly, but relating each line to the others may cause problems.

Figure 4.14 Pseudo-logarithmic scale

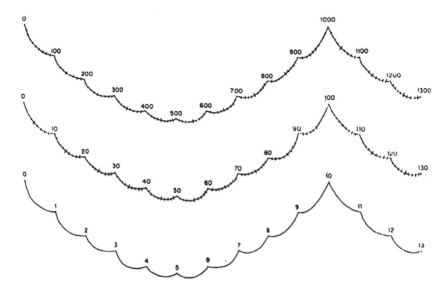

Figure 4.15 Number lines with periodic curves

On the number blocks in Figure 4.16, the positions and the numbers are quite clear. However, the number 1000 cannot be included on the same diagram.

The diagram, or combination of diagrams, which a child follows most easily is again the best alternative. All this is of course preceded by work using as many concrete materials as appropriate (e.g. money, Dienes, metre rule). The diagrams are somewhat demanding conceptually, but they do summarise a concept and spatial presentation that is difficult to do otherwise.

1	2	3	4	5	6	7	8	9	10
20	19	18	17	16	15	14	13	12	11
21	22	23	24	25	26	27	28	29	30
40	39	38	37	36	35	34	33	32	31
41	42	43	44	45	46	47	48	49	50
60	59	58	57	56	55	54	53	52	51
61	62	63	64	65	66	67	68	69	70
80	79	78	77	76	75	74	73	72	71
81	82	83	84	85	86	87	88	89	90
100	99	98	97	96	95	94	93	92	91
101	102	103	104	105	106	107	108	109	110
120	119	118	117	116	115	114	113	112	111
121	122	123	124	125	126	127	128	129	130
140	139	138	137	136	135	134	133	132	131
141	142	143	144	145	146	147	148	149	150
160	159	158	157	156	155	154	153	152	151

1, 2, 3, 4, 5, 6, 7, 8, 9, 10, 11, 12, 13, 14, 15, 16

Figure 4.16 Number blocks

Summary

This chapter has looked at the concept of numbers and their values, concentrating on place value. The remaining chapters will continue to develop number concept and facility by extending the child's experiences into the interrelationships of numbers. What is important at this stage is that the child has some clear ideas as to the values of the low numbers, an understanding of number bonds in the light of conservation of number and the commutative law, and a clear concept of place value. This knowledge will form a good base for the remaining development, the foundations of the developmental programme.

Chapter 5
Addition and Subtraction: Basic Facts

Introduction

If you ask dyslexic children to add 8 and 7 and explain how they reached their answer you will get a selection of methods depending on each child's experiences and idiosyncratic ideas (Ackerman et al., 1986, call them inconsistent), for example:

- Counting on: the child simply starts at 8 and counts on 7 (using his fingers or counting on objects in the room) or starts at 1, counting through 8 to 15.
- Using 10: the child breaks 7 into 2 + 5, uses the 2 with the 8 to make 10, then adds on 5, or works via 7 + 3.
- Using doubles: the child uses $(2 \times 8) - 1$ or $(2 \times 7) + 1$.
- Straight recall: the child 'just knows'.

In this chapter we will look at strategies for working out basic facts efficiently and in a way that enhances number concept and facility with number. We are assuming that a child will have great difficulty in rote learning of facts and, if he should succeed, he will have difficulty holding those facts for more than a few hours. Each child therefore needs strategies to use when his memory fails him and leaves him with no way to obtain an answer. Some strategies are going to be used in their entirety, but others can be mastered to the stage where they become memory 'hooks' and are only used in part to supplement a half-known fact.

The strategy of counting on is not an effective strategy beyond counting on 1 or 2. It is a method that requires too much time to operate and it tends, therefore, to be susceptible to poor short–term memory. It is also susceptible to counting errors. Furthermore, it does not support number concept nor the relationships between and patterns of, numbers. Strategies which use number relationships are advocated wherever possible. Chinn (1994) looked at the knowledge of basic

addition facts presented at 4–second intervals and 12–second intervals
to a dyslexic population of 11– to 13–year–olds and found that, although
they scored significantly less well than a mainstream population in the
4–second task, their scores in the 12–second task were virtually equivalent. This is not surprising as one would expect any of the facts asked to
be accessible in 12 seconds by finger counting (although other strategies
were used by both groups).

It easy to underestimate just how much early experience and information a dyslexic student has missed, which makes it difficult to know
how far back to go when starting a teaching programme. One of the key
ideas advocated in this chapter is the breaking down and building up of
numbers. So, if a child did not receive and absorb work such as looking
at 6 as in Figure 5.1, then strategies which suggest that 8 + 6 can be
added as (8+ 2) + 4 will be less easy to teach (or learn). As ever, you
have to 'read' the child to know how much material to provide. (Ashlock
et al., 1983, provide an excellent range of teaching ideas to develop and
reinforce algorithms and concepts.)

Figure 5.1

Strategies for Learning/Remembering the Addition and Subtraction Facts

The basic addition facts (which are also the basic subtraction facts) from
0 to 10 can be arranged in a square (Figure 5.2; see also times–table
facts). This gives the child a task of rote–learning 121 addition and 121
subtraction facts or developing strategies for as many of these facts as
possible.

The procedure for addressing the addition/subtraction facts task is
similar in technique to that used for times tables. It uses patterns, the
interrelationships between numbers and the ability to break down and
build up numbers. It builds on strategies which children themselves use,
but organises and rationalises idiosyncratic ideas; it adds structure. The
presentation as a square of facts gives some motivation in that initial
gains can be shown quickly and strategies are less individual, that is, they
can be more flexible, applicable and extensible.

Even though we discuss subtraction after work on the addition aspect of these facts, we feel it is most important to emphasise the subtraction 'side' of the addition fact as each fact is discussed.

The zero facts: + 0

$n + 0$ and $0 + n$ can be established using, for example, counters in boxes.
- An empty box is shown to the child and, after discussion about the contents and zero, 0 is written on the board or a sheet of paper.
- Five counters are added to the box. + 5 is written on the board/paper, giving $0 + 5$.

+	0	1	2	3	4	5	6	7	8	9	10
0	0	1	2	3	4	5	6	7	8	9	10
1	1	2	3	4	5	6	7	8	9	10	11
2	2	3	4	5	6	7	8	9	10	11	12
3	3	4	5	6	7	8	9	10	11	12	13
4	4	5	6	7	8	9	10	11	12	13	14
5	5	6	7	8	9	10	11	12	13	14	15
6	6	7	8	9	10	11	12	13	14	15	16
7	7	8	9	10	11	12	13	14	15	16	17
8	8	9	10	11	12	13	14	15	16	17	18
9	9	10	11	12	13	14	15	16	17	18	19
10	10	11	12	13	14	15	16	17	18	19	20

Figure 5.2 The square of addition facts

- The child counts the number of counters in the box, 5.
- The written form now has $0 + 5 = 5$.

A similar procedure may be used to deduce $5 + 0 = 5$. Careful and emphasised use of language is needed if later confusion with $\times 0$ facts is to be pre–empted.

This establishes 21 facts, although, as is ever the case, an unusual presentation of a 'known' fact may confuse the child. A typical error occurs in addition sums such as

$$\begin{array}{r} 356 \\ +\ \ 30 \\ \hline 380 \end{array}$$

Remember to discuss the subtraction of zero.

Adding on 1 (and 2)

This can be introduced by asking the child to look at a number line and handle counters, so that he sees, say, 4 + 1 as one move on the number line, i.e. a move to the next number. He can also experience a move to the next number by counting the addition with counters or, say, unifix cubes. The child has to 'see' the process as simply moving to the next number (and the reverse for subtraction).

A very similar argument applies to adding 2, although the child may have to physically count on the two numbers. This should still be quick and accurate. A knowledge of the even and odd numbers will support this operation. The child can practise counting in twos, starting from different numbers. The child will then need to spend some time looking at facts such as 1 + 9 and 2 + 7, with the teacher talking him into the commutative property of $1 + n = n + 1$ and teaching that it is quicker, less prone to error and more effective to count the smaller onto the bigger number.

If this can be accomplished, then 36 more addition fact squares can be shaded in, making a total of 57, leaving 64 to go.

Adding to 10; adding on 10

It is often the case when working with dyslexics that a lesson has more than one goal. The subsidiary goal is usually a review of a previously 'learned' (and perhaps 'forgotten') fact or concept. In this case the forgotten concept is likely to be that 10 represents 1 in the tens place–value column and zero in the units place–value column (i.e. it is an empty column). If this is re–established, then adding on to 10 is taking the child back to the first family of basic addition facts, i.e. $n + 0$ and $0 + n$ and extending it to $n + 10$ and $10 + n$.

A teaching idea is to use a place–value card and discuss and do the addition in symbols and with counters. There is some benefit in using 1p and 10p coins or base–ten 'longs' and 'units' because they clearly illustrate the difference between unit and ten values.

The visual pattern is

10 + 1 = 11
10 + 2 = 12
10 + 3 = 13
10 + 4 = 14, etc.

The tens digit (1) does not change, but the units digit becomes the same as the added number, 10 + d = 1 d (not algebra!). An extra difficulty sometimes arises from the unfortunate fact that the names of the numbers from 11 to 19, unlike subsequent decades, have the unit digit named first, e.g. seventeen. This also makes the aural pattern less consistent.

If this series of facts is understood then the task has reduced to 49 facts.

Use of doubles

For addition facts, children often know the doubles (similarly, in multiplication they often know the squares) and also use them to derive other addition facts, for example, 8 + 7 is often seen as double 8 less 1 (and sometimes as double 7 plus 1).

Two columns of counters provide a good representation of the derivation of these facts. Cuisenaire rods are also useful, e.g. two seven rods are placed side by side and 7 + 7 is written and discussed as being equal to 14. A one rod is placed on the end of a seven rod, increasing the sum to 15 (adding on 1 takes you to the next number). The seven and one rods are exchanged for an eight rod and the addition 7 + 8 = 15 is discussed:

$$(2 + 2) + 1 = 2 + 3 = 5$$
$$(3 + 3) + 1 = 3 + 4 = 7$$
$$(3 + 3) - 1 = 3 + 2 = 5$$
$$(4 + 4) + 1 = 4 + 5 = 9$$
$$(4 + 4) - 1 = 4 + 3 = 7$$
$$(5 + 5) + 1 = 5 + 6 = 11$$
$$(5 + 5) - 1 = 5 + 4 = 9, \text{ etc.}$$

This gives seven facts for the doubles and 12 facts for doubles ± 1. The task is down to 30 facts, half of which are commutative, so there are 15 different facts to go.

Number bonds for 10

These facts are extensible facts, that is, they can have significant uses in other situations to solve other problems. They are therefore important facts to learn.

There are a variety of concrete images which can be used to illustrate the number bonds to 10.

- Cuisenaire rods (Figure 5.3) give a colourful image of the linear relationship.
- A pile of poker chips (good because they are thick) can be used to show one pile growing as the other decreases as chips are transferred from one pile to the other.
- The number bonds can be written graphically (Figure 5.4).

Whatever materials the child handles, you must make sure that the digits are presented with each manipulative aid.

Although this section collects together the number bonds for 10, only 6 + 4, 4 + 6, 7 + 3 and 3 + 7 are 'new' facts—so, 26 to go.

Figure 5.3 Cuisenaire rods

Figure 5.4 Number bonds written graphically

Number bonds for 9

These follow on from the number bonds for 10. They are important as part of the strategy for the 9 times–table facts. The child has to see that 9 is one less than 10, so the two sets of number bonds need to be compared and the consistent relationship emphasised.

Adding on 9

This also follows on from the equivalent 10 facts, which are useful as an introduction to estimation. The child is learning again that 10 is one more than 9 and that 9 is one less than 10.

The child can practise the addition with coins or base–ten blocks, comparing adding 10 with adding 9, looking at adding 9 by adding 10 then subtracting 1, or using the added number to provide 1 to make the 9 up to 10 (and the added number one less), e.g. $9 + 6 = 10 + 6 - 1$ or $9 + 6 = (9 + 1) + (6 - 1)$.

These two groups of nine facts add 12 more facts, leaving 14 to go.

Sharing doubles

$n + n$ is the same as $(n - 1) + (n + 1)$. There are six of these facts:

$3 + 5$ and $5 + 3$ are the same as $4 + 4 = 8$
$5 + 7$ and $7 + 5$ are the same as $6 + 6 = 12$
$8 + 6$ and $6 + 8$ are the same as $7 + 7 = 14$

(The others are: $2 + 4$ and $4 + 2$; $4 + 6$ and $6 + 4$; $7 + 9$ and $9 + 7$.)

Again these facts can be experienced by moving counters between two initially equal piles. The strategy is an example of the conservation of number and is worth including for learning this alone.

There are eight facts to go. The commutative property reduces this to four: $8 + 3$, $8 + 4$, $8 + 5$, $7 + 4$.

Adding onto 8 can be achieved via 10, e.g. $8 + 5$ becomes $(8 + 2) + 3$. And $7 + 4$ can be seen as one more than the number bond $7 + 3$.

Summary

Some of the facts described in this chapter fall into more than one strategy group. As flexibility is important, this gives the child some choice of method. Shading squares on the addition square for families of strategies emphasises the pattern of each relationship.

In each strategy there is ample scope to have the child use concrete manipulative materials. These materials must be used *and* used in conjunction with showing the child the written numbers. The child has to learn to progress from the concrete to the symbolic and the process has to be multisensory. Again, with each strategy, the child must practise using the digits. Kirby (1989, 1992, 1993a; see Appendix 1) has some useful games to add variety and motivation to the practice (and which may help to reduce the frequency of transpositions, such as 42 for 24).

Subtraction Facts

Although the subtraction facts should be discussed alongside the addition facts, there will probably be a need to reinforce this material. From informal surveys when lecturing to adults on teaching arithmetic, we know that the perception of subtraction is that it is a harder operation than addition.

When writing and talking about the addition facts, you must use more than one format, for example, $4 + 6 = 10$ can be phrased as:

- What is 4 add 6?
- What adds on to 4 to make 10?
- Can you find the 'right' number to fit into the box:

$$4 + 6 = \Box \qquad 4 + \Box = 10 \qquad \Box + 6 = 10?$$

The latter two examples are leading the child to see subtraction as 'adding on'; $4 + 6 = \Box$ is a straight addition fact. The child is, however, learning that 10 can be split into two constituent parts, in this case 4 and 6. With $4 + \Box = 10$ and $\Box + 6 = 10$ the child still has to know that we are looking at two parts, but he now knows the total and only one of the parts. We are changing the frame of reference, not the knowledge. The child is learning the adaptability of mathematics facts.

Further examples and the introduction of the vocabulary of subtraction (minus, subtract, –, etc.) should lead the child to transfer his addition facts into subtraction facts. The idea of a total or sum and two parts or addenda will be used in 'harder' subtraction problems in the next chapter.

The child needs to learn that addition and subtraction are variations of the same process (Ashcroft and Chinn, 1992). The ideas above provide the framework which can be used and developed into an instructional format.

Extension

Ashcroft and Chinn (1992) advocate the use of patterns and sequences. For example, addition facts can be extended to the sequence/pattern which shows the consistent contribution of $4 + 7$ to a sequence of sums. The dyslexic child often needs the aspects of this pattern (and similar patterns) pointed out to him. In doing this, you are also leading the child towards addition sums, where he will be using the addition facts and, hopefully, reinforcing his knowledge of these facts.

$$
\begin{aligned}
4 + 7 &= 11 & 4 + 7 &= 11 \\
4 + 17 &= 21 & 14 + 7 &= 21 \\
4 + 27 &= 31 & 24 + 7 &= 31 \\
4 + 37 &= 41 & 34 + 7 &= 41 \\
4 + 47 &= 51 & 44 + 7 &= 51, \text{ etc.}
\end{aligned}
$$

Chapter 6
Times Tables

Introduction

Whenever there is a back–to–basics movement in education, the issue of learning times tables (and other basic facts) arises. To a large extent this argument is irrelevant for dyslexics. In our combined experience of over 30 years of teaching mathematics to dyslexics, we have found that the rote learning of times tables is a frustrating exercise for both learner and teacher (see also Miles, 1983; Pritchard et al., 1989; Chinn, 1994; Turner Ellis et al., 1996). As Ginsburg (1997) says

> ...that deficit seems to be the major feature differentiating children with and without learning disabilities.

We believe that there is an effective alternative solution to this problem. Although we suggest an effective rote learning technique, we believe that strategies based on patterns and the interrelationships of numbers are effective in learning how to work out times–table facts. These strategies give the learner routes to an answer, as opposed to him or her relying on memory which gives no possibility of obtaining a correct answer when he or she forgets the fact (Chinn, 1994). Again, our experience is that many children already use strategies (Bierhoff, 1996, p. 32–33) which they have devised for themselves, although often these strategies are neither consistent nor organised mathematically.

Siegler (1989) writes that

> Children often know and use many strategies for solving a class of problems. Knowing diverse strategies adds to the children's flexibility in solving problems.

and

> Children's strategy choices may be less subject to conscious, rational control than often thought.

Our experience is that strategies need to be taught and organised, although often working from what the child already knows and uses. We have tried to use strategies which are developmental, for example, the strategy used to work out 7×8 by breaking down the single step to 5×8 plus 2×8 will be used for products such as 23×54 and later for algebraic expressions (Wigley, 1995).

Rote Learning with Tape Recorders

Use of music

There are tapes of times tables set to music. The rhythm and the tune help some children to learn tables but, in our experience, only a few.

The ARROW technique

The learner can use the ARROW technique (Lane and Chinn, 1986; Lane, 1992), as described in Chapter 4. This is a multisensory method using the learner's own voice recorded on tape. Tape recorders with a review button are easiest to use.

1. The child copies out the table facts he wishes to learn.
2. He records them onto tape, in groups of about four facts at a time, leaving a three to five second gap between each fact.
3. He puts on headphones and listens to the first fact. He stops the tape.
4. He says the fact and writes it. He rewinds the tape back to the start of the fact.
5. He listens again to the fact. He repeats steps 4 and 5 three or four more times.
6. He repeats steps, 3, 4 and 5 with the next fact.

The learner should experiment within this basic structure to find which multisensory procedure is the most effective. The listening frequency encourages sub–vocalising, which also reinforces learning. This can be a very effective method for many people, but not for all.

The process should be repeated several days in a row for the same set of facts. The learner will probably find that five to ten facts per session are enough, but success has a great motivating effect, so more may be possible.

Learning by Understanding

There are many advantages in learning times–table facts by understanding. The methods we advocate provide memory 'hooks' on which to hang several connected facts and some of them are introductions to procedures used later on in mathematics, such as in estimation, long multiplication and algebra (part of the developmental aspect of the programme). The strategies suggested here encourage the learner to look for patterns and interrelationships between numbers; they help develop a facility with numbers and an understanding of algorithms.

It is our experience that the basic structure for the strategy approach uses the times–table square, even though initial work is with separate tables. The square gives an overview of the task, encourages interrelating and can be used to illustrate gains in an encouraging way.

There are 121 facts in the table square (Figure 6.1). The size of this task can be reduced quite quickly and easily. This progress can be readily shown to the learner and contrasts with the normal approach of, 'Which tables do you know?'.

The teacher should ask the child to look at the table with him, to see several helpful things.

×	0	1	2	3	4	5	6	7	8	9	10
0	0	0	0	0	0	0	0	0	0	0	0
1	0	1	2	3	4	5	6	7	8	9	10
2	0	2	4	6	8	10	12	14	16	18	20
3	0	3	6	9	12	15	18	21	24	27	30
4	0	4	8	12	16	20	24	28	32	36	40
5	0	5	10	15	20	25	30	35	40	45	50
6	0	6	12	18	24	30	36	42	48	54	60
7	0	7	14	21	28	35	42	49	56	63	70
8	0	8	16	24	32	40	48	56	64	72	80
9	0	9	18	27	36	45	54	63	72	81	90
10	0	10	20	30	40	50	60	70	80	90	100

Figure 6.1 The times–table square

There are patterns, e.g. the column and row for the 10–times facts is 10, 20, 30, 40, 50, 60, 70, 80, 90, 100, the numbers from 1 to 10 with an extra digit, a 0, at the end (see also place value). If information can be seen to be in patterns or if it can be organised in patterns, it is easier to learn. There is also a sound pattern for the 10–times facts which links to the numbers one to nine: ten, twenty, thirty, forty, fifty, sixty, seventy, eighty, ninety – one of us (S.C.), uses 'tenty' as well as one hundred to reinforce the pattern, to emphasise the place value need for a special word for 100 and to refer to when in subtraction a hundred is renamed as 10 lots of 10 — 'tenty'. It's also fun.

There are other patterns in the square which the child can look at later. At this stage you are introducing an idea. You must use your professional judgement to see how far you can go at this stage without becoming counter–productive.

Numbers which do not appear

Not all the numbers between 0 and 100 appear, e.g. 43. This does not mean they are not important, just less used in this area of work.

Limiting the task

The numbers have a lowest value of 0, and a highest value of 100. So the child has some limits for the task and the task can be made to appear possible and, with a little understanding of how numbers relate to each other, even more possible. Indeed there is benefit in referring to the 100 square to put the values in context (for example, $7 \times 7 = 49$ which is 1 less than half of 100).

Remember that each time the child learns a set of facts, the task gets smaller. Furthermore, when he learns a fact from say the 5 times table, e.g. $5 \times 7 = 35$, he also learns $7 \times 5 = 35$, two facts for the price of one. This commutative property can be introduced quite early in the work.

You will note that the square does not include 11 times or 12 times. This is deliberate. Both can be taught, if deemed necessary, by strategies based on $11 = 10 + 1$ and $12 = 10 + 2$.

The Order in which to Learn the Facts

It seems sensible to learn first the facts which lead to the quickest gains and therefore encourage confidence. You may wish to change the order given in Table 6.1, but we suggest that the first three remain set as shown. Our order is based on:

- The facts that a dyslexic pupil is most likely to know ($1 \times$, $2 \times$, $5 \times$ and $10 \times$).
- The type of strategy advocated.

So by the time the child has learnt the times tables listed in Table 6.1, he has reduced his task from 121 facts to learn down to 25. These first 96 facts are the easiest to learn and you can quickly demonstrate how the child can start to make rapid gains.

Quick check–backs

Constant reviews are important. You are dealing with severe short–term, long–term and retrieval memory deficits. It is beneficial to revise and review material with the child quite often and, as with all skills, a lack of practice will reduce the skill level. This is especially so with dyslexics. We maintain that learning–check charts with headings 'Taught, Revised, Learnt' should also have a fourth column for use with dyslexics, 'Forgotten'.

Table 6.1 Times-table learning

Times table	Number of facts left to learn
0's	100
1's	81
10's	64
2's	49
5's	36
4's	25
9's	16
3's	9
6's	4

The Commutative Property

The commutative property is expressed algebraically as:

$$a \times b = b \times a$$

It can be introduced to a child as a way of getting double value for most of the times–table facts that he learns (not the squares).

One of the models or pictures for 'times' is area. Squared paper is useful for this model. To illustrate the commutative property a learner can draw a rectangle of 4×10, oriented to have the side of 10 units horizontal, then he can draw a second rectangle, 10×4, with the side of 10 units vertical. These areas can represent rooms or carpets. If it is not obvious that the two areas are the same, then the learner can count the squares or, if prone to miscounting, cut out the two rectangles and place them on top of one another to show they are the same size (Figure 6.2).

Another illustration of the same property can be achieved with Cuisenaire rods. So for 3×5 and 5×3, three five rods (yellows) can be put down to make a rectangle and then five three rods (light green) can be placed next to them to show that 3×5 and 5×3 cover the same area (and that three lots of five and five lots of three are the same) (Figure 6.3). Area is a powerful model for the developmental aspect of this work.

Another effective demonstration which focuses on the 'lots of' version of 'times' is to use counters in rows and columns. This additional 'picture' reinforces and develops further understanding of the concept of multiplication. For example, 12 counters can be placed down as three rows of four or as four rows of three (Figure 6.4).

Each of these methods looks at a different facet of multiplication and each has future currency; this suggests that all three should be used to demonstrate and reinforce the concept. Examples of future currency are using area to provide a picture of multiplications such as $(a + b)(a + 3b)$, and extending 5×8 from five lots of eight to six lots of eight.

You have then demonstrated that 4×10 is exactly the same as 10×4, that $3 \times 8 = 8 \times 3$, that $3 \times 4 = 4 \times 3$, and so on. Each fact the child learns can have the order changed round, giving him another fact—free! You may wish to digress to discuss squares, such as 4×4—judge the readiness of the learner(s).

Figure 6.2 Using area

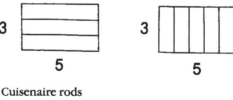

Figure 6.3 Using Cuisenaire rods

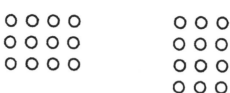

Figure 6.4 Using counters

Learning the Table Square

Zero: 0

Zero is an important concept, so time should be spent establishing that the child has some understanding of zero; zero, nought, nothing—as ever, the language should be varied.

In later numeracy work the child will meet examples such as 304×23 or $406 \div 2$, where the process of multiplying a zero, multiplying by zero or dividing into zero is used. You can start by explaining the meaning of 3×0 and so on: 3×0 means:

- 3 times 0.
- Three lots of 0 giving the answer 0.
- 0×3 is the same, zero lots of 3 is also zero.

Two suggested teaching models

- Talk about having nothing in one pocket, nothing in two pockets and so on.
- Use empty 35 mm film tubes and discuss how much in one empty tube, two empty tubes and so on.

The child should then realise that any number times 0 equals 0 and 0 times any number equals 0. So

$$1 \times 0 = 0 \qquad \text{and} \qquad 0 \times 1 = 0$$
$$2 \times 0 = 0 \qquad\qquad\qquad 0 \times 2 = 0$$
$$3 \times 0 = 0 \qquad\qquad\qquad 0 \times 3 = 0$$

Children like massive examples such as a million lots of zero or zero lots of a million—it impresses much more than zero lots of two, even if the result is the same!

Now you can tell the child to look at the table square, and can say,

'You will see a row of 0s across the top, and a column of 0s down the left hand side. You have just learnt your first 21 facts.'

Progress check

If you want the child to keep a check on his progress use the table square in Figure 6.1, copy it and hand it to the child to act as his record of progress. Tell him to shade in all the zero facts—the top row and the first column. You will probably find the child needs a second table square to keep as a 'clean' copy.

One: 1

One is the basic unit: 4×1 means:

- 4 times 1.
- or 4 lots of 1 gives the answer 4.
- 1×4 is the same.
- Any number times 1 equals that number.
- 1 times any number equals that number.

Counters are quite a good manipulative aid for demonstration (they can also be used on an overhead projector), or for the child to use to understand 'one lot of' or 'n lots of'. Money can also be introduced here in the form of pennies. So $7 \times 1 = 7$ (seven lots of one) and $1 \times 6 = 6$ (one lot of six) and so on.

The concept being introduced here is summed up by the equations:

$$n \times 1 = n \text{ and } 1 \times n = n$$

Again tell the child to look back at the table square and see that the 1 times–table facts appear twice, first written across, second row down; then written down, second column in.

$$
\begin{aligned}
1 \times 0 &= 0 \\
1 \times 1 &= 1 \\
1 \times 2 &= 2 \\
1 \times 3 &= 3 \\
1 \times 4 &= 4 \\
1 \times 5 &= 5 \\
1 \times 6 &= 6 \\
1 \times 7 &= 7 \\
1 \times 8 &= 8 \\
1 \times 9 &= 9 \\
1 \times 10 &= 10
\end{aligned}
$$

Again explain and demonstrate the important fact that the number you multiply by 1 does not change in value (the use of the phrase 'in value' could be considered pedantic, but it is important not to teach information which has to be 'unlearned' at a later date, e.g. in fractions). When 1 multiplies a number it leaves that number with the same value it had before.

$$
\begin{aligned}
0 \times 1 &= 0 \\
1 \times 1 &= 1 \\
2 \times 1 &= 2 \\
3 \times 1 &= 3 \\
&\vdots \\
10 \times 1 &= 10
\end{aligned}
$$

The child has now learnt 19 new facts (he had already learnt 0×1 and 1×0), making a total so far of 40 out of 121—almost one–third.

Progress check

The child can now shade in the $1 \times$ facts. He shades in the second row and the second column. These are the numbers 1 to 10 across and down.

Ten: 10

1, 2, 3, 4, 5, 6, 7, 8, 9 are single digits, 10 has two digits, a 1 followed by a 0. The 0 means no units, and the 1 means 1 ten. Hopefully the child has retained earlier work on place value from Chapter 4. A moment's reinforcement will check this.

Ten is a key number in this chapter. The 10 times–table facts will be extended to teach the child how to work out the 5 times facts and the 9 times facts. Thus it is well worth reviewing the child's understanding of 10 and place value.

So explain that 20 has a 0 for 0 units and a 2 for 2 tens, 2×10 means:

- 2 times 10 equals 20.
- 2 lots of 10 are 20.

There is an easy pattern to show:

A	BB
1×10	$= 10$
2×10	$= 20$
3×10	$= 30$
4×10	$= 40$
5×10	$= 50$
6×10	$= 60$
7×10	$= 70$
8×10	$= 80$
9×10	$= 90$
10×10	$= 100$

- The numbers under A are the first 10 units.
- The numbers under BB are the first 10 tens.

Get the child to listen to the pattern as he says the 10 times table and sees the connection: e.g. six tens are sixty, and nine tens are ninety. Even two tens are twenty gives a two–letter clue. We find that a brief digression to 'twoty', 'threety' and 'fivety' reinforces rather than confuses.

This pattern can be practised with trading money, always remembering to have the child say as he trades one 1p coin for one 10p coin, 'one times ten is ten'. He then trades two 1p coins for two 10p coins, and says 'two times ten is twenty'. This continues until he trades 10 times 10p coins for ten 10p coins, and says 'ten times ten is tenty'; there is no such word of course and a special word is used instead—hundred. A hundred, 100, has three digits, the only number with three digits in the table square. A hundred pence has its own coin, a pound, so $10 \times 10p = 100p = £1$.

There are other ways to practise the units/tens relationship.

- Single cocktail sticks, and bundles of 10 cocktail sticks:

  1 stick × 10 = 1 bundle = 10
  2 sticks × 10 = 2 bundles = 20
  3 sticks × 10 = 3 bundles = 30

each time '10 times bigger' means exchanging a 10–stick bundle for a single stick.

- Cuisenaire rods:

  1 unit × 10 = 1 of ten strips = 10
  2 units × 10 = 2 of ten strips = 20
  3 units × 10 = 3 of ten strips = 30
  and so on (Figure 6.5).

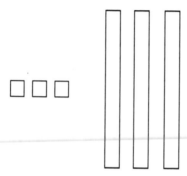

Figure 6.5

- Base–ten (Dienes) blocks or a metre rule can be used to add to the development of the idea of the 10 times table.

A useful illustration from the child's (probable) experience is the idea of change machines, one giving 1p coins and one giving 10p coins and pressing, for example, the '4' button on each; one gives 4p, the other gives 40p.

Remember that some materials are proportional in size to their value, e.g. Cuisenaire rods; some are proportional in number, e.g. bundles of sticks; some are proportional by volume, e.g. base–ten blocks; some are proportional by length, e.g. a metre rule; some are representative of value, e.g. 1p and 10p coins. Using a mixture of these *and the numbers themselves* ensures development from concrete to symbolic under-standing.

Some 'everyday' examples may be used to provide reinforcement:

- How many legs on 10 cows?
- How many wheels on 10 bikes?
- How many pence in 10 5p coins?
- How many legs on 10 spiders?
- How many sides on 10 50p coins?

Progress check

If the child thinks that he has learnt the 10 times facts then he can shade in the end column and the bottom row of his table square, the 10 times facts. Filling in the tens column and the tens row should remind the child that for each times fact he can write the numbers in either order, so, for example, $2 \times 10 = 10 \times 2$. This means that, if he remembers that $10 \times 3 = 30$, then he knows $3 \times 10 = 30$, one fact from the 3 times table and one fact from the 10 times table—two for the price of one! The commutative property should be reinforced frequently.

So far the child has learnt 57 facts, almost one–half. He has 64 to learn.

Two: 2

First, as for each number, the lessons should look at the concept of the number and its interrelationships with other numbers. There can be some demonstrations and discussions and some information on 2, such as:

- Two is one more than one.
- It is twice as big as one.
- It is an even number.
- Even numbers are numbers that share into two equal parts, e.g.

    8 divides (shares) into two lots of 4:
    $8 \div 2 = 4$ or $8 = 4 + 4$.
    20 divides into two lots of 10:
    $20 \div 2 = 10$ or $20 = 10 + 10$.

Each child can try equal sharing with a random pile of pennies, sharing them out, one at a time, into two piles. If the two piles are equal, then the child started with an even number. If there is one penny left over, then he started with an odd number.

- Even numbers from 1 to 10 are 2, 4, 6, 8, 10.
- Odd numbers from 1 to 10 are 1, 3, 5, 7, 9.

A useful extra fact (generalisation) here is that any even number ends in 2, 4, 6, 8, or 0, and any odd number ends in 1, 3, 5, 7, or 9. Some review/revision questions can be used, such as:

- Which of these numbers is even? 2341, 4522, 57399, 34, 70986, 11112, 335792.
- Which of them divides evenly by two?
- If the pattern for even numbers is
  2 4 6 8 10 12 14 16 18 20 22 24 26 28 30,

  continue the pattern to 102.

The 2 times table

1×2	=	2
2×2	=	4
3×2	=	6
4×2	=	8
5×2	=	10
6×2	=	12
7×2	=	14
8×2	=	16
9×2	=	18
10×2	=	20

Notice:

- The end number pattern repeats 2, 4, 6, 8, 0.
- The answers are the same as in the even number table the child did earlier.

The first four facts can be learnt as a chant:

- Two, four, six, eight, who(m) do we appreciate?

This chant brings the child to almost half way in learning the 2 times table.

Often it is useful to have reference points in calculations. The child already has a start reference point, $1 \times 2 = 2$, and an end reference point, $10 \times 2 = 20$. The middle reference point has its value on the child's hands—two hands, each with five fingers, two lots of five fingers, ten fingers, $2 \times 5 = 10$ or $5 \times 2 = 10$. It also is illustrated by $5 \times 2p = 10p$, a trading operation, where five 2p coins are traded for one 10p coin. So $5 \times 2 = 10$ is the middle reference point on which to build the remaining facts 6×2 to 10×2.

The answers for 6×2 to 9×2 have the same last digits as the first four facts, 12, 14, 16, 18—the child needs to be shown the pattern. They have the same digit pattern because 6×2 is one more 2 than 5×2 and 7×2 is two more 2s than 5×2, etc., and because 5×2 has 0 in its units digit column. This is the first use of the strategy of a middle reference point, which in this case combines with the strategy of breaking down numbers to build up on known facts.

Therefore, if the child can remember the reference value $5 \times 2 = 10$, he can quickly work out, say, 8×2. If 8 is $5 + 3$, so 8×2 is five lots of 2 plus three lots of 2, so $8 \times 2 = (5 \times 2) + (3 \times 2) = 10 + 6 = 16$.

There are three useful and regularly occurring strategies here:

- Breaking down a number into numbers from the child's repertoire (usually 1, 2, 5, 10) e.g. 8 into 5 and 3, so that these facts are used and extended.
- The use of a reference point in the middle of the task. A child will claim to 'know' the 2 times table. When asked for 7×2 he begins at 2 and works up 2, 4, 6, 8, 10, 12, 14. A middle reference point means that the child can start at 10.

- The use of 'lots of' for times leads to six lots of 2 being seen as one more lot (of 2) than five lots of 2. This mixed image of multiplication to include repeated addition and clustered addition will be used again later.

Strategies need practice and reinforcement

Some practical work can be built around coins and trading, using a 10p coin for tens and 2p coins for two. The learner trades five lots of 2p for a 10p coin to reinforce the middle reference point and the repeating 2, 4, 6, 8 pattern. An example with 8×2 is to take eight 2p coins, take out five of these and trade them for a 10p coin. This leaves one 10p coin and three 2p coins, which combine as 10 and 3×2 to make 16. This reinforces the image of 8×2 breaking into clusters of 5×2 and 3×2. Trading is a procedure used again in addition and subtraction.

Five: 5

As with all the times tables, the first step is to establish a basic understanding of the number, in this case 5.

Some information about 5

- The key fact is that five is half–way from zero to ten. The learner can be reminded how five was used as a half–way reference point in the 2 times table, i.e. five is half of ten.
- Ten divided by two is five. It can be written in numbers as: $10 \div 2 = 5$.
- Five is an odd number.
- Five can look like 5 or 11111 or V or $^{10}/_2$ or $10 \div 2$.

The 5 times table

		Notice:
1×5	$= 5$	• The child knows the start reference point $1 \times 5 = 5$,
2×5	$= 10$	and the end reference point $10 \times 5 = 50$.
3×5	$= 15$	• There is a pattern in the last 5 digits: 5, 0, 5, 0, 5, 0,
4×5	$= 20$	5, 0, 5, 0.
5×5	$= 25$	
6×5	$= 30$	• This means another pattern: an odd number times
7×5	$= 35$	five gives an answer which ends in 5 and an even
8×5	$= 40$	number times five gives an answer which ends in 0.
9×5	$= 45$	
10×5	$= 50$	

It is useful to set up a comparison of the 10 and 5 times tables by writing the answers side by side. Looking at the answers illustrates the relationship between them, i.e. each 5 times answer is half of each 10 times answer, e.g. $6 \times 5 = 30$ and $6 \times 10 = 60$, and 30 is half of 60. It is possible to work out the fives by taking the tens and halving the answers. So, for 8 $\times 5$: $8 \times 10 = 80$ and half of 80 is 40. As a check, 8 is even, so the answer ends in 0. Again, for 5×5: $5 \times 10 = 50$ and half of 50 is 25. As a check, 5 is odd, so the answer ends in 5.

This strategy of looking at the last digit helps reinforce the child's attention on reviewing an answer and its validity.

Some practical work

The learner can practise halving tens by trading 10p and 5p coins; for each 10p trade one 5p. Each time you must help the child rehearse the process:

> Seven times five. Start at seven times ten. Half of seventy is thirty plus five, that is thirty–five. Seven was odd. The answer ends in a five. That checks.

This can be reinforced by taking seven 5p coins and explaining that they are worth half as much as seven 10p coins.

If the child has difficulty in dividing 30, 50, 70 and 90 by 2, remind the child how to break numbers down, e.g. 50 is $40 + 10$. Halve 40 (answer 20) and halve 10 (answer 5), so that $20 + 5 = 25$.

Again you may have to remind the child how it is sometimes easier to use two small, quick steps than to struggle with one difficult step.

Other materials may be used to reinforce this relationship between five and ten; these include Cuisenaire rods, 5p and 10p coins and 35mm film tubes with 5 or 10 items inside. This last material emphasises the 'lots of' aspect of multiplication, used when extending knowledge of, say five 'lots of' to six or seven 'lots of'.

As before, the target is for the learner to be able to recall a 5 times table fact from memory or work out an answer quickly. Starting from 1×5 and counting up to the required answer is not the target. When the learner can remember or work out the 5 times facts, then he can shade in the five row and column on his table square. The times–table task is reduced to 36 facts.

Four: 4

You should give an overview of the properties of four, relating four to other numbers. The most important of these relationships are:

- $4 = 2 \times 2$.
- Four is twice two.
- Four is four units, 4, IV, 1111.
- Four is two times two.

This last relationship is the basis of the method advocated for the 4 times table. The method is building on knowledge the child has already learnt and makes use of the interrelationships of numbers. The child is taught to double the 2 times table. We have found that effective memory triggers have been to call this the 'two–two' method or the 'double–double' method. You have to establish the strategy using materials such as 2p coins, set up to show the 2 times table alongside the 4 times table, e.g.

- 2×2 compared with 2×4.
- 3×2 compared with 3×4.

The 2 times table is shown with single piles of 2p coins and the 4 times table is shown with double piles of 2p coins. Also, 35 mm film tubes may be used to reinforce the idea of comparing three lots of 2 with three lots of 4. The child can see 'three lots of' and it should be possible to convince him that he ends up with twice as much from three tubes with 4p in as he does from three tubes with 2p in. (This is a similar strategy to comparing the 5 times and 10 times tables.)

Once the idea of the strategy is established, you can move on to comparing the answers to the 2 times and 4 times tables in the same way that the 5 times and 10 times tables were compared.

1×2	=	2	4	=	1×4
2×2	=	4	8	=	2×4
3×2	=	6	12	=	3×4
4×2	=	8	16	=	4×4
5×2	=	10	20	=	5×4
6×2	=	12	24	=	6×4
7×2	=	14	28	=	7×4
8×2	=	16	32	=	8×4
9×2	=	18	36	=	9×4
10×2	=	20	40	=	10×4

(It is worth reminding the learner that he already knows 0×4, 1×4, 2×4, 5×4, 9×4 and 10×4 from the tables he has learned previously.)

1×4 to 5×4 are achieved by doubling within the known range of the 2 times table, e.g. the learner can manage 4×4 as $2 \times 4 = 8$ and $2 \times 8 = 16$ and thus $4 \times 4 = 16$. Some practice to reinforce this 'known' pattern may be needed.

6×4 and 7×4 are relatively easy since there is no carrying to complicate the second doubling:

6×2	= 12	12×2	= 24
7×2	= 14	14×2	= 28

The second doubling of 8×4 and 9×4 can be done via breakdown strategies, using 8 as $5 + 3$ and 9 as $5 + 4$ or $10 - 1$. Alternatively, 9×4 can be done as 4×9 from the 9 times table.

It may be good practice for the learner to give you the middle step in practice sessions so that 7×4 is delivered in two stages: 14 then 28.

When the 4 times facts are shaded in on the table square the learner has just 25 facts to learn.

Three, six, seven and nine: 3, 6, 7 and 9

The strategy used for these times–table facts is the same and is very much a part of the developmental nature of this programme. The strategy is to break down a 'difficult' number into two 'easier' numbers. So 3 becomes $2 + 1$, 6 is $5 + 1$, 7 is $5 + 2$ and 9 is $10 - 1$. This procedure is used in long multiplications such as 35×78, where 35 is broken down to $30 + 5$ and two partial products are then recombined for 35×78. Whilst this example is the procedure advocated by many texts, most people do not need to use it for easier numbers such as 6 or 7. We have extrapolated the method back to help with basic fact knowledge. This also serves as a first introduction to the area model for partial products in multiplication and hopefully sets this idea for future work in other multiplications such as fractions and quadratic equations. The figures 6.7 to 6.10 illustrate the model and its developmental property.

Nine: 9

There is an easy method to work out the 9 times facts using fingers. If we were being rigidly principled, we might not mention a method which is radically different from the other methods and strategies mentioned in this book. However, working with dyslexics can make you very pragmatic and eclectic, on the basis that the gains in the child's self–confidence may outweigh any doubts about the academic validity of a particular technique.

So, if you want to know the answer to 4×9, for example, put the fingers of both hands down on a surface and tuck back the fourth (4) finger from the left (Figure 6.6). The answer lies each side of this fourth finger, the tens to the left, three fingers means 30, and the units to the right, six fingers, giving an answer of 36.

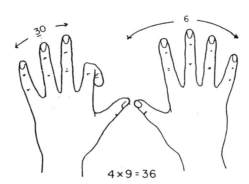

$4 \times 9 = 36$

Figure 6.6

However, we prefer a strategy with potential for further use. Therefore, the strategy we advocate is based on estimation, the particularily useful estimation of ten for nine, and the subsequent refinement of this estimation. The strategy could also be perceived as a break down/partial products method, with a subtraction of the partial products rather than the normal addition.

The first step is to establish the principle of the method, that is that nine is one less than ten. This is helped by examining nine.

- Nine is nine units.
- Nine is one less than ten.
- $9 = 10 - 1$ and $10 = 9 + 1$.

The closeness in value of nine and ten can be demonstrated by showing the child a pile of ten 1p coins and asking him to say, without counting them, if there are nine or ten. It does not matter which the child guesses. It is the uncertainty that is important; the nearness of nine and ten makes it hard to give an answer with certainty. The demonstration can move on to Cuisenaire rods. A ten rod (orange) and a nine rod (blue) are placed side by side. A one rod (white) is added to the nine rod to show that the difference is one. This is presented in numerals as

$$9 + 1 = 10 \qquad 10 - 1 = 9$$

This demonstration is now extended to show how to estimate and refine from the 10 times table to the 9 times table.

Two nine rods are placed on a flat surface. Two ten rods are placed alongside and two whites are added to the nine rods to show that the difference in value is two. The process is repeated to develop the pattern that n nine rods are n ones less than n ten rods. In numbers:

$$2 \times 10 = 20 \qquad 20 - 2 = 18 \qquad 2 \times 9 = 18$$
$$3 \times 10 = 30 \qquad 30 - 3 = 27 \qquad 3 \times 9 = 27$$
$$4 \times 10 = 40 \qquad 40 - 4 = 36 \qquad 4 \times 9 = 36$$

Thus any 9 times fact can be worked out from a 10 times fact, for example, 6×9 is worked out as:

$$6 \times 10 = 60 \qquad 60 - 6 = 54 \qquad 6 \times 9 = 54$$

This is verbalised as

Six times nine is six less than six times ten. Six times ten is sixty, so, six times nine must be fifty something.

The 'something', the unit digit, can be found by subtracting 6 from 60, or 6 from 10, using number bonds for 10. It can be found by counting backwards from 60, although this is a very difficult task for some dyslexics, or a further pattern can be used:

$1 \times 9 = 9$
$2 \times 9 = 18$
$3 \times 9 = 27$
$4 \times 9 = 36$
$5 \times 9 = 45$
$6 \times 9 = 54$
$7 \times 9 = 63$
$8 \times 9 = 72$
$9 \times 9 = 81$
$10 \times 9 = 90$

Notice:
The units column digits go from 9 to 0, whilst the tens column digits go from 0 to 9. This results in the sum of the two digits in each answer always being 9, e.g. for 63, $6 + 3 = 9$.

So the child can work through the following process for, say, 4×9.

$4 \times 10 = 40$
4×9 is smaller and must be 'thirty something';

the 'something' must be the number which adds on to 3 to make 9, that is 6. So the answer is 36. For 6×9, again.

$6 \times 10 = 60$
$6 \times 9 = 5\square$
$5 + \square = 9$
$\square = 4$ so $6 \times 9 = 54$

The child may think that this is a long process, but with regular practice it becomes quicker. Also, as the child becomes more adept, he starts to short–circuit the process and use it to top off a half–known answer. In other words, the strategy provides a memory hook for the child so that he is not left floundering when faced with an 'impossible' question.

When the child has grasped this strategy, he may shade in the 9 times column and row. He now has 16 facts left to attack.

10×7 -1×7 $=$ 9×7

9 x
= 10 x minus 1 x

Figure 6.7

Three: 3; Six: 6

The 3 times and 6 times tables share the same, important strategy. The 3 times is broken down into 2 times plus 1 times and the 6 times is broken down into 5 times + 1 times. Later on, when the student has to calculate products such as 23×45, the breaking down strategy (23 times as 20 times + 3 times) will be the most likely procedure for all students, that is including those who can answer 6×7 in one go.

The language of multiplication can be quite abstract. 'Four times three' requires the student to know the code. An alternative wording, 'four lots of three' is more concrete. This latter wording also lends itself to the concept of $3n = 2n + n$ and $5n + n = 6n$.

(The same concept applies for $5n + 2n = 7n$ and $5n + 3n = 8n$.)

$2 \times 4 + 1 \times 4 = 3 \times 4$

$2 \times 8 + 1 \times 8 = 3 \times 8$

3 x
= 2 x plus 1 x

Figure 6.8

$5 \times 6 + 1 \times 6 = 6 \times 6$

6 x
= 5 x plus 1 x

Figure 6.9

So the 3 times table is calculated by taking a 2 times–table fact and adding on one more multiplicand, for example

$3 \times 6 = 2 \times 6 + 6 = 12 + 6 = 18$
$3 \times 8 = 2 \times 8 + 8 = 16 + 8 = 24$

and the 6 times table takes a 5 times–table fact and adds on one more multiplicand, for example;

$6 \times 6 = 5 \times 6 + 6 = 30 + 6 = 36$
$6 \times 7 = 5 \times 7 + 7 = 35 + 7 = 42$

Seven: 7; Eight: 8

The target has now been lowered to four facts or three separate facts:

$7 \times 7, 7 \times 8$ and 8×8.

These three are often perceived as the hardest to learn, but there are some helpful strategies here, too. The 5 times facts are extended to 7 times facts by adding on the relevant 2 times fact.

- Show, using counters, that 8×5 (via 8×10 as revision) is the same as 5×8.
- Use film tubes or Cuisenaire rods to show that seven lots of 8 are two more lots of 8 than five lots of 8.

The film tubes emphasise the move from 'five lots of' to 'seven lots of' whilst the contents (8) are seen to be what is added on to the 40. This should help explain the strategy and avoid the child obtaining 47, the most likely error.

There is a pattern for the hardest fact, 8×7. This pattern, which appeals more to adults than to children, is seen if the normal order of presentation is reversed:

5678 $56 = 7 \times 8$

(This order occurs one other time in the table square with $12 = 3 \times 4$.)

We hypothesise that children do not relate to $56 = 7 \times 8$ because facts are normally presented in the $7 \times 8 = 56$ direction. The $56 = 7 \times 8$ direction makes the fact more of a division fact than a multiplication fact. If we expect children to adapt to division and include it in their repertoire of mathematical concepts, it might be wise to teach times–table facts in this reverse format as well.

7×7 and 7×8 can be taught by a similar sequence, that is $5 \times 7 = 35$ and $2 \times 7 = 14$, so $7 \times 7 = 35 + 14 = 49$ and $5 \times 8 = 40$ and $2 \times 8 = 16$, so $7 \times 8 = 40 + 16 = 56$.

5x8   + 2x8 =   7x8

$7 \times$
$= 5 \times$ plus $2 \times$

Figure 6.10

The comparison of $7 \times 7 = 49$ (1 less than 50, which is half a 100) with $10 \times 10 = 100$ is interesting, and makes a useful cutting up exercise with squared paper. This can be extended to build up 7×7 from $5 \times 5 + 2$ $(5 \times 2) + 2 \times 2$, although $5 \times 7 + 2 \times 7$ is likely to be easier.

Again, you are showing how to build up and break down an answer.

Final notes

The squares, 3×3, 4×4, 5×5, 6×6, 7×7, and 8×8 are connected to the products of the numbers 'each side' of them, that is 2×4, 3×5, 4×6, 5×7, 6×8 and 7×9 respectively by

$a \times a = (a - 1)(a + 1) + 1$

$3 \times 3 = (2 \times 4) + 1$;	$3 \times 3 = 9$;	$2 \times 4 = 8$
$4 \times 4 = (3 \times 5) + 1$;	$4 \times 4 = 16$;	$3 \times 5 = 15$
$5 \times 5 = (4 \times 6) + 1$;	$5 \times 5 = 25$;	$4 \times 6 = 24$
$6 \times 6 = (5 \times 7) + 1$;	$6 \times 6 = 36$;	$5 \times 7 = 35$
$7 \times 7 = (6 \times 8) + 1$;	$7 \times 7 = 49$;	$6 \times 8 = 48$
$8 \times 8 = (7 \times 9) + 1$;	$8 \times 8 = 64$;	$7 \times 9 = 63$

8×8 can be explored in terms of powers of 2:

$8 \times 8 = 8 \times 4 \times 2 = 4 \times 4 \times 2 \times 2 = 16 \times 2 \times 2 = 32 \times 2 = 64$

6×6 can be explored in terms of three dozen:

$6 \times 6 = 3 \times 2 \times 6 = 3 \times 12 = 36$

In these strategies you are introducing factors, as you did with the two–two method.

Summary

In this chapter we have introduced the idea of teaching strategies to learn/work out the times–tables facts. We believe that this approach is pragmatic, since few dyslexics can rote–learn this information. It has the added bonus of teaching several useful mathematical processes and concepts, which include estimation, factors, that number values are interrelated, and partial products, that is the strategy of breaking down numbers into convenient and appropriate parts. We hope that a child may, through these strategies, learn to produce quick answers for the times–table facts, whilst having a back–up strategy for those occasions when the mind goes blank. We have also tried to introduce some flexibility in the methods described, ever mindful of our basic premise that all children do not learn in the same way.

It is worth repeating the cautionary note concerning division facts. We think that so many children perceive these facts as the *times* table facts that they forget that they are also the basic *division* facts.

A fuller treatment of these methods is covered in What to do When you can't Learn the Times Tables by Steve Chinn which is also available on CD-Rom (see Appendix 1).

Chapter 7
Computational Procedures for Addition and Subtraction

The child's knowledge of basic facts concerning addition and subtraction can now be extended to longer computations. Good teaching will always help a dyslexic, at least to reduce learned difficulties (rather than learning difficulties), but you still need to understand and adjust to your pupil to maximise the chances of effective learning (Miles and Miles, 1992).

Our experience of dyslexics leads us to think that some apparent deficits occur because a procedure appears to have no reference or rationale which makes the knowledge seem relevant or distinguishable. For example, directions which rely solely on 'left' and 'right' instructions are less likely to be remembered than directions which include landmarks. The landmarks make the directions more 'real' and concrete.

Addition and subtraction can be taught by multisensory methods and these methods should achieve a double aim. First, the child has the benefit of input through more than one sense and, second, the child has concrete experiences to which he can relate the abstract symbols called numbers. Thus the child may learn to understand an algorithm rather than just to apply it mechanically. Kennedy (1975) refers to research which supports the seemingly obvious statement that children perform better when using algorithms which they understand. Madsen et al. (1995) refer to the benefits of teaching concepts. The use of mulltisensory teaching in mathematics makes understanding more likely, especially if the materials are used so as to give concrete meaning to the concept.

There have been, however, some cautionary words. Hart (1989) warns that children do not always relate the 'bricks' to the 'sums'. Indeed some may not be ready for this transition. Thus the concrete materials must be accompanied by the written symbols and the teacher must look for the connection being taken on board. Teachers must also remember that children do not all have the same cognitive style and therefore should be encouraged to use global overviews, estimates, detailed algorithms, documentation and evaluation (checking), remembering that some of these operations are more related to one end of the learning and cognitive style spectrum than to the other.

Finally, we believe there is great value in teaching addition and subtraction together. We feel that the two procedures reinforce the understanding of the algorithms, especially the renaming process.

Estimation

Estimates and evaluations should be encouraged as they serve several purposes.

- Some dyslexics are likely to transpose numbers so that, for example, 39 becomes 93. Estimates and evaluations reinforce the need to check answers (before and after they have been calculated) and help the pupil to see his possible errors. We have found that checks made after a break from the work are often more effective than immediate checks.
- Estimates and evaluations should be used to check results from calculators, where dyslexics are prone to press the wrong keys (possibly also in the wrong sequence).
- Estimates are often a real–life mathematics calculation. For example, a driver may only need to know roughly how many litres of petrol he can buy for £10 rather than to have an answer to three decimal places.
- Estimates can (and should) use less threatening numbers, requiring the learner to interrelate numbers again.

Addition

Work on the computational procedures for addition should be preceded by a review of place value. You need to remember the dyslexic's need for continual reminders and memory refreshers. Overlearning is an important part of any long–term tuition plan and re–establishing the precursors of a new topic reduces the sources of potential failure. An example is:

$$
\begin{array}{r}
38 \\
+\ 27 \\
\hline
515
\end{array}
$$

The child adds the unit digits to obtain 15, but fails to realise that the 1 represents a 'ten' and should be added into the tens column. Errors such as these are less likely if the child is taught to preview and review the value of his answers. Again, you should be trying to encourage the child to be flexible in his cognitive processes.

The use of concrete materials adds a multisensory dimension to the teaching. Teachers need to keep in mind the level of abstraction of the materials being used and to remember to link the concrete to the symbols.

A developmental programme for teaching addition and subtraction

The programme is illustrated by two problems:

253 + 312   and   458 + 376

which are added and then used as subtractions;

565 – 253   and   834 – 458

Start with 253 + 312.

Stage 1. You need a place column card, some base–ten blocks and a sheet of paper on which to write the sum as it progresses.

Set the numbers up on a place–value board in base–ten blocks (Figure 7.1a). Write the sum on the paper. Tell the child to add (combine/put together) the unit blocks (3 + 2), which gives him 5 unit blocks. Write 5 in the units column of the written sum.

Now tell the child to add the ten blocks (5 + 1), which gives him 6 ten blocks in the tens column. Write 6 in the tens column of the written sum.

Move to the hundred blocks and tell the child to add/put together the hundred blocks (2 + 3), which gives him 5 hundred blocks. Write 5 in the hundreds column of the written sum.

Look at the whole answer and identify it as 565.

Stage 2. Repeat the process with coins, again writing each step of the sum on the paper, identifying the answer as 565.

You can discuss the idea of adding and putting together, leading the discussion into the idea of taking apart, subtracting the numbers, in this case back to the original two (unequal) parts.

Set up the problem 565 – 253.

Stage 1. Set up the 565 on a place value card in base–ten blocks. Tell the child that he is going to take away 253 from the 565. Write the problem on paper. The answer to the subtraction will be the number left behind. Take 3 unit cubes down the card, leaving 2 unit cubes. Write this on the paper. Now tell the child to take away/subtract 5 ten blocks, leaving 1 ten block. Write down this step. Then the child takes away 2 hundred blocks, leaving 3 hundred blocks. Write down this step.

The child should look at the card and the paper and see that there is 253 in base–ten blocks at the bottom and that there is 312 left at the top of the place value card and that the written sum mirrors this.

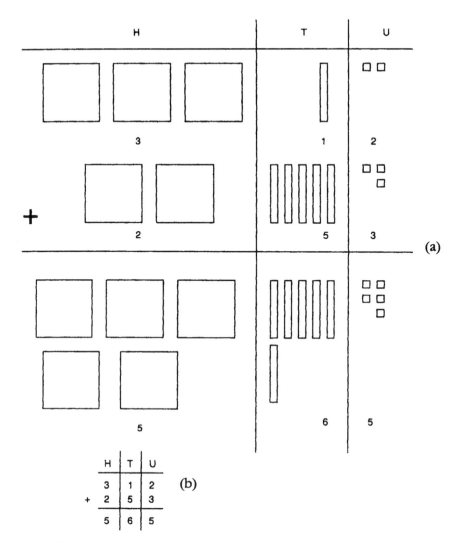

Figure 7.1

Stage 2. The same procedure is followed using coins instead of base–ten blocks. The subtraction problem and its answers should be reviewed and related to the equivalent addition problem.

Now set up the second problem, 458 + 376.

Stage 1. Set the numbers up on a place–value board in base–ten blocks (Figure 7.2a). Tell the child to add (combine/put together) the unit blocks (8 + 6), which gives him 14 unit blocks. You can then discuss this, looking at 14 as four units and one ten. The ten unit blocks can be traded for one ten block. This is also shown in symbols, so the child relates the written algorithm to the blocks (Figure 7.2b). Write this step on paper.

Then tell the child to add the 10 blocks (5 + 7 + 1). Encourage the same type of discussion, i.e. the child has 13 ten blocks, which should be viewed as 100 and 30, i.e. one 100 and three 10s. The 10 ten blocks are traded for 1 hundred block and the operation is written in symbols (digits) so that the child relates the written algorithm to the concrete manipulative aids (Figure 7.2c). Write this step on paper.

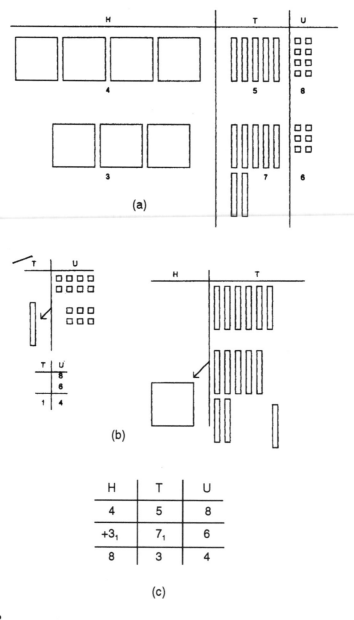

H	T	U
4	5	8
+3₁	7₁	6
8	3	4

(c)

Figure 7.2

Finally, the hundred column is considered. The blocks show 4 + 3 + 1 in 100 square blocks, giving a total of 8 hundred blocks. Then, take the child through the algorithm again, just in symbols, reminding him of the blocks as each place value is added. Write this step on paper.

Look at the answer and identify it as 834.

Stage 2. Repeat the process with coins, explaining how a maximum of 9 pennies is allowed in the units column and the consequent need to trade lots of 10 × 1p for 1 × 10p and 10 × 10p for 1 × 100p (£1) (Figure 7.3).

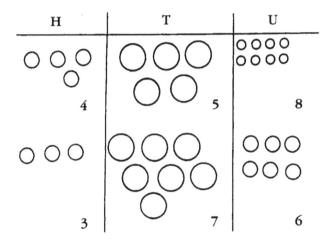

Figure 7.3

Now the addition can be reversed as an example of subtraction. The problem is 834 – 458.

Stage 1. Set up the problem on a place value card with base–ten blocks, so there are 8 hundred blocks, 3 ten blocks and 4 unit blocks. Tell the child that he has to take away 458, that is 4 hundred blocks, 5 ten blocks and 8 unit cubes and identify the number left. Each step with the blocks should be written (as numbers) on paper.

Tell the child to start in the units column and take away 8 unit cubes. Obviously he cannot do this with only 4 unit cubes available. The subsequent discussion can look back at the addition when 10 unit cubes were traded for 1 ten block and the need to reverse this for this subtraction which is the reverse of addition. (Sometimes S.C. keeps the traded blocks from the addition ready to use in the subtraction, adding further evidence to the interconnection). Thus a ten block is traded for 10 unit cubes and the written version mirrors this.

A similar process deals with the subtraction in the tens column. The trading is now to take 1 hundred block and trade it for 10 ten blocks (a 'tenty'). The subtraction in the hundreds column is straightforward. For both these steps the written version should mirror the concrete materials.

It is also a method which enables the breakdown/conservation of the number to be discussed. Thus, the 834 has become

7 hundreds	700
12 tens	120
14 units	14
which add up to	834

Stage 2. The procedure is followed using coins.

A final example addresses one of the most frequent sources of error, that is problems which include a zero. For example, 507 + 322 and 603 – 247. The reader will be able to extend the previous examples to cover this important extension.

Estimation

In an addition problem like the one above (458 + 376) the child can be taught various accuracy levels of estimation. At the simplest level the sum is reduced to the hundred digits (400 + 300). At a more sophisticated level the sum can be presented as 450 + 350 + 30, with the child seeing 458 as approximately 450, but with 8 left over. The 376 is seen as 350 and 25. The 8 from 458 and the 25 from 376 are combined to give an estimate of 30 and the total 450 + 350 + 30 =830.

The grasshopper (see Chapter 2) may even tackle the complete calculation along these lines, combining convenient parts of the two numbers and mopping up the remainders. For example, he may take 24 from the 458 to make 376 into 400, then add on the 434 which is left. He may take out 350 from 376, 450 from 458 and combine these to make 800, which can be put to one side in short–term memory. Only 8 + 26 is left, which can be added via bonds for 10 as 26 + 4 + 4 = 34. This is added onto the 800 to make 834.

Similar principles apply to estimating subtractions. For example, 834 – 458 might be seen as close to 858 – 458 or 834 – 434, both giving an answer of 400. Then, if the pupil can decide whether the adjustment made the estimate high or low, he can say that the answer is a little less than 400. If an accurate answer is needed, then it could be by looking at the adjustment, say, in the 858 – 458 version it was to add on 24, then the actual answer is 400 – 24.

These methods illustrate the advantages of breaking down and building up numbers.

Column addition

The addition of a column of numbers requires somewhat different techniques and can be a daunting task. There are two low–stress

Figure 7.4 Using tally marks for 10's (and 100's) thereby adding only one-digit sub-sums

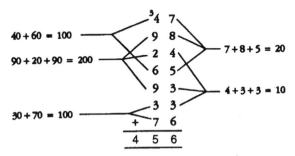

Figure 7.5 Casting out 10's (or 20's) using again number bonds for 10

algorithms (Ashlock, 1982, p. 21) which may help. One (Figure 7.4) is more likely to appeal to inchworms and the other (Figure 7.5) to grasshoppers.

In Figure 7.4, addition starts at the top of the units column with 7 + 8 giving 15. The stroke through the 8 is the tally for the 10 in 15, leaving the 5 units to add to the 4, making 9. The 9 is added to 5 to make 14 and the stroke through the 5 is the tally for the 10 in 14. This leaves 4 units to add to the 3, making 7, which is added to the next 3, making 10. The stroke through the 3 is the tally for 10. The last unit digit, the 6, is written at the bottom of the sum. The tallies in the units column are counted. There are 3, so 3 is written at the top of the tens column. The same procedure is now used to add down the tens column.

In Figure 7.5 combinations which make 10 or 20 are 'cast out', thereby reducing the addition task.

Mental arithmetic

An extreme inchworm will probably try to visualise a written procedure, so that 330 + 97 becomes

```
    330
+    97
```

which is then added as though on paper, whereas a grasshopper will try to use numbers near to 10, 100 and 1000 or clusters of other numbers which make up 10, 100, 1000, etc. Thus 330 + 97 becomes 330 + 100 = 430, then 430 – 3 takes the grasshopper to the right answer, 427. It can be helpful for less skilled grasshoppers to ask themselves whether the answer will be less or more than that obtained when adding a 100 so that the correct adjustment is made with the 3.

The latter process is usually a lesser strain on short–term memory, and requires less knowledge of basic facts.

The same processes apply to subtraction, for example 578 – 299. The inchworm will visualise the sum rewritten as

$$
\begin{array}{r}
578 \\
-\ \ 299 \\
\hline
\end{array}
$$

which is a daunting task for those with memory problems!

The grasshopper will round the 299 up to 300, subtract to get 278, add on 1 to obtain the final answer of 279. As with addition, some may need to decide whether the final answer will be bigger or smaller than the intermediate answer before dealing with the 1 used for rounding up the 299.

Teaching Subtraction as a Separate Exercise

Even though we feel there are many advantages to teaching subtraction and addition together, there may be situations where subtraction has to be approached separately.

It may be necessary for you to start by providing an overview to remind or re–establish the concept and vocabulary of subtraction before teaching specific algorithms. Some examples to which the child can relate, such as change from shopping and/or examples using manipulative aids, are suitable.

The teacher should be trying to establish in the child's mind a clear picture of the component parts of the subtraction. It is usually unnecessary to use the mathematical terms minuend, subtrahend and remainder, but the child needs to understand the consequences of subtraction and be able to relate it to addition.

Subtraction without regrouping

This is the easiest process and acts as a good introduction as well as reinforcing the concept of subtraction and the identification of the component parts of the sum. Thus a subtraction such as

$$
\begin{array}{r}
79 \\
-\ \ 34 \\
\hline
45
\end{array}
$$

may be used to practise the use of manipulative materials such as money or base–ten blocks. Such manipulative work may have to use a place value card. There is, as ever, a need to teach estimating and to re–emphasise its value as a way to minimise errors.

Subtraction with regrouping: the decomposition method

This method is a relatively recent introduction to teaching and is well illustrated by base–ten blocks (and money). As with so much in mathematics, the work here relies on previous concepts and therefore these concepts may need attention before the main agenda is started. The main review here is to look again at the regrouping of numbers, e.g. 72 is also 60 + 12 (as spoken in French) or at the renaming (a more descriptive term) of numbers such as 742 to the specific format 600 + 130 + 12.

Work on renaming three–digit numbers into this format can be investigated and the consequent patterns derived. Examples are:

$$543 = 400 + 130 + 13$$
$$754 = 600 + 140 + 14$$
$$865 = 700 + 150 + 15$$
$$976 = 800 + 160 + 16$$

The application of this renaming process should lead on to subtraction examples set up on a place–value board with the teacher talking the child through the algorithm. For example:

$$\begin{array}{r} 742 \\ - \ 386 \\ \hline \end{array}$$

The blocks (Figure 7.6a) used first, followed by money, should be moved by the child and progression should be from base–ten blocks to money, each time writing the numbers as the manipulatives are moved. If the child seems to be understanding the work, then you may take the child to working with just the digits. The child may well need to start this stage with place–value columns drawn on the paper.

Spatial and organisational problems may make the traditional layout too confusing, at least at first, so an intermediate presentation may help. A separate middle line is set up with all the renaming done at one time and before the actual subtraction (Figure 7.6c).

Finally the place–value columns can be removed and the child works on squared or lined paper (Figure 7.6d).

As in the addition/subtraction programme, examples which include zeros should be demonstrated.

The equal–additions method

The method is based on the equation $a - b = (a + 10) - (b + 10)$, with 10 added to both a and b, which keeps the difference, $a - b$, the same. It is a harder method to explain to a child than the decomposition method,

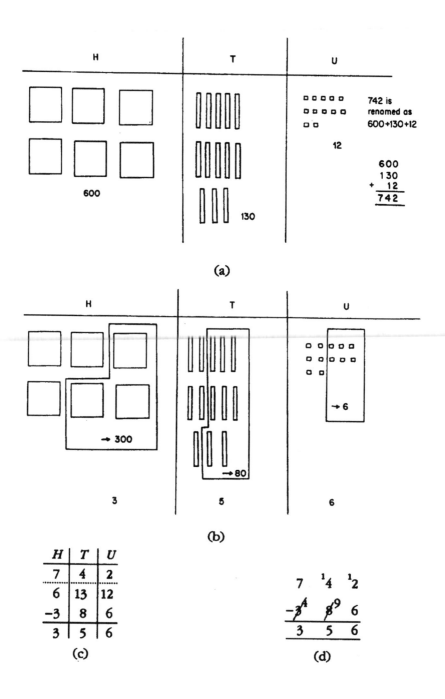

Figure 7.6

and Kennedy (1975) quite rightly pointed out that children have more difficulty remembering an algorithm they do not understand. It is also harder to provide multisensory experiences which clearly illustrate this algorithm. Despite these reservations, if the process can be mastered it is easy to reproduce. An 'easy' example may clarify the process, for example

$320 - 90$ becomes $(320 + 10) - (90 + 10) = 330 - 100$

The explanation could be developed from such examples.

Subtraction by equal additions is quicker, and probably easier, than decomposition as a mechanical process, but Kennedy's comment should be remembered as being particularly apposite for dyslexics, who often need a concrete base on which to build their understanding and memory.

Mental arithmetic

The method of equal additions adjusts the numbers in the calculation and this adjusting strategy can be extended into mental arithmetic. For example, $342 - 197$ can be made an easier calculation by adding 3 to both numbers:

$342 - 197 = 345 - 200$

This method is easier for some children than a similar procedure where the 197 is rounded up to 200, 200 is subtracted from 342 and 3 is added back onto the resultant 142.

A subtraction such as $411 - 115$ does require the latter strategy. The difference is approximately 300 but is less than 300 (this evaluation as to whether the answer is more than 300 or less than 300 is fundamental to the success of this strategy). If 4 is added on to 411, then the subtraction gives an answer of 300. The added-on 4 now needs compensation, so $300 - 4 = 296$ is the correct answer.

As before, the ability to perform mental arithmetic with facility is greatly enhanced by an understanding of the interrelationships between numbers and the relationship between addition and subtraction, so that $411 - 115$ is seen to be close to, but less than 300 and 197 is seen to be 3 short of 200. Such calculations also involve and develop estimation skills.

Chapter 8
Multiplication

Introduction

Multiplication will be used to illustrate the use of a full programme of instruction. The principles of this programme are applicable to other topics. The work moves from a manipulative aid, which is a direct representation of the problem, to a model (in this case, area), to purely written symbols and an algorithm which links back to the concrete model. Whenever possible, more than one written method is given, so as to acknowledge the spectrum of cognitive styles. The multisensory introduction is used to lead into flexible cognitive processes and to give an introductory overview.

The Special Case of Multiplying by 10 and Powers of 10

The first stage is to secure estimation skills. Estimation skills in multiplication (used, for example, to back up calculator work) centre on an ability to multiply by tens, hundreds, thousands, etc. In our experience this relatively basic operation needs frequent review (see Chapter 15 on the spiral construction of the Mark College mathematics programme).

The pattern of multiplying by ten must be explained in terms of the basic concept and the implication on place value, rather than solely in terms of the purely mechanical action of 'adding on' zeros, a procedure which generates horror in the minds of mathematicians, yet is readily adopted by children (who tend to act so pragmatically).

The objective is to explain that multiplying by 10, 100, 1000 and so on moves numbers up in place value, but that the digits themselves do not change. To illustrate this, consider 536×10:

- 6×10. Use a place–value board and put six unit cubes in the units column. Remind the child of the 10 times table and the exchanging of ten blocks for unit cubes. Then ask the child to exchange each unit cube for a ten block, placing the ten blocks in the tens column. Give the child a sheet of paper with place–value columns on it and ask him to write in numerals the 6 and the 60. Discuss the 60 being ten times bigger than the 6 and emphasise that the 6 has moved from the units column to the tens column (Figure 8.1a).

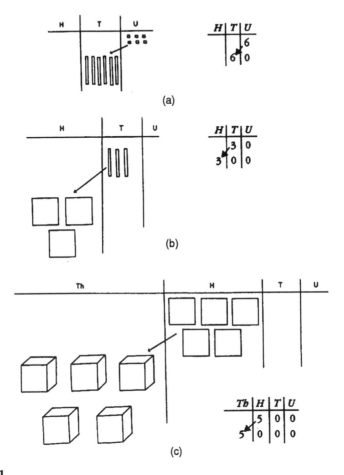

Figure 8.1

- 30 × 10. Repeat the process, but exchange three hundred blocks (squares) in the hundreds column for three ten blocks in the tens column (Figure 8.1b).
- 500 × 10. Repeat the process again, exchanging five thousand blocks (cubes) for five hundred squares (Figure 8.1c).
- 536 × 10. Repeat the process all in one example (Figure 8.2). Then discuss what has happened to each digit, the relevance numerically, the pattern, and what has and has not changed in the process. The procedure can be illustrated with place–value number arrows (Figure 8.3) as a further reinforcement of the concept.

Figure 8.2

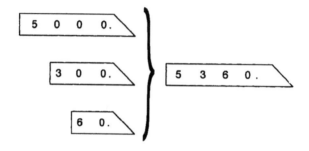

Figure 8.3

It should now be possible for the child to explain equations such as 849 × 10 = 8490, including the significance of the zero in the units column, and to restate that the order of digits remains the same. As ever, this work includes a significant element of revisiting previous work and ideas.

A similar process can be used to teach × 100 and × 1000 and other powers of 10. Although not mathematically as sound as we would normally prefer, the relationship between the number of zeros in the multiplier and the number of extra zeros in the result should be pointed out. The child should also relate the number of place–value moves to the number of zeros in the multiplier.

The child should practise the work, using the base–ten blocks for some examples, place–value columns and (squared) paper for others. He should be encouraged to articulate his work and to review the under-lying significance of the procedure.

It may be useful to extend multiplication by powers of 10 to examples such as × 20, × 60, × 300 and so on. The method advocated is a two–stage process, so that × 20 is done as × 2 then × 10 (or × 10 then × 2).The child should compare the results of × 2 with × 20 by using base–ten blocks, e.g. 42 × 20:

$42 \times 10 = 420$ (Figure 8.4a)
$42 \times 2 = 84$ (Figure 8.4b)
giving
$42 \times 20 = 42 \times 2 \times 10 = 840.$

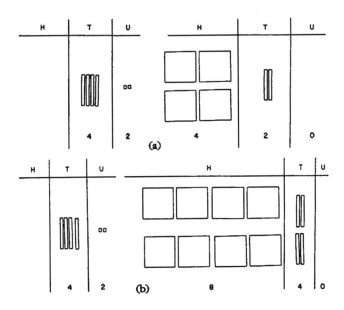

Figure 8.4

The child needs to realise that, if the multiplier is ten times bigger, then the result is ten times bigger. This procedure is, of course, similar to the times–table strategy for × 4 of using × 2 twice.

Multiplication

Times–table facts are one digit times one digit operations. This chapter extends this to two digit times one digit and then to two digit times two digit and thus, by using the same models, to any multiplication. The model of multiplication used is area. This model is advocated because it can be extended into other aspects of multiplication (such as fraction times fraction) (Sharma, 1988b).

Introducing the model

The child needs some square counters (Figure 8.5). The three piles illustrate three lots of four. This can be discussed as repeated addition, 4 + 4 + 4 leading to the more economical representation 3 × 4. The counters are then rearranged to represent area.

The concept of $a \times b$ as area can be discussed in real–life terms, such as carpet tiles, areas of wall for painting, etc.

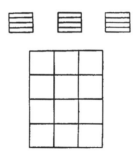

Figure 8.5

Two digit times one digit

Consider 23 × 4. As with × 20, the child is going to learn a two–stage procedure (not the same one). This procedure was used in the times–table chapter (Chapter 6) for the 7 times table, where, for example 7 × 2 was treated as (5 × 2) + (2 × 2), a process of breaking down followed by building up again.

Set up the multiplication with base–ten blocks (Figure 8.6a). The area divides up into two sub–areas. One area is made up from tens blocks and the other area from unit blocks. The two areas can be physically separated to show 20 × 4 (Figure 8.6b) and 3 × 4 (Figure 8.6c). The two areas can then be brought back together to show 23 × 4 (Figure 8.6d).

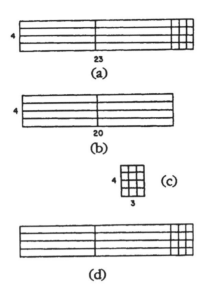

Figure 8.6

At each step the written symbols are shown to the child. The demonstration shows and separates the two partial products. The child should set up some areas for himself and show the partial products both as blocks and as written digits.

Two digit times two digit

The model is again area. Consider the example 22×31. The inefficiency of repeated addition could be reviewed for this example:

22 + 22 + 22 + 22 + 22 + 22 + 22 + 22 + 22 + 22 + 22 + 22 + 22 +22 + 22 + 22 + 22 + 22 + 22 + 22 + 22 + 22 + 22 + 22 + 22 + 22 + 22 + 22 + 22 + 22 + 22.

Indeed, this overwhelming presentation would suggest some grouping and could be another route into the area model and the final algorithm.

- Set up the multiplication in base–ten blocks (Figure 8.7a). The blocks illustrate area. They are movable, so that the four sub–areas can be separated (Figure 8.7b). These partial products allow a difficult problem to be broken down into smaller, easier steps. The child can handle the blocks and physically break down the problem with the blocks, as well as with the written digits.
- The four constituent areas are discussed, starting with the largest area, the area formed by the 'hundred squares'. This offers a first estimate. The blocks provide a very real model of this (Figure 8.7c). The estimation sum is written by the child in digits ($30 \times 20 = 600$).

- The four areas are examined (Figure 8.7b). They are:

30×20, 1×20, 30×2, 1×2.

30×20	tens × tens	= 600
1×20	ones × tens	= 20
30×2	tens × ones	= 60
1×2	ones × ones	= 2
	[total =	682]

This algorithm is $(a + b)(c + d) = ac + ad + bc + bd$.

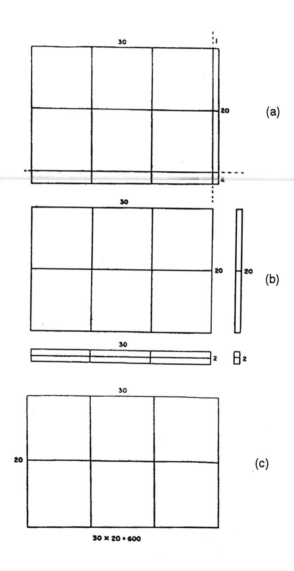

Figure 8.7

The child needs to see and handle each partial product in order to see that the area does break down into constituent parts. Each partial product should be written down in digits.

- The problem is drawn to scale on squared paper by the child, and this will look like Figure 8.8b. The sub–divisions are drawn in, and the relationship between the areas and the numbers in the partial products is explained.
- A problem is presented as numbers, e.g. 22×31. The partial products are written down and calculated. The child is asked to identify the 'estimate' partial product.
- The problem is drawn to scale again on squared paper and only one sub–division is made, leaving two areas (Figure 8.9). In numbers the two areas are 20×31 and 2×31. The algorithm is based on $(a + b) c = ac + bc$.

The calculation becomes:

$$
\begin{array}{cc}
31 & 31 \\
\times 20 & \times 2 \\
\hline
620 & 62
\end{array}
\qquad
\begin{array}{ll}
31 & \\
\times 22 & \\
\hline
620 & (31 \times 20) \\
62 & (31 \times 2) \\
\hline
682 & (31 \times 22)
\end{array}
$$

Figure 8.8

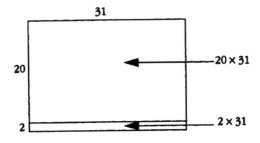

Figure 8.9

The child is still doing four multiplications as before, but he is combining two on each line of the calculation.

Compare the two methods as used for another example, 54×23:

$$
\begin{array}{rl}
54 & \\
\times 23 & \\
\hline
1000 & (50 \times 20) \\
80 & (4 \times 20) \\
150 & (50 \times 3) \\
12 & (4 \times 3) \\
\hline
1242 &
\end{array}
\qquad
\begin{array}{rl}
54 & \\
\times 23 & \\
\hline
1080 & (54 \times 20) \\
162 & (54 \times 3) \\
\hline
1242 &
\end{array}
$$

The child should chose the method which best helps his short–term memory, organisation and spatial problems.

Mnemonics may help the child

- FOIL (Figure 8.10)
  The First two digits are multiplied together: 50×40.
  The Outer two digits are multiplied together: 50×3.
  The Inner two digits are multiplied together: 2×40.
  The Last two digits are multiplied together: 2×3.
- The smiley face (Figure 8.10). The lines join the numbers which have to be multiplied together. There can, however, be place–value problems with this mnemonic.

Figure 8.10

Estimation

While calculators provide a relatively stress–free way of multiplying, dyslexics have a tendency to press the wrong number keys, get the numbers in the wrong order, use the wrong operation key or use the right operation key at the wrong time. A pre–estimate and a post–evaluation are, therefore, important.

The area model provides a good picture of how to estimate, based on the biggest sub–area plus or minus the other sub–areas. It also allows the child to evaluate his estimate and see if it is high, low or fairly accurate. Some examples will explain this.

- 33×54 (Figure 8.11a). This is estimated at $30 \times 50 = 1500$ and can be seen to be an underestimate, but reasonably close to the accurate answer.
- 42×78 (Figure 8.11b). Subtract and add to refine the estimate. Note that the 78 has been estimated up to 80 so that the length of the rectangle drawn is longer. The shaded part has to be subtracted if refined estimates are required. This, then, is estimated at $40 \times 80 = 3200$ and can be seen to be very close to the accurate answer with the extra 2×40 (which has to be subtracted) not quite compensating for the 2×78 (which has to be added).
- 51×92 (Figure 8.11c). Subtract and add to refine the estimate. Note that the 92 has been estimated up to 100. This is estimated at $50 \times 100 = 5000$ and can be seen to be an overestimate with 8×50 (which has to be subtracted) bigger than 1×92 (which has to be added).

Figure 8.11

Extension

The principle of the algorithm for a two digit times two digit calculation can be readily extended to three digit times three digit calculations and so on. The spatial organisation problems may require the child to work on squared paper (see Chapter 15), and in earlier examples the child may benefit from writing or articulating what each partial product means. Equally the principle of developing work from manipulative aids, through visual models, to symbol work is applicable to 'harder' examples.

These procedures integrate multisensory experiences with sound mathematical algorithms and provide the child with some concrete experiences and pictures which will help him to remember what might otherwise seem to him to be a meaningless random process. The structure provided by the identification of the partial products (and the number of partial products involved) helps the child and should help the teacher with diagnosis of errors and subsequent remedial input.

Chapter 9
Division

Introduction

In this chapter, suggestions for teaching the concept of division, division by single–digit numbers and division by powers of ten are discussed. For more complex divisions, estimation followed by the use of a calculator is recommended, although an alternative algorithm to the traditional one is discussed, should you want to leave the child with at least one method for calculations.

The actual process of long division is very demanding on many of the skill areas that dyslexic students find most difficult. The algorithm traditionally used for long division requires good skills in sequencing, memory, knowledge of basic facts and spatial organisation.

It is worth considering the problems dyslexic pupils face in this particularly difficult topic. The extent of these difficulties may be alleviated by references to and building on other work the child has covered and by interrelating concepts (such as subtraction and division) so as to try and make old and new work mutually supportive. Once again, the child's existing knowledge makes a good baseline. You need to capitalise on existing knowledge and thus should begin with informal diagnostic work, which is intended to find out what the child knows and which examples and illustrations he relates to.

The language of division can lead to early problems and can be an initial block to understanding of the concept and processes of division. A typical early question could be, 'Divide 36 by 6' or '36 ÷ 6'. The order in which the numbers are stated is the opposite to the demands of the algorithm, $6\overline{)36}$.

Furthermore, 'divide' is an abstract word and children are more likely to be familiar with phrases such as, 'How many 6s in 36?' or 'Share 36 between 6 people'. These phrases relate more readily to the manipulative materials and are easier for the child to grasp, so the move from concrete to symbolic requires the teacher to be aware of these language needs of the child, as well as of any lag in his conceptual development.

The spatial and organisational demands of division algorithms are considerable. The traditional algorithm for $6\overline{)378}$ requires the child to work from left to right, writing the answer at the top, working from the hundreds to the tens and then to the units and carrying down numbers as the problem proceeds. These requirements are almost directly opposite to those for addition, subtraction and multiplication. Furthermore, to help meet these directional demands, the child may well need support in getting the correct place values on the answer line. Extra support for this accuracy can be provided by teaching estimating skills and by encouraging the child to overview the question (which may include rephrasing it).

Introduction to Division

The initial aims are to introduce (or review) division in at least four ways: as sharing out or dividing up into parts; as finding out how many numbers in; as the converse of multiplication; and as repeated subtraction. An introductory activity of taking (small) numbers of counters and dividing them up into groups helps the child to see the processes of division in action and the interrelationship between division and subtraction. The teacher can then extend the child's perception of the activity by structured questions and representation of the 'dividing up' actions.

- Take 12 counters and place them randomly on a table (Figure 9.1). Ask the child to count them. (Some children will group the counters automatically when they do this.) Then ask the child to share/divide them into three groups.

Figure 9.1

- Ask the child to reorganise the groups into rows and columns. Then the following relationships can be examined as manipulatives and as equations:

Four lots of 3. (How many 3s in 12?)
Three lots of 4. (How many 4s in 12?)
3 goes into 12 four times.
12 divided by 3 gives 4.
Repeated subtraction of 3 from 12.

This work can be related back to the table square, so that its use as a division square can be taught. Repeated subtraction relates division to subtraction and acts as a first exposure to a later algorithm:

$$4 \times \square = 12 \qquad\qquad 12 \div 3 = 4$$
$$3 \times \square = 12$$

$$12 = 4 \times 3 \qquad\qquad \frac{4}{3 \overline{)12}}$$

$$12 - 3 = 9$$
$$9 - 3 = 6$$
$$6 - 3 = 3$$
$$3 - 3 = 0$$

Thus the child is seeing the relationship between division and multiplication, the idea of dividing up, the phrasing 'How many x in y?', the concept of division as repeated subtraction and the idea of sharing equally. Simple division facts can be presented as multiplication facts with 'gaps' and the child can be shown how to use a table square to obtain division facts. Again the child is taught to use the interrelationships between numbers and operations in a way that makes maximum use of known facts, rather than the rote learning of seemingly unrelated facts.

Obviously many other examples besides 12 should be used, with the possibility of phasing out the (multisensory) manipulative aids as the child becomes more confident in his knowledge and understanding.

The relationship between the size/value of the divided number, divisor and answer can be shown by examples such as dividing 12 by a series of divisors: 12, 6, 4, 3, 2, 1. Work of this type (using, as ever, written presentation alongside manipulative work) leads the child towards estimation skills. At the least, the child is learning that the bigger the divisor, the smaller the answer and vice versa.

Dividing two–digit numbers by one–digit numbers, with remainder

Although the work described so far could be used to introduce a child to the topic of division, it is best considered as an early stage of remediation. For these early confidence–building stages, remainders provide less confusion than decimal or fraction answers. Thus $14 \div 4$ is presented with counters (Figure 9.2). It is apparent that the answer is 3 and that there are two counters left over or remaining. 'Remainder' seems to be a reasonable name for these counters.

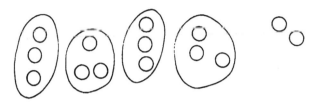

Figure 9.2

Dividing two– and three–digit numbers with renaming (of tens and hundreds)

65 ÷ 5

An efficient procedure for dividing 65 into five equal parts requires the child to progress from just counting out 65, unit by unit, into five groups. He has to learn how to start with 'How many tens will be in each of the five parts?', then 'What do you do with the 10 left over and where do you bring in the 5 units from the 65'. In other words, this is quite a leap in skill and understanding. The demands of the division algorithm on deficit areas are significant (see the Introduction section in this chapter). Again the principle is to relate the symbols to a concrete base and make the algorithm relate to a manipulative procedure. A structured approach that pre–empts as many of the difficulties as possible and creates this concrete image for the child is advocated:

* 65 is presented in base–ten blocks (Figure 9.3a).
* Five 10s are taken out, one to each of the 5 parts (Figure 9.3b).
* The 'left over' 10 is traded for 10 unit cubes and added to the existing 5 unit cubes (Figure 9.3c).
* The 15 unit cubes are shared out, adding 3 unit cubes to each of the 5 parts making 10 + 3, an answer of 13 (Figure 9.3d).

At each stage the written algorithm matches the base–ten manipulatives. You can explain the significance of each move and can relate it back to other work. For example, the need to trade tens for units is used in subtraction.

504 ÷ 4

* A similar structure is presented, with 504 shown in base–ten blocks. This time the first move is to take out four hundred blocks and place one in each part (Figure 9.4a).
* This leaves one hundred block, which is traded for 10 ten blocks, which are placed in the tens column. This highlights the previously

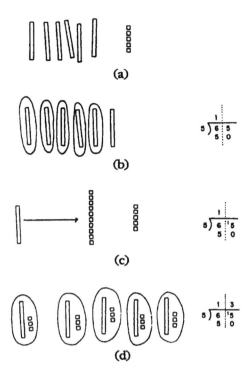

Figure 9.3

empty tens column and emphasises the need to mark its presence in the answer line. Eight ten blocks are removed, two for each part (Figure 9.4b).
- The two remaining ten blocks are traded for unit cubes, giving 24 unit cubes to share into the four parts, six in each (Figure 9.4c).
- The final answer is 126.

Note the use of place–value columns in the written version (given along-side the blocks in the parts of Figure 9.4). (Other suitable manipulative aids are money and bundles of cocktail sticks.)

Other examples should be used to consolidate this method. When the manipulative–aid stage is phased out, the use of the place–value lines should remain as it tends to eliminate the common errors of starting the answer in the wrong place or missing out a place as in 2)408 (often erroneously answered as 24).

Some alternative algorithms

Ashlock et al. (1983) offer two interesting alternatives, both based on repeated subtraction. Both require careful presentation. One is quite demanding on directional skills, but both offer a method which helps the child who cannot work out where to start. Both methods are based on subtracting multiples of the divisor. The pyramid algorithm (Figure 9.5a) allows the child to choose any estimate for his multiples. It also acts as a half–way house to the traditional algorithm, if that is the goal.

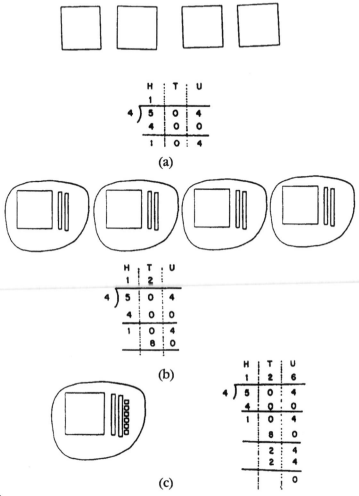

Figure 9.4

The other algorithm has been adapted by Chinn to utilise the facts dyslexics can calculate readily, that is multiples of 1, 2, 5, 10, 20, 50, 100 etc., followed by repeated subtraction. The algorithm also fits into the developmental aspects of the programme.

The first step is to set up a table of multiples, based on an easy pattern and using the facts most likely to be easy for a dyslexic pupil. (Figure 9.5b).

Once 1x, 2x, 10x and 5x are written, the other multiples follow a pattern which is the same for any division problem. This step also provides an estimate. In this case the answer lies between 200 and 500 and since 5024 is nearer to 3200 than to 8000, the estimate must be closer to 200 than 500. Thus the procedure encourages the evaluation of the answer, too.

1 ×	16	
2 ×	32	
5 ×	80	
10 ×	160	
20 ×	320	
50 ×	800	
100 ×	1600	
200 ×	3200	
500 ×	8000	

```
49
 4 ········
 5 ········
20 ········
20 ··
6) 294
-120 ·
174
-120 ········
 54
- 30 ········
 24
-24 ········
  0
```

20 + 20 + 5 + 4 = 49

```
5024
-3200    200
1824
-1600    100
 224
-160     10
  64
 -32      2
  32
 -32      2
   0     314
```

(a)   (b)   (c)

Figure 9.5 (a) The pyramid algorithm, (b) 16 × fact table for division by repeated subtraction, (c) Division by repeated subtraction

The division is then tackled by subtraction of these multiples of 16 (Figure 9.5c). The method is related to our procedures for multiplication, showing division to be the reverse operation. It can be illustrated by partitioning off an area (Figure 9.6) in line with the subtractions as documented in Figure 9.5c.

Figure 9.6

The authors' experience of this method is that our Year 7 pupils can do this procedure with concrete materials (which act as an introduction to the method), but usually find the digits too difficult. By Year 9 the upper groups adapt to it readily. This method provides a good illustration of 'readiness' (see Chapter 15 on time) and the teacher should watch the class carefully to ensure understanding is achieved.

Estimating

The ability to multiply the divisor by powers of 10 can be used to act as another useful and consistent estimating aid.

$3285 \div 5$

The divisor is multiplied by increasing powers of 10 and the product is compared with 3285:

$5 \times 10 = 50$
$5 \times 100 = 500$
$5 \times 1000 = 5000$

So the answer will lie between 100 and 1000. It is, therefore, a three–digit answer and by comparing/evaluating 3285 with 500 and 5000 it can be seen that the quotient will be closer to 1000 than to 100. Again the link between division and multiplication is made and there is another chance for the child to reinforce his ability to multiply by powers of 10.

Dividing by Powers of 10

This requires an understanding of place value, so a review of this concept can be a precursor to the topic. The child needs to remember that the place a digit holds in a number controls its value by a power of 10 (for example, in 58725, the 7 is the third number in, it is in the hundreds column and its value is 7×100 or 700).

Division by powers of 10 produces a pattern which can be illustrated by activities where the pupil uses base–ten blocks to divide numbers into 10 parts and thus is drawn to the conclusion that (as with multiplying by powers of 10) the numbers do not change, only their place value. At this early stage it is advisable to avoid answers which are decimals. A series of base–ten block activities leads to series such as:

$400 \div 10 = 40$	$400 \div 100 = 4$	$4000 \div 1000 = 4$
$440 \div 10 = 44$	$4000 \div 100 = 40$	
$4000 \div 10 = 400$	$4400 \div 100 = 44$	
$4400 \div 10 = 440$		
$4440 \div 10 = 444$		

It will almost certainly be necessary to use place–value columns to emphasise the way the numbers move. A structured programme of manipulative aids (base–ten blocks and/or money) and written digits should establish the idea of movement and values in the child's mind and lead him to some mnemonics. If this is so, then the move on to quotients that are decimals does not present such a difficult hurdle (see Chapter 12).

Division by Multiples of Powers of 10

Examples such as 4000 ÷ 20, 3000 ÷ 2000, 4500 ÷ 50, etc., can be solved by teaching the child to take a two–stage approach: dividing first by 10 and then by 2; by 1000 then by 2; by 10 then by 5. This can be a multisensory activity with base–ten blocks. (It also relates to the making of fractions such as ⅙ by a two–stage process: ÷ 2 and ÷ 3.)

Conclusions

Further work should probably use calculators, providing that, as ever, there is an ability to estimate and check the answers. The work outlined in this chapter provides the child with the basic concept and the skills of division, and the ability to estimate.

Chapter 10
Fractions, Decimals and Percentages:
An Introduction

Introduction

If mathematics is generally concerned with using numbers to describe things, then this chapter is about describing *parts* of things with numbers. There are important differences among the three alternative forms, otherwise fractions, decimals and percentages would not have evolved. Each of the three forms is described in subsequent chapters, its independent characteristics being covered in detail. The first aim is to help you establish, with the child, a good understanding of each form, and to avoid the possible misconceptions, many of which are specifically covered.

Of course, there are many similarities and equivalences between fractions, decimals and percentages—some text–books still refer to 'vulgar fractions' and 'decimal fractions'. Methods are covered for converting each form into each of the others, and in these the key values, such as

$\frac{1}{2}$ = 0.5 = 50%, will be highlighted.

Fractions

Fractions are the most basic way of describing parts of things. Thus, they are and have been taught in primary schools and there is an expectation from parents and perhaps some teachers that children should find fractions easy. Memories are being selective here, since fractions always were exceptionally difficult in their written form.

Many teachers and children use folding paper to establish how fractions work. It makes them easy to understand. In this book, this idea is taken further. The easy, folded–paper methods are allowed to dictate how fraction questions and answers should be written down. The written versions should then be just as easy to understand.

Drawings of folded fractions provide a means of recording and communicating a point understood from the paper version. They form a step between between the folded–paper fractions and the written fractions.

We recommend that roughly square shapes are folded and drawn at all times. The practice of using thin strips of paper masks the relationship, which it is invaluable to exploit, between forming fractions and multiplication of fractions (interpreted as two–dimensional in Chapter 11). That other popular alternative, the use of circles (or circular cakes), requires the understanding of harder concepts, such as angles and circle terms; also, how, for example, can a circular piece of paper be folded easily into equal fifths?

Terminology

A fraction such as $^4/_5$ will be referred to as 'part' of a whole thing. The fraction is made up of equal fifths, which will be referred to as 'segments', rather than parts of the fraction. This avoids the duplicate use of the word 'parts', and children will be familiar with the notion of segments of an orange.

The terms 'denominator' and 'numerator' should not be used with children, and will only be used in this book where they avoid clumsy circumlocutions.

What is a fraction?

Part of a whole thing

- The piece of paper in Figure 10.1a has one fifth shaded in. It is divided into five equal segments and one is shaded, so the fraction is written as $^1/_5$.

- The fraction in Figure 10.1b shows three quarters. The written version is $^3/_4$.

Children can be asked to give the written form for other fractions, such as those shown in Figure 10.1c.

Whole things divided into equal segments

- Figure 10.2a shows a whole square of paper is five fifths (that's why they are called fifths). This is written as $^5/_5 = 1$ whole square. The number on the bottom of the fraction indicates both the number of segments and the size of the segments.

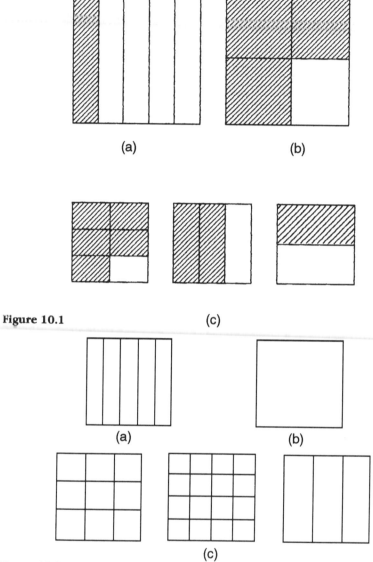

Figure 10.1

Figure 10.2

- The square in Figure 10.2b has been left whole. It can be written as $\frac{1}{1} = 1$ and called 1 whole.

Children can be asked to write down the fraction for given examples, such as those shown in Figure 10.2c.

- The special name for the segments in Figure 10.3a—halves—should be highlighted.
- The segments in Figure 10.3b are usually known as quarters, but

calling them fourths at the beginning tells children more about them.
- The version of fourths/quarters shown in Figure 10.3c should also be recognised.

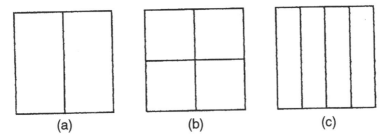

(a)   (b)   (c)

Figure 10.3

More than one whole thing

- Figure 10.4a shows two squares left whole. This can be written as $^2/_1$.
- Figure 10.4b shows two whole squares divided into quarters. This can be written as $2 \times {}^4/_4 = {}^8/_4$.

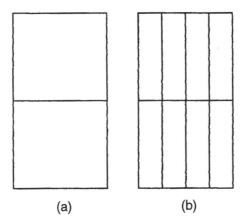

(a)   (b)

Figure 10.4

Making fractions

It is of the greatest importance that children make fractions themselves, by folding paper squares. This will help in the avoidance of such fundamental misconceptions as the idea that halving, halving and halving again will produce sixths. Demonstrably, it produces eighths. It will also help at future points of difficulty, if children can recall how the fractions were made.

Halving procedure

Figure 10.5a shows the folding procedure which produces halves. If the procedure is repeated, halving and halving again makes quarters (Figure

10.5b). Repeated halving produces a family of fractions, whose subsequent members are eighths, sixteenths, etc.

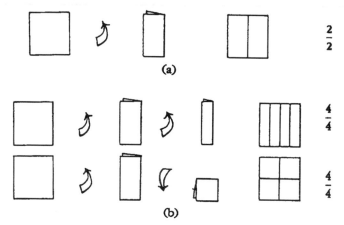

(a)

(b)

Figure 10.5

Other fractions require different folding procedures.

Thirding procedure

Figure 10.6a

The procedure shown in Figure 10.6a produces thirds. Repeating the procedure will produce a family of fractions, the next member of which is ninths.

Fifthing procedure

Figure 10.6b

The procedure shown in Figure 10.6b produces fifths and repeats to produce twenty–fifths, etc.

Other procedures

A new procedure is required every time the number of segments is prime: $2/2$, $3/3$, $5/5$, $7/7$, etc.

In practice, halves, thirds and fifths are sufficient, because sevenths, elevenths, etc., are very rarely needed—and never desirable at the learning stage.

Some teachers refer to these folding procedures as 'machines'.

Other fractions

Other important fractions must be made using a combination of folding procedures.

* Sixths—made by halving and thirding in either order.
* Tenths—made by halving and fifthing in either order.
* Twelfths—made by halving, halving and thirding in any order.
* Twentieths—made by halving, halving and fifthing in any order.

Table 10.1 summarises how to make all the fractions it is worthwhile considering at this stage.

Table 10.1

Fractions	Procedures						
	Half	*Half*	*Half*	*Half*	*Third*	*Third*	*Fifth*
Halves	*						
Thirds					*		
Fourths/quarters	*	*					
Fifths							*
Sixths	*				*		
Eighths	*	*	*				
Ninths					*	*	
Tenths	*						*
Twelfths	*	*			*		
Sixteenths	*	*	*	*			
Twentieths	*	*					*

Equal or equivalent fractions

Fractions are equal (or equivalent) if they cover the same amount/area of a paper square. For example, Figure 10.7 shows that

$$\frac{3}{4} = \frac{6}{8}.$$

Figure 10.7

The extra (horizontal) fold has produced twice as many segments and twice as many are shaded. The written format which gives the same effect is

$$\frac{3}{4} = \frac{3 \times 2}{4 \times 2} = \frac{6}{8}.$$

Formally, it is permissible to multiply the top and bottom by the same number. There are many different forms of exercise for establishing this concept.

Children can be asked the following questions.

- Give the written form for the two equal fractions shown in Figure 10.8a.

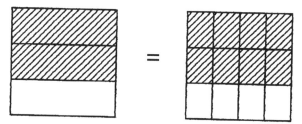

Figure 10.8a

- Draw in the extra fold lines in Figure 10.8b to show that $1/2 = 3/6$.

Figure 10.8b

- Write the correct numbers in the empty boxes:

$$\frac{1}{3} = \frac{1 \times 5}{3 \times 5} = \frac{\square}{\square}$$

$$\frac{3}{5} = \frac{3 \times \square}{5 \times 2} = \frac{6}{\square}$$

$$\frac{3}{8} = \frac{3 \times \square}{8 \times \square} = \frac{9}{\square}$$

$$\frac{3}{4} = \frac{3 \times \square}{4 \times \square} = \frac{\square}{16}$$

Simplifying fractions

Example

In the example shown in Figure 10.9, it is possible to divide all the tenths into groups of two, as shown. The shaded four are divided into groups of two in the same process. The written format which gives this effect is:

$$\frac{4}{10} = \frac{4 \div 2}{10 \div 2} = \frac{2}{5}$$

Formally, it is permissible to divide the top and the bottom by the same number.

Figure 10.9

A practical problem, here, is to decide what number to use for dividing the top and the bottom, i.e. into what size groups can the segments be divided. Prime factors can be used, or trial and error (based on a knowledge of the multiplication/division facts), but the method consistent with the philosophy of this book is to try the numbers used in forming the original segments by folding.

In the example above, tenths would have been formed by folding into halves and fifths. Therefore, dividing into groups of two or five should be tried. Of these, only the groups of two work for the shaded segments, and so the fraction is in its 'lowest terms', when this has been done.

Example

Simplify $^8/_{12}$. For this example, the twelfths would be formed by folding into halves, halves and thirds. Therefore, dividing by 2, 2 and 3 should be attempted:

$$\frac{8}{12} = \frac{8 \div 2}{12 \div 2} = \frac{4}{6}$$

$$= \frac{4 \div 2}{6 \div 2} = \frac{2}{3}$$

Dividing top and bottom by 3 does not work, so the fraction is as simple as it can be made.

Since halving and halving again produces quarters, a short cut would be to try dividing directly into groups of four, as illustrated in figure 10.10.

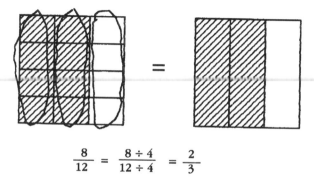

$$\frac{8}{12} = \frac{8 \div 4}{12 \div 4} = \frac{2}{3}$$

Figure 10.10

There are many different forms of exercise for establishing this concept.

• What are the folding steps which would make the following fraction in Figure 10.11?

Figure 10.11

- Write the correct numbers in the empty boxes:

$$\frac{5}{10} = \frac{5 \div 5}{10 \div 5} = \frac{\square}{\square}$$

$$\frac{4}{12} = \frac{4 \div 4}{12 \div \square} = \frac{1}{\square}$$

$$\frac{2}{6} = \frac{2 \div \square}{6 \div \square} = \frac{1}{\square}$$

$$\frac{8}{20} = \frac{8 \div \square}{20 \div \square} = \frac{4}{\square} = \frac{4 \div \square}{\square \div \square} = \frac{\square}{5}$$

$$\frac{6}{10} = \frac{6 \div \square}{10 \div \square} = \frac{\square}{\square}$$

Decimals

Decimals are parts of a whole thing.

Where a number also contains some whole things, the decimal part is separated by a decimal point, e.g. 37.651.

There is a sense in which decimals are just specific fractions—the first column after the decimal point representing tenths, the second representing hundredths, etc. However, because of this, each column is ten times the previous column, and so decimals are a continuation of the whole number system. They demonstrate this property when a number is carried in an addition, for example, or when a decimal is multiplied by 10.

First place as tenths

This can be demonstrated well with a measuring exercise. Consider the following length *AB* marked against a scale (Figure 10.12).

Figure 10.12

- Each large unit on the scale (cm) is divided into 10 smaller units (mm).
- Each smaller unit will be $1/10$ of a large unit.
- The length AB is 53 small units and 5 $3/10$ large units.
- If AB is written as 5.3 large units, then .3 means $3/10$ and the first number after the decimal point represents tenths.

This convention can be established and reinforced for children by having them measure a series of modest lengths and write their answers in centimetres as both fractions and decimals. If centimetres and millimetres are too small, a ruler graduated in inches and tenths of an inch will give a useful increase in size.

Second place as hundredths

This can be demonstrated with a money example.

$$100p = £1$$

$$10p = £\frac{1}{10}$$

$$1p = £\frac{1}{100}$$

Almost all children will accept and understand the above equivalents for money units. The amount of money illustrated in Figure 10.13 is written in pence at the top and pounds at the bottom.

100	10	1	
4	2	3	p

	1	$\frac{1}{10}$	$\frac{1}{100}$
£	4	2	3

Figure 10.13

With the amount of money in pounds, the decimal point takes up its familiar position. Figure 10.13 confirms that the first column after the decimal point represents tenths and shows that the second column represents hundredths.

A good exercise for establishing and reinforcing this convention is to ask children to convert various quantities of pennies into pounds, written as both decimals and fractions, e.g.

$$587p = £5.87 = £5 \frac{87}{100}$$

Fractions which simplify should be avoided at this stage, because, after simplification, they would produce something other than hundredths.

Further decimal places

Once the fraction equivalents are established for the first and second places of decimals, it is relatively easy for children to accept the next place as thousandths, and so on. A reminder that the familiar whole number column headings are Ones, Tens, Hundreds, Thousands, etc., is usually helpful.

It is worthwhile emphasising here that decimal place–value difficulties (like difficulties with whole number place values) are dramatically reduced if children can be persuaded to write their examples down in columns with headings.

Converting decimals to fractions

As was outlined earlier, decimals are composed of the specific fractions $\frac{1}{10}$, $\frac{1}{100}$, $\frac{1}{1000}$, etc., depending on the column(s) in which they are written. To convert them back to fractions, it is necessary simply to read off which of these columns they reach. Examples are given in Figure 10.14.

$\frac{1}{10}$	$\frac{1}{100}$	$\frac{1}{1000}$	
3			$\frac{3}{10}$
3	7		$\frac{37}{100}$
0	9		$\frac{9}{100}$
7	8	9	$\frac{789}{1000}$
0	0	7	$\frac{7}{1000}$
0	2	3	$\frac{23}{1000}$

Figure 10.14

For those children who, during this last example, question why the 2 (in the second column) is not seen as $^2/100$, there follows an explanation (which slightly anticipates addition of fractions).

$$.023 \; = \; \begin{array}{c} \dfrac{2}{100} \\[4pt] + \\[4pt] \dfrac{3}{1000} \end{array} \; = \; \begin{array}{c} \dfrac{20}{1000} \\[4pt] + \\[4pt] \dfrac{3}{1000} \end{array} \; = \; \dfrac{23}{1000}$$

Examples which can be simplified

After some decimals have been converted into fractions, they can be simplified.

$\frac{1}{10}$	$\frac{1}{100}$	$\frac{1}{1000}$				
8			$=$	$\frac{8}{10}$ $=$	$\frac{8 \div 2}{10 \div 2}$ $=$	$\frac{4}{5}$
4	5		$=$	$\frac{45}{100}$ $=$	$\frac{45 \div 5}{100 \div 5}$ $=$	$\frac{9}{20}$
0	0	4	$=$	$\frac{4}{1000}$ $=$	$\frac{4 \div 4}{1000 \div 4}$ $=$	$\frac{1}{250}$

Use of the number 25

In many cases, where decimals have been converted into fractions, and are to be simplified, the ability to divide (top and bottom) by 25 is very useful, as a short cut. There are two in 50, three in 75, four in every 100 and so 40 in every 1000, e.g.

$$.375 \; = \; \frac{375}{1000} \; = \; \frac{375 \div 25}{1000 \div 25} \; = \; \frac{15}{40} \; = \; \frac{15 \div 5}{40 \div 5} \; = \; \frac{3}{8}$$

Special decimals

A few decimals convert and simplify to very important fractions. It is desirable for these to be remembered by heart:

$$.1 \; = \; \frac{1}{10} \qquad .01 = \frac{1}{100} \qquad .001 = \frac{1}{1000}$$

$$.5 \; = \; \frac{1}{2} \qquad .25 \quad \frac{1}{4} \qquad .75 \; = \; \frac{3}{4} \quad .2 \; = \; \frac{1}{5}$$

The significance of zeros

Zeros in certain positions are very important, whereas others are unimportant or optional. As with whole numbers, it is the zeros that hold other numbers in their right places which have significance. The following pairs of examples can be used to demonstrate the possibilities:

$\frac{1}{10}$	$\frac{1}{100}$		
7		$=$	$\frac{7}{10}$
0	7	$=$	$\frac{7}{100}$

The zero in .07 gives it a different value from .7.

$\frac{1}{10}$	$\frac{1}{100}$	$\frac{1}{1000}$		
1	0	9	$=$	$\frac{109}{1000}$
1	9		$=$	$\frac{19}{100}$

The zero in .109 again affects its value, because it pushes the 9 into a different place.

$\frac{1}{10}$	$\frac{1}{100}$		
3		$=$	$\frac{3}{10}$
3	0	$=$	$\frac{30}{100} = \frac{3}{10}$

The zero in .30 makes no ultimate difference to its value, although there are ways in which it can sometimes be made useful, as will be shown later.

When a decimal, such as .92 has no whole number part, it is usually written in the form 0.92, with an optional zero at the front, as a matter of style. As long as children are having difficulty with decimals, simplicity is more important than style, so this should be avoided. In this chapter, such zeros have been omitted, for this reason.

In general, just as for whole numbers, the significant zeros are located between other numbers, or between a number and the decimal

point. The unimportant or optional zeros are to be found beyond those
numbers furthest from the decimal point.

Comparing decimals

'Which decimal is bigger .87 or .135?' In answer to this question, many
children will answer .135, because they see 135 as bigger than 87. Of
course, they are not comparing like with like, because the 135 are
thousandths whereas the 87 are hundredths. By way of explanation, all
that is necessary is to write the decimals in their columns and make them
the same 'length' by using optional zeros:

$\frac{1}{10}$	$\frac{1}{100}$	$\frac{1}{1000}$
8	7	0
1	3	5

This process has the same effect as making segment sizes the same for
fractions. Now the 870 is clearly bigger than the 135.

Some children have a similar problem understanding why .25 is half
way between .2 and .3, both of which may seem smaller. The column
headings and optional zeros can help again:

$\frac{1}{10}$	$\frac{1}{100}$
2	0
2	5
3	0

Quite clearly, 25 hundredths is half-way between 20 hundredths and 30
hundredths.

Another approach to these and other similar problems is to explain
with a decimal number line, such as is shown in Figure 10.15. This
number line shows quite clearly that .87 is bigger than .135. The equivalent fractions above the line provide further justification. It also shows
that .25 lies half-way between .2 and .3, another such situation being
observable at .865, which is half-way between .86 and .87.

Decimal number sequences

Decimal number sequences can be regarded as extended extracts from a
number line, such as that above. If the extracts are selected carefully,
they can provide a very convincing alternative way of looking at problem

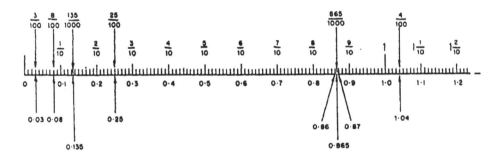

Figure 10.15 Number line for decimals

areas that have not been fully understood. One such problem area is tackled below. Consider the following sequence:

2.97, 2.98, 2.99,

Those children who have not properly taken on board the message that decimals behave in their columns, just like ordinary whole numbers, may make the mistake of supposing that the next decimal in the sequence is 2.100. They have not understood that the 1 from the 100 will be carried across the decimal point to produce 3.00. One way of clarifying this situation is to suggest that the decimal point could be temporarily ignored, whereupon the 299 would naturally be followed by 300. Perhaps a more satisfactory method, and certainly more interesting method for the children, is to challenge them with a decimal number sequence where the missing number is in the middle of the sequence. The above sequence might become:

2.97, 2.98, 2.99,　　,3.01, 3.02, 3.03

The opportunity now exists to find the missing decimal more easily, by approaching it from the other direction. Working towards it downwards gives 3.03, 3.02, 3.01, and then quite naturally 3.00. Furthermore, all kinds of very sound ideas about checking answers by working backwards and the reciprocity of addition and subtraction are being quietly covered.

Each of the following sequences straddles a different awkward region, where the numbers in parentheses would be left out for the children to find:

1.7, 1.8, 1.9, (2.0), (2.1), 2.2, 2.3
7.3, 7.2, (7.1), (7.0), 6.9, 6.8
8.8, 8.6, 8.4, 8.2, (8.0), 7.8, 7.6, 7.4
39.7, 39.8, 39.9, (40.0), (40.1), 40.2, 40.3
20.03, 20.02, (20.01), (20.00), 19.99, 19.98, 19.97.

Converting fractions to decimals

Some fractions are very simple to convert into decimals, because they are already tenths, hundredths or thousandths. They slot into the decimal columns immediately, like the examples below:

	$\frac{1}{10}$	$\frac{1}{100}$	$\frac{1}{1000}$
$\frac{1}{10}$ =	1		
$\frac{23}{100}$ =	2	3	
$\frac{7}{100}$ =	0	7	
$\frac{3}{1000}$ =	0	0	3
$\frac{29}{1000}$ =	0	2	9
$\frac{527}{1000}$ =	5	2	7

There are other fractions, which can easily be made into tenths, hundredths or thousandths, as shown with the following examples:

					$\frac{1}{10}$	$\frac{1}{100}$	$\frac{1}{1000}$
$\frac{2}{5}$ =	$\frac{2\times2}{5\times2}$ =	$\frac{4}{10}$ =			4		
$\frac{3}{4}$ =	$\frac{3\times25}{4\times25}$ =	$\frac{75}{100}$ =			7	5	
$\frac{1}{20}$ =	$\frac{1\times5}{20\times5}$ =	$\frac{5}{100}$ =			0	5	
$\frac{7}{8}$ =	$\frac{7\times125}{8\times125}$ =	$\frac{875}{1000}$ =			8	7	5

The final example $^7/_8$ in the table above, depends for its conversion on the knowledge that $8 \times 125 = 1000$. The likely absence of this knowledge would push this conversion into the most difficult category, along with fractions like $^5/_9$. There is no way in which $^5/_9$ can be converted into tenths, hundredths or thousandths. For such an example, it is necessary to regard $^5/_9$ as $5 \div 9$, and to perform a decimal division, which is beyond the scope of this chapter, so such conversions are covered in Chapter 12.

Percentages

Percentages are another way of describing parts of whole things.

'Per cent' means 'out of a hundred'. For example, 1 per cent means 1 out of a 100, which can also be written as 1/100. In essence, 'percentages are hundredths'. The sign for per cent, %, seems to be constructed from a 1, a 0 and another 0, so it behaves as a perpetual and valuable reminder of the importance of 100. Clearly, since percentages are hundredths, it is a simple matter to convert between percentages and fractions. Moreover, since hundredths constitute one of the decimal column headings, it is also relatively easy to convert between percentages and decimals.

Percentages and whole things

Writing down whole things in terms of percentages is slightly more difficult with fractions or decimals, where whole numbers are just written separately, in front. However, there is subsequently much less need to manipulate the percentages, so the difficulty carries no further.

A whole thing is $^{100}/_{100}$, which is 100%. Every whole thing is 100%, and so, for example, the whole number 5 is 500%.

A Global Model for Percentages, Fractions and Decimals

Figure 10.16 shows a whole square divided into 100 equal segments. Each segment is $^1/_{100}$, or 1%, or .01 (1 in the hundredths column). These can be represented physically by the unit bricks in Dienes apparatus. Each column is $^1/_{10}$, or 10%, or .1 (1 in the tenths column). These can be represented by 'longs'. The whole square is 100%, or 1 whole number, and could be represented by a 'flat'.

Figure 10.16

Percentages are a rather more palatable way of expressing parts of whole things, for most people.

- Because they are so small, any part of a whole thing will contain a workable number of them.
- Understood to be hundredths, they are fractions written without a denominator, or decimals without the need for the decimal point.
- More generally, it seems easier for most people to visualise 39%, for example, as 39 out of *their* picture of 100, rather than $^{39}/_{100}$ or .39.
- Percentages are much easier to compare.

Comparing percentages

Unlike fractions, which can have segments of any size, or decimals, which can be tenths, hundredths, thousandths, etc., percentages all have the same segment size—they are all hundredths. Their numerical values can therefore be compared in a straightforward way—the bigger the number, the bigger the percentage (and the bigger the part that it represents).

Examples

- 38% is bigger than 26% (by 12%) (Figure 10.17).
- 19% is smaller than 82% (by 61%).
- 31% is bigger than 7.25%.
- 135% is bigger than 87%.

Figure 10.17

Converting percentages to fractions

Percentages are 'understood' to be hundredths, so converting them to fractions is simply a matter of writing them with 100 on the bottom.

Examples

- 27% = $\dfrac{27}{100}$ (Figure 10.18).

- $127\% = 1\dfrac{27}{100}$

- $91\% = \dfrac{91}{100}$

- $9\% = \dfrac{9}{100}$

Figure 10.18

Sometimes the fraction obtained can be simplified.

Examples

$$45\% = \frac{45}{100} = \frac{45 \div 5}{100 \div 5} = \frac{9}{20} \qquad \text{(Figure 10.19)}$$

Figure 10.19

$$62\% = \frac{62}{100} = \frac{62 \div 2}{100 \div 2} = \frac{31}{50}$$

$$70\% = \frac{70}{100} = \frac{70 \div 10}{100 \div 10} = \frac{7}{10}$$

$$75\% = \frac{75}{100} = \frac{75 \div 25}{100 \div 25} = \frac{3}{4}$$

$$5\% = \frac{5}{100} = \frac{5 \div 5}{100 \div 5} = \frac{1}{20}$$

Some percentages produce fractions that take many steps to simplify. Such simplifications rarely occur elsewhere, and so they are covered here.

Example

$$12.5\% = \frac{12.5}{100} = \frac{12.5 \times 10}{100 \times 10} = \frac{125}{1000}$$

$$= \frac{125 \div 25}{1000 \div 5} = \frac{5}{40}$$

$$= \frac{5 \div 5}{40 \div 5} = \frac{1}{8}$$

(see Chapter 12 for multiplying decimals by 10.)

Example

$$33\tfrac{1}{3}\% = \frac{33\tfrac{1}{3}}{100} = \frac{33\tfrac{1}{3} \times 3}{100 \times 3} = \frac{\frac{100}{3} \times 3}{300}$$

$$= \frac{100}{300} = \frac{100 \div 100}{300 \div 100}$$

$$= \frac{1}{3}$$

(See Chapter 11 for multiplication of fractions.)

Converting fractions to percentages

When fractions are hundredths, a % can replace the 100 in the denominator.

Examples

$$\frac{83}{100} = 83\%$$

$$2\frac{83}{100} = 283\%$$

$$\frac{7}{100} = 7\%$$

Some fractions have first to be changed into hundredths. (A similar step was necessary in converting fractions to decimals.)

Examples

$$\frac{1}{2} = \frac{1 \times 50}{2 \times 50} = \frac{50}{100} = 50\% \text{ (Figure 10.20)}$$

$$\frac{2}{5} = \frac{2 \times 20}{5 \times 20} = \frac{40}{100} = 40\%$$

$$\frac{12}{25} = \frac{12 \times 4}{25 \times 4} = \frac{48}{100} = 48\%$$

$$\frac{37}{50} = \frac{37 \times 2}{50 \times 2} = \frac{74}{100} = 74\%$$

Figure 10.20

At times, children will be unable to change the fraction into hundredths, because they do not know the multiplier that will make the denominator 100. Finding this multiplier becomes the first step. Consider $^{17}/_{20}$:

$$\frac{17}{20} = \frac{17 \times ?}{20 \times ?} = \frac{?}{100}$$

It is required to identify how many 20s in 100. Put this way, it becomes evident that 100 needs to be divided into 20s. Since 100 ÷ 20 = 5, it is now possible to multiply top and bottom by 5 and obtain hundredths:

$$\frac{17}{20} = \frac{17 \times 5}{20 \times 5} = \frac{85}{100} = 85\%$$

Sometimes there is no whole number that will multiply the denominator to produce 100. The required multiplier is a decimal. Proper consideration for decimals is given in Chapter 12, but an example is dealt with here, for completeness. Consider $^{5}/_{16}$. Now 100 ÷ 16 = 6.25, and so this is the required multiplier:

$$\frac{5}{16} = \frac{5 \times 6.25}{16 \times 6.25} = \frac{31.25}{100} = 31.25\%$$

$5/16$ is a very simple fraction, which has become the rather clumsy percentage 31.25%. Nevertheless, this form will give some people a much better understanding of the part of a whole thing represented.

Converting percentages to decimals

Percentages are understood to be hundredths, and the second column of decimals is understood to be for hundredths. Therefore it is a simple matter to write a whole–number percentage in the decimal columns. It is required to finish in the hundredths column.

Examples

	$\frac{1}{10}$	$\frac{1}{100}$	$\frac{1}{1000}$	$\frac{1}{10000}$
28% =	2	8		(Figure
72% =	7	2		10.21)
50% =	5	0		
=	5			
8% =	0	8		
31.25% =	3	1	2	5

The final example above shows the harder decimal percentage which was converted from $5/16$. Exceptionally, it does not finish in the hundredths column, because of the .25% on the end. This needs extra decimal places, reaching to the ten thousandths, because

$$.25\% = \frac{0.25}{100} = \frac{0.25 \times 100}{100 \times 100} = \frac{25}{10000}.$$

Figure 10.21

Converting decimals to percentages

The second column of decimals is for hundredths. Therefore, any decimal, which can be 'lifted' entirely out of the first two columns of decimals, can be written immediately as a percentage.

Examples

	$\frac{1}{10}$	$\frac{1}{100}$	$\frac{1}{1000}$	
	2	5		= 25%
	9	7		= 97%
	0	5		= 5%
	1	0		= 10%
so	1	8		= 18%

If the decimal contains more than two places, then the percentage will have to be extended to contain them.

Examples

	1	$\frac{1}{10}$	$\frac{1}{100}$	$\frac{1}{1000}$	$\frac{1}{10000}$	
		6	6			= 66%
so		6	6	6	6	= 66.66%
		3	7			= 37%
so		3	7	5		= 37.5%
		1	8			= 18%
so	4	1	8			= 418%

Special percentages

The following list shows the equivalent percentages, fractions and decimals for the most important parts of a whole thing:

$\frac{1}{2}$ = 50% = .5

$\frac{1}{4}$ = 25% = .25

$\frac{3}{4}$ = 75% = .75

$\frac{1}{10}$ = 10% = .1

$\frac{1}{5}$ = 20% = .2

$\frac{1}{3}$ = 33⅓%

= 33.3% = .333

$$\frac{2}{3} \quad = \quad 66^2/_3\%$$

$$= \quad 66.6\% \quad = \quad .666$$

$$\frac{1}{100} \quad = \quad 1\% \quad = \quad .01$$

A Global Exercise with Fractions, Percentages and Decimals

In order to practise the various conversion processes detailed in this chapter, the child should give the written forms of the shaded parts on the diagrams, such as those shown in Figure 10.22. He should write percentages, decimals and fractions (simplified where possible)

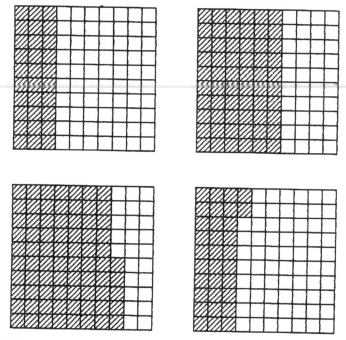

Figure 10.22

Chapter 11
Operating with fractions

Introduction

Work with simple fractions epitomises the argument 'Mathematics is easy, only writing it down is hard'. For example, as we shall show, it is very easy to make $3\frac{1}{4} + 1\frac{1}{2}$ into $4\frac{3}{4}$ using the paper–folding model advocated in this book for introducing fractions, but the written version, which carries with it a complex and virtually unjustifiable algorithm, seems very difficult indeed by comparison. The work in this chapter is designed to link the 'doing' with the 'writing down' with the aim of making them equally easy. The paper–folding model also provides a visual and kinaesthetic image to help the child recall and use the algorithm correctly.

As in Chapter 10, the ideas illustrated and substantiated by paper folding show the child what the written–down version should be, so that the written version of the problem relates directly to the concrete model. Thus, at a point of difficulty with a written problem there will be a parallel paper–folding procedure to support memory (or conceptual difficulties).

Here, as elsewhere in this book, the structure brought by these models and the procedures are intended to contribute towards the pupil's overall understanding of the algorithms and concepts. The use of folded–paper fractions is often clear enough for the diagrams or examples to speak for themselves, and thus the minimum amount of explanatory text is needed. As in other chapters, you must use your experience of the child to blend the work to suit the individual. The basic structure is, however, best left intact.

Making Segment Sizes the Same

It will become apparent at points in this chapter that if two or more fractions are to be compared, added or subtracted, their segments must be the same size. Generally, their segments will not be the same size, but there is a method of making them so, which is fully consistent with the philosophy of this book. It depends on the argument that for segments to be made the same size, the fractions must be made to undergo the same paper–folding steps. Each fraction must be given the folds it does not already share with the others. The folding can be real, drawn, imagined or written, but the objective will be a situation where all fractions have been through the same folding steps. The experience gained earlier, in actually making fractions, will be valuable here.

Examples

- Consider the fractions $\frac{7}{8}$ and $\frac{3}{4}$ (Figure 11.1a).

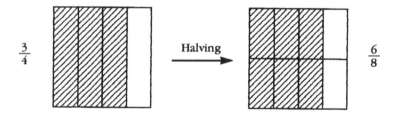

Figure 11.1a

		Folding it has had	Folding it now needs
	$\frac{7}{8}$	Halving, halving, halving	–
	$\frac{3}{4}$	Halving, halving	Halving

The written version is shown in Figure 11.1b. The folded–paper diagram and the written version are now showing eighths as the segment size for both fractions.

Figure 11.1b

- Consider the fractions ¾ and ⅔ (Figure 11.2a). ¾ has been through halving and halving and ⅔ has been through thirding. ⅔ now needs thirding; ⅔ now needs halving and halving.

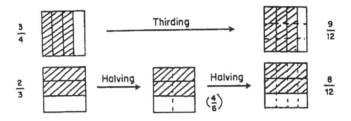

Figure 11.2a

The written version which gives this effect is shown in Figure 11.2b. Now twelfths is the segment size for both fractions. Notice that it is unnecessary to know in advance that the shared segment size will be twelfths.

$$\frac{3}{4} \quad \text{ₘ} \quad \frac{3 \times 3}{4 \times 3} \quad \text{ₘ} \quad \frac{9}{12}$$

$$\frac{2}{3} \quad \text{ₘ} \quad \frac{2 \times 2}{3 \times 2} \quad \text{ₘ} \quad \frac{4}{6} \quad \text{ₘ} \quad \frac{4 \times 2}{6 \times 2} \quad \text{ₘ} \quad \frac{8}{12}$$

Figure 11.2b

- Consider ⅚ and ⁹⁄₁₀ . After considering how they were formed, it is evident that ⅚ now needs fifthing and ⁹⁄₁₀ needs thirding. This time using the written form only gives

$$\frac{5}{6} = \frac{5 \times 5}{6 \times 5} = \frac{25}{30}$$

$$\frac{9}{10} = \frac{9 \times 3}{10 \times 3} = \frac{27}{30}$$

In later examples, where this procedure is taking place, the region of working will be highlighted within a dotted rectangle as it has been in these examples. Of course, this is not necessary outside this book.

Comparing Fractions

Examples

- Which is bigger: ³/₅ or ²/₃?

Some children would say ³/₅, because there are more segments, whereas others would say ²/₃ because the segments are bigger. Even a picture of the folded–paper version leaves some doubt (Figure 11.3a).

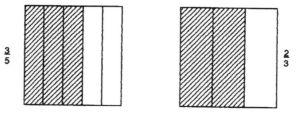

Figure 11.3a

Fractions can be compared best when their segments are the same size. This can be achieved by the procedure detailed in the previous section, which involves further folding, real, drawn, imagined or written. Again, the objective is a situation where both fractions have been through the same folding procedure. ³/₅ has been through fifthing. ²/₃ has been through thirding.

Therefore, ³/₅ now needs thirding and ²/₃ needs fifthing (Figure 11.3b).

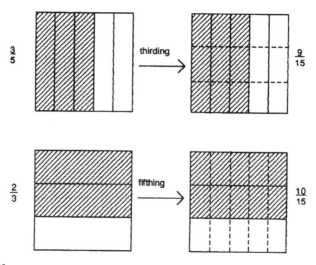

Figure 11.3b

The written version of this would be as shown in Figure 11.3c. Both the folded and written versions show $\frac{2}{3}$ to be bigger (by $\frac{1}{15}$).

$$\frac{3}{5} \quad = \quad \frac{3 \times 3}{5 \times 3} \quad = \quad \frac{9}{15}$$

$$\frac{2}{3} \quad = \quad \frac{2 \times 5}{3 \times 5} \quad = \quad \frac{10}{15}$$

Figure 11.3c

- Compare $\frac{9}{16}$ and $\frac{5}{8}$.

After considering how these fractions would be folded, it is evident that all that is now needed is for the $\frac{5}{8}$ to undergo another halving process. Using only the written form:

$$\frac{9}{16} \quad = \quad \frac{9}{16}$$

$$\frac{5}{8} \quad = \quad \frac{5 \times 2}{8 \times 2} \quad = \quad \frac{10}{16}$$

which makes $\frac{5}{8}$ bigger (by $\frac{1}{16}$).

Converting mixed fractions to top-heavy fractions

$2\frac{1}{4}$ is called a mixed fraction, because it has a whole number part and a fraction part. It is frequently necessary to convert all of this mixed fraction into segments (in this case quarters). Figure 11.4 shows the

Paper version | Written/spoken version

$$2\frac{1}{4} \;\; = 2 \times 1 + \frac{1}{4}$$

$$= \frac{2 \times 4 \text{ quarters}}{+\, 1 \text{ quarter}}$$

$$= \frac{8 \text{ quarters}}{+\, 1 \text{ quarter}}$$

$$= 9 \text{ quarters}$$

$$= \frac{9}{4}$$

Figure 11.4

paper and written/spoken versions. The result is known as a top–heavy fraction for obvious reasons. The careful use of words in the written/spoken version is deliberate and necessary at first. This is because many children who have seen this work before remember incorrect methods. They remember a rule which says, 'Multiply something by something and add something', but unfortunately mix up their somethings. Until they understand why they are multiplying and adding, they are likely to produce $2 \times 1 + 4$ or $4 \times 1 + 2$ rather than $2 \times 4 + 1$.

Subsequently they will perform the correct calculation in their heads, or write a variant of

$$2\tfrac{1}{4} \quad = 2 \times {}^4\!/_4 + {}^1\!/_4$$
$$= {}^8\!/_4 + {}^1\!/_4$$
$$= {}^9\!/_4.$$

Converting top–heavy fractions to mixed fractions

Top–heavy fractions have been called 'improper' fractions, a name which suggests it is undesirable to leave them in this form. They can be converted into mixed fractions as follows.

Example

-     ${}^{14}\!/_3$

As the segments are thirds, they must be grouped in threes to form whole numbers (Figure 11.5). Any remainders will stay as thirds. The essential working is a division by three:

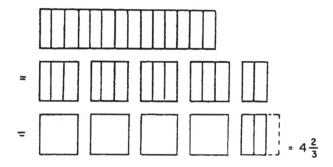

Figure 11.5

$$\begin{array}{r} 4\text{r}2 \\ 3\overline{)14} \end{array}$$

The results may be interpreted as follows:

Spoken version	*Written version.*
Fourteen thirds	$^{14}/_3$
equals four times three thirds plus two thirds	$= 4 \times {}^3/_3 + {}^2/_3$
equals four whole numbers plus two thirds	$= 4 \times 1 + {}^2/_3$
equals four and two thirds	$= 4\,{}^2/_3$

Combining Fractions

Vertical and horizontal presentation of fraction problems

We believe that a major cause of misunderstanding and confusion with fractions derives from the radical differences between the procedures used for addition and subtraction and those used for multiplication (and division). These differences are summarised in Table 11.1.

Table 11.1

Addition/Subtraction	Multiplication
Addition and subtraction cannot take place until there are common denominators (i.e. equal segment sizes)	Multiplication can take place without common denominators
The denominators are neither added nor subtracted	The denominators (and numerators) are multiplied
Simplification is left to the end	Simplification is done as early as possible
Whole numbers are treated separately	Whole numbers are combined with fractions (to make mixed fractions)

Paper folding is used as the (two–dimensional) model to illustrate the combining of fractions. This easy demonstration can be shown to dictate and therefore relate directly to the written algorithm. It simplifies each operation and provides a solution to the problem summarised in Table 11.1. It leads naturally to a vertical layout for addition and subtraction, which contrasts with the horizontal presentation suggested for multiplication. Further advantages of this will be discussed later in this chapter.

The difficult concept of division of and, especially, division by fractions is also discussed later in the chapter. The 'normal' algorithms that are used to solve fraction–division problems must seem totally irrational and bizarre to many children (and adults). Some explanation is given, along with two methods, one vertical, one horizontal.

Adding Fractions

This section starts by using paper folding to provide a concrete image of the operation. The explanation then moves to a more conceptual level in order to extend the child's performance and streamline his work. The initial descriptions progress from the easiest operation on fractions with the same denominator (segment size) to problems which involve mixed fractions.

Fractions where the segments are the same size

Example

- $\frac{1}{5} + \frac{3}{5}$

Paper, written and spoken versions are given in Figure 11.6. The reference to a 'spoken version' introduces another two senses, oral and aural, and emphasises that adding fifths to fifths produces fifths, that is, there is no change in segment size (or name), just as adding a number of marbles to another number of marbles still produces marbles. Thus examples of this type are used to establish that segments must be the same size before addition can proceed. You can judge how many examples of this type are needed to establish this fundamental precept.

Paper version	Written version	Spoken version
	$\frac{1}{5}$	one-fifth
	$+\ \frac{3}{5}$	plus three-fifths
	$\frac{4}{5}$	four-fifths

Figure 11.6

Adding fractions where the segments are of different size

Example

- $\frac{1}{2} + \frac{2}{5}$

Again the different versions are given, in Figure 11.7. The paper–folding version signals a problem since the segments of the two pieces of paper in this type of problem are of different sizes. The spoken version confirms that like is not being added to like. Furthermore, if such an addition were to proceed, you could speculate about the problem with the child, 'What would be the segment size of the result?'.

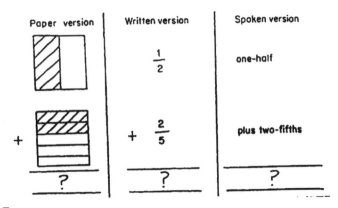

Figure 11.7

The child's attention should be focused on the segments, which are not the same size (nor have the same name) and this is the reason why addition cannot proceed without some modification to one or both of the segment names. The modification is to make the segments the same size (or give them the same name).

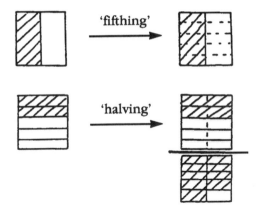

Figure 11.8

In this example the new segment size is tenths, because both halves and fifths can be renamed to this segment size (see Chapter 10). Both existing segments are folded again (Figure 11.8). The written version:

$$\frac{1}{2} = \frac{1 \times 5}{2 \times 5} = \frac{5}{10}$$

$$+ \frac{2}{5} = \frac{2 \times 2}{5 \times 2} = \frac{4}{10}$$

$$\frac{9}{10}$$

follows the steps shown in Figure 11.8 with the paper and extends the method described in Chapter 10, which makes segments the same size.

Adding more than two fractions

The same method, of making segment sizes the same, can be extended. Again the principle is to obtain the same segments for each fraction. Since more fractions are being added there is a likelihood of larger answers, possibly resulting in a top–heavy fraction.

Example

• $3/4 + 1/6 + 2/3$

The common segment size is twelfths (Figure 11.9). The written version is:

$$\frac{3}{4} = \frac{3 \times 3}{4 \times 3} = \frac{9}{12}$$

$$\frac{1}{6} = \frac{1 \times 2}{6 \times 2} = \frac{2}{12}$$

$$+ \frac{2}{3} = \frac{2 \times 4}{3 \times 4} = \frac{8}{12}$$

$$\frac{19}{12} = \frac{12}{12} + \frac{7}{12} = \frac{19}{12} = 1\frac{7}{12}$$

Adding mixed fractions

Mixed fractions with segments that are the same size

The procedure is similar to the addition of simple fractions, but the child is learning to treat the whole numbers and fractions separately.

Example

• $2^{1}/5 + 3^{2}/5$

The folded–paper version (Figure 11.10) shows the answer clearly and also relates well to the written version:

$2^1/5$		
$3^2/5$	compare with	32
$5^3/5$		53

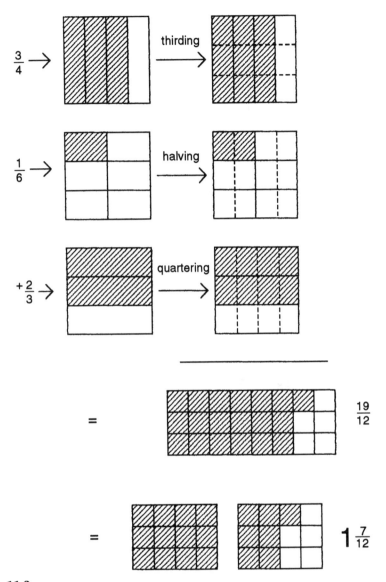

Figure 11.9

It demonstrates the need to deal separately with the whole numbers and the fractions in the same way that tens and units are dealt with separately in whole–number addition.

Mixed fractions with different segment sizes

Once again the child has to focus on the size of the segments and remember from the example above to deal with the whole numbers and fractions separately. Thus the exercise can be used to reinforce previously learnt skills.

$$2\tfrac{1}{5} + 3\tfrac{2}{5}$$

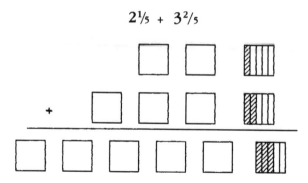

Figure 11.10

Example

- $2\tfrac{1}{4} + 1\tfrac{2}{3}$

The written version is

$$2\ \frac{1}{4} = \frac{1\times3}{4\times3} = \frac{3}{12}$$

$$+1\ \frac{2}{3} = \frac{2\times2}{3\times2} = \frac{4}{6} = \frac{4\times2}{6\times2} = \frac{8}{12}$$

$$3 \qquad\qquad\qquad\qquad\qquad \frac{11}{12}$$

It would be simple to use paper folding to demonstrate the above steps, confirming the algorithm and the answer:

$$2\tfrac{1}{4} + 1\tfrac{2}{3} = 3\tfrac{11}{12}$$

Subtracting Fractions

The basic principle is the same as for addition. The child has to learn that the segments have to be the same size (same name) before subtraction can proceed. As with addition, a series of progressively more complex examples is given.

Fractions where the segments are the same size

Example

- $\tfrac{3}{5} - \tfrac{1}{5}$

Paper, written and spoken versions are given in Figure 11.11. The

Paper version	Written version	Spoken version
	$\dfrac{3}{5}$	three-fifths
	$-\dfrac{1}{5}$	minus one-fifth
	$\dfrac{2}{5}$	two-fifths

Figure 11.11

spoken version confirms that the segments are the same size (have the same name) for the subtraction process.

Fractions with different segment sizes

Example

- $^4/_5 - {}^2/_3$

The paper version (Figure 11.12) shows that the problem is impossible to complete in this form (by showing different segment sizes). The spoken version confirms this because the segments have different names. The problem requires, as with addition, that the segments should be made the same size, in this case fifteenths. Again the concrete example of the paper folding focuses attention on the critical part of the algorithm, the need to work with segments which are the same size:

$$\frac{4}{5} = \frac{4 \times 3}{5 \times 3} = \frac{12}{15}$$

$$-\frac{2}{3} = \frac{2 \times 5}{3 \times 5} = \frac{10}{15}$$

$$\frac{2}{15}$$

Subtracting mixed fractions

Mixed fractions where the segments are the same size

Example

- $3^5/_9 - 2^1/_9$

Paper version	Written version	Spoken version
	$\frac{4}{5}$	four-fifths
−	$-\ \frac{2}{3}$	minus two thirds
?	?	?

Figure.11.12

The paper version is shown in Figure 11.13. The answer is quite clearly $1^4/_9$, and it is also clear that the whole numbers should be treated separately. The written version is as follows:

$$
\begin{array}{r}
3^5/_9 \\
-\ 2^1/_9 \\
\hline
1^4/_9
\end{array}
\qquad \text{compare with} \qquad
\begin{array}{r}
35 \\
-\ 21 \\
\hline
14
\end{array}
$$

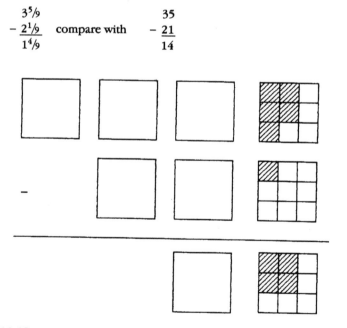

Figure 11.13

Mixed fractions with different segment sizes

Again the child has to focus on the segment sizes. The segments must be adjusted to be the same size (and to have the same name) and the whole numbers and parts must be dealt with separately. The child can use paper folding for all parts or just the fraction part of this problem. For the convenience of brevity only the written version is shown for this example:

- $5\frac{5}{6} - 2\frac{1}{4}$

$$5 \quad \frac{5}{6} = \frac{5 \times 2}{6 \times 2} = \frac{10}{12}$$

$$-2 \quad \frac{1}{4} = \frac{1 \times 3}{4 \times 3} = \frac{3}{12}$$

$$3 \qquad\qquad\qquad\qquad\qquad \frac{7}{12}$$

Mixed fractions where a bigger fraction part is subtracted from a smaller fraction part

Example

- $4\frac{1}{2} - 2\frac{2}{3}$

Since $\frac{2}{3}$ is bigger than $\frac{1}{2}$ the problem requires an adjustment not dissimilar to a whole–number subtraction such as $374 - 158$, where 8 is bigger than 4. The solution to the difficulty with fractions is very similar to that used with whole numbers. The child has to go to a whole number and convert it to a fraction in the same way as a child doing a whole–number subtraction has to go to the tens column to obtain units.

Thus the algorithm is not another new, unrelated idea to learn. You are showing the child the wide applicability of mathematical procedures. The action of paper folding provides a concrete model for the algorithm and a multisensory input to the memory. The paper–folding procedure also confirms for the child that $\frac{2}{3}$ is bigger than $\frac{1}{2}$. The paper version is given in Figure 11.14.

The written version is as follows:

$$4\frac{1}{2} = 4\frac{3}{6} = \quad 3 \quad \frac{6}{6} \quad \frac{3}{6}$$

$$-2\frac{2}{3} = 2\frac{4}{6} = \quad 2 \quad \frac{4}{6}$$

$$\overline{\qquad\qquad\qquad 1 \quad \frac{5}{6}}$$

Figure 11.14

Combined Additions and Subtractions

Both addition and subtraction of fractions require:

* Segments of the same size (same name).
* Whole numbers to be treated separately from parts.

Consequently, it is possible to perform both operations in the same calculation without a change of algorithm.

The child may need to use paper folding, but by now he may be able to move straight to the written algorithm.

Example

* $2\frac{1}{8} + 3\frac{1}{2} - 1\frac{1}{4}$

$$
\begin{array}{llll}
2\ \frac{1}{8} & & = & \frac{1}{8} \\[2mm]
+3\ \frac{1}{2} & = \dfrac{1\times 4}{2\times 4} & = & \frac{4}{8} \\[2mm]
-1\ \frac{1}{4} & = \dfrac{1\times 2}{4\times 2} & = & \frac{2}{8} \\[2mm]
\hline
4 & & & \frac{3}{8}
\end{array}
$$

It may be advantageous to show the child why the addition and subtraction of fractions have been presented in a vertical format. The following summarises the advantages.

Advantages of the vertical layout for addition and subtraction of fractions

* It signals the need to make segment sizes the same.
* There is less likelihood of adding or subtracting the denominators.
* It allows room horizontally to change the segment sizes.

- It lines up fractions and whole numbers separately and encourages the child to deal with them separately.
- Numbers are added and subtracted vertically which is more familiar and easier for most children.

This layout is a well–established method of presentation in the USA.

Multiplying by Fractions

The language of multiplication should be established first. As with percentages, the word 'of' is frequently used to mean multiply. For example $\frac{3}{4}$ of 8 means $\frac{3}{4} \times 8$. If the child needs to be convinced of this use, then refer back to whole number examples such as, 'How many sweets in 7 packets of 10?' or 'If a pen costs 20p how much will I pay for 8 of them?' may help.

Fraction times fraction

The multiplication of whole number by whole number (Chapter 8) used area as a model. Area is a two–dimensional model. The paper–folding model for fraction times fraction does the same.

Finding the fraction of a square of paper was explained earlier. Multiplication repeats the process in a second dimension. So one dimension represents a and the other dimension represents b in $a \times b$.

Example 1

- $\frac{1}{2} \times \frac{1}{3}$

This multiplication is carried out by using a square of paper to find one half of one third of the square.

Figure 11.15

Figure 11.15 shows $\frac{1}{3}$ shaded. A vertical fold gives one half of this third. The part shaded twice is one half of one third. There are six segments in all, so one segment is $\frac{1}{6}$.

This was the method used earlier to fold $\frac{1}{6}$, acknowledging the interrelationship among the fractions $\frac{1}{2}$, $\frac{1}{3}$ and $\frac{1}{6}$.

The application of two fraction operations to the same square has two major implications:

- The change in segment size is seen to be inevitable. It should be obvious to the child that the answer will have a new segment size (and that it will be smaller).
- The *horizontally* written layout of this multiplication reflects the difference of this operation and its model from that used for addition and subtraction.

The written form of the example above is:

$\frac{1}{2} \times \frac{1}{3} = \frac{1}{6}$

Example 2

- $\frac{2}{3}$ of $\frac{4}{5}$

$$\frac{2}{3}$$

$$\frac{4}{5}$$

Figure 11.16

The square is folded into fifths in one direction and four of these fifths are shaded (Figure 11.16). The square is then folded into thirds in the opposite direction to give a grid with 15 segments, i.e. fifteenths. Two of the thirds are shaded (in the opposite direction) and the child should see the answer, $\frac{8}{15}$, shaded twice.

The concrete operation of folding and shading the square relates directly to the written form:

$$\frac{2}{3} \text{ of } \frac{4}{5} = \frac{2}{3} \times \frac{4}{5} = \frac{2 \times 4}{3 \times 5} = \frac{8}{15}$$

The child is multiplying top and bottom parts of the fractions, which is easier to remember if the fractions are written side by side. The folding shows why 3 and 5 are multiplied together to make 15 segments and why 2 and 4 are multiplied together to give 8 of these segments.

Example 3

- $\frac{1}{2}$ of $\frac{4}{5}$

This results in an answer which can be simplified or reduced. The paper–folding procedure is the same as in example 2, leading to an answer of ⁴/₁₀. Although this is not wrong, it would be more elegant to obtain ²/₅.

The written version may be used to explain cancelling before and after the multiplication. This offers an opportunity to remind the child that fractions are about division and that a fraction may have more than one 'name'.

Fraction times whole number

Example 1 (Figure 11.17a)

- ¼ of 1

Figure 11.17a

Example 2 (Figure 11.17b)

- ¼ of 3

Figure 11.17b

The child should see that ¼ of 3 is ¼ three 'times', relating 'times' and 'of' once again. The written version relates exactly to fraction times fraction if 3 is written as ³/₁:

$$\frac{1}{4} \text{ of } 3 = \frac{1}{4} \times \frac{3}{1} = \frac{1 \times 3}{4 \times 1} = \frac{3}{4}$$

Example 3 (Figure 11.17c)

* $\frac{2}{5}$ of 2

The written version is:

$$\frac{2}{5} \text{ of } 2 = \frac{2}{5} \times \frac{2}{1} = \frac{2 \times 2}{5 \times 1} = \frac{4}{5}$$

$$\frac{2}{5} \text{ of } 2 = \qquad\qquad = \frac{4}{5}$$

Figure 11.17c

Multiplying Mixed Fractions

Example

* $3\frac{1}{2} \times 2\frac{1}{4}$

The most probable error in this type of calculation arises when the child separates the fractions from the whole numbers, following an addition algorithm, and simply multiplies 3×2 and $\frac{1}{2} \times \frac{1}{4}$.

A consistent application of the area model for multiplication shows the need for four separate multiplications (see Chapter 8).

$3\frac{1}{2} \times 2\frac{1}{4}$ gives four areas, A, B, C and D (Figure 11.18).

Figure 11.18

A is $3 \times 2 = 6$ (which provides a simple estimate)
B is $2 \times \frac{1}{2} = 1$
C is $3 \times \frac{1}{4} = \frac{3}{4} = \frac{6}{8}$
D is $\frac{1}{2} \times \frac{1}{4} = \frac{1}{8}$
Total $= 7\frac{7}{8}$

Although this provides a method consistent with that used for two digit times two digit whole–number multiplications, it is somewhat complex for fractions, so a procedure that is usually less open to errors is recommended. The mixed fractions are converted to top–heavy fractions, which can then be multiplied together as for simple fractions:

$$3\tfrac{1}{2} \times 2\tfrac{1}{4} = \frac{7}{2} \times \frac{9}{4} = \frac{7 \times 9}{2 \times 4} = \frac{63}{8} = 7\tfrac{7}{8}$$

Figure 11.19

A new diagram can be drawn to illustrate this written method (Figure 11.19). This rectangle shows there are halves (seven of them) and that there are fourths (nine of them). The unit square shows the answer will be in eighths and the 7×9 grid shows there are 63 of these eighths.

With these larger numbers there is more encouragement to cancel prior to multiplication, in examples where this is possible.

Example

• $2\tfrac{2}{3} \times 2\tfrac{1}{10}$

$$2\tfrac{2}{3} \times 2\tfrac{1}{10} = \frac{8}{3} \times \frac{21}{10} = \frac{^4\cancel{8} \times \cancel{21}^7}{_1\cancel{3} \times \cancel{10}_5} = \frac{28}{5} = 5\tfrac{3}{5}$$

The advantages of a horizontal layout for multiplication

• It prompts the child to multiply the top numbers together and then to multiply the denominators together.
• It encourages simplifying (cancelling) at the beginning.
• There is less temptation to treat whole numbers in isolation.
• It distinguishes between addition/subtraction and multiplication.

The advantages of different presentations for addition/subtraction and multiplication are best illustrated with an example which combines addition and multiplication.

Many children will want to begin by inappropriate separation of the portions of the problem. You should encourage the child to read the problem and analyse its demands. The layout shown presents the problem clearly and logically.

The structured layout for the operations has extra advantages in this type of problem. It also follows the rules for the order of operations BOMDAS (Brackets Of Multiply Divide Add Subtract), where multiplication precedes addition.

Example

- $3\frac{1}{2} \times 1\frac{1}{2} + 1\frac{2}{3} \times 2\frac{1}{5}$

$$3\frac{1}{2} \times 1\frac{1}{2} = \frac{7}{2} \times \frac{3}{2} = \frac{7 \times 3}{2 \times 2} = \frac{21}{4} = 5\frac{1}{4} = \frac{3}{12}$$

$$+ 1\frac{2}{3} \times 2\frac{1}{5} = \frac{5}{3} \times \frac{11}{5_1} = \frac{1 \times 11}{3 \times 1} = \frac{11}{3} = 3\frac{2}{3} = \frac{8}{12}$$

$$8 \qquad \frac{11}{12}$$

multiplication $\longrightarrow$

addition $\downarrow$

Dividing with fractions

A sequence of divisions may be used to introduce the child to this difficult concept (Ashcroft and Chinn, 1992):

$20 \div 4 = 5$
$20 \div 2 = 10$
$20 \div 1 = 20$
$20 \div \frac{1}{2} = 40$

This may help the child to learn to rephrase the question, a strategy that has quite extensive value. Thus $20 \div 1/2$ becomes 'How many halves in 20?'. A square of paper may be folded to make two halves, followed by the question 'How many halves in one?'. It can be halved again, leading to the question 'How many quarters in one?'. The process can be continued through 1/8, 1/16, 1/32 to show the answer becoming bigger as the fraction becomes smaller.

Divison by fractions

Two methods are described here. The first deals with simple examples and establishes a concrete image for this difficult concept. It is harder to explain the second method in this way, but it is the expedient way for those who progress to algebra.

The first method is set out vertically whereas the second method is presented horizontally (it being more akin to multiplication).

Division by making the segments the same size

Example

- $^7/_{10} \div {}^1/_{10}$

The spoken version of this problem needs a flexibility of mathematical vocabulary again. It could be read as 'Seven tenths divided by one tenth', but the child is more likely to understand 'How many tenths in seven tenths?'. Again the ability to rephrase a question can take the child a long way towards the answer of seven.

Example

- $^3/_4 \div {}^1/_8$

The use of the same spoken version leads to 'How many (one) eighths in three quarters?. This makes about as much sense as 'How many cars in a pencil?'. However, the alternative interpretation 'Divide three quarters into eighths' indicates more positively that the segment sizes should be made the same. So the first step is to make the segment sizes the same. Figure 11.20 shows the paper, written and spoken versions.

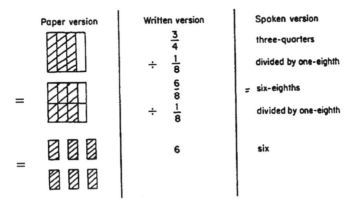

Figure 11.20

Example

- $^3/_5 \div {}^7/_{10}$

This is shown in the written version only:

$$\frac{3}{5} = \frac{6}{10}$$

$$\div \frac{7}{10} = \frac{7}{10}$$

$$= \frac{6}{7}$$

Examples with mixed fractions

The initial step of the method advocated is to convert the mixed fraction into a top–heavy fraction.

Example

• $3^3/_4 \div {}^3/_4$

Since the segments are already the same, the division proceeds immediately. The three versions are shown in Figure 11.21. The question is interpreted and illustrated as, 'How many groups of 3 (quarters) in 15 (quarters)?'.

Paper version	Written version	Spoken version

$$3\frac{3}{4}$$

$$\div \quad \frac{3}{4}$$

$$\frac{15}{4}$$

fifteen quarters
divided by
three quarters

$$\div \quad \frac{3}{4}$$

$$= \quad 5$$

Figure 11.21

Example

• $5^2/_3 \div 2^1/_2$

This is shown in written version only, because by now the child should have a well–established model of fractions:

$$5^2/_3 \ = \ \frac{17}{3} \ = \ \frac{17 \times 2}{3 \times 2} \ = \ \frac{34}{6}$$

$$\div \ 2^1/_2 \ = \ \frac{5}{2} \ = \ \frac{5 \times 3}{2 \times 3} \ = \ \frac{15}{6}$$

$$\frac{34}{15} \ = \ 2^4/_{15}$$

Dividing fractions by inverse multiplication

This method is quicker, but asks the child to remember a seemingly inexplicable rule. So $4 \div {^2/_3}$ is calculated as $4 \times {^3/_2}$. Some children will be happy enough to accept the explanation (rationalisation) that since multiplication is the opposite of division then there is a need to do an opposite thing with the fraction, that is, to turn it upside down.

An explanation for the algorithm can be developed for the child by a series of paper–folding exercises.

- $1 \div {^1/_3}$

By definition, one whole number divided into thirds gives 3 (Figure 11.22a).

$$1 \div \frac{1}{3} = \ 3$$

Figure 11.22a

- $4 \div {^1/_3}$

Four whole numbers divided into thirds will give $4 \times 3 = 12$ (Figure 11.22b).

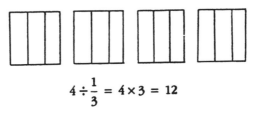

$$4 \div \frac{1}{3} = 4 \times 3 = 12$$

Figure 11.22b

• $4 \div \frac{2}{3}$

4 divided into groups of two thirds will give (Figure 11.22c):

$4 \times 3 \div 2$ or $\dfrac{4 \times 3}{2}$ or   6

$$4 \div \frac{2}{3} = \frac{4}{1} \times \frac{3}{2} = \frac{\overset{2}{4} \times 3}{1 \times \underset{1}{2}} = \frac{6}{1} = 6$$

Figure 11.22c

Since $\frac{2}{3}$ is twice as big as $\frac{1}{3}$, then the child should expect the answer to be half that of the previous example, that is, the previous answer has to be divided by 2. However you choose to justify the rule, it remains a case of inverting the fraction, then multiplying:

$$y \div \frac{a}{b} = y \times \frac{b}{a}$$

Chapter 12
Decimals

Introduction

It is the very great importance of the decimal point which engenders puns such as 'What's the point?' and visual jokes suggesting 'It's only a little dot'. Indeed, it is mainly the necessity to manoeuvre the decimal point into its correct position that differentiates decimal calculations from whole number calculations. Apart from the decimal point, the processes of addition, subtraction, multiplication and division are identical to those covered for whole numbers in Chapters 7 and 8. The decimal point adds another 'dimension' to place value, and another potential source of errors.

It will be evident from the other chapters in this book that we are wary of teaching dyslexic children too many rules, because they are likely to forget or confuse them. However, this situation is an exception, largely because the rules for positioning the decimal point, once properly justified and established, are simple enough to make alternative procedures seem clumsy and pedantic. Indeed, ultimately, for all except multiplication, the rules boil down to keeping the decimal points under each other in a vertical line. Thus using a rule becomes pragmatically the best route.

Addition and Subtraction

Addition

Common errors tend to be due to misalignment of the decimal point—that is, incorrectly lining up the place values of the numbers involved (Ashlock, 1982). The following errors demonstrate confusion over the positioning of the numbers in their columns and consequently of the decimal point. Reinstating column headings can help, but the tendency persists to line up the numbers from the right, irrespective of place value.

1.23 + 5   becoming   1.23
                                + 5
                                1.28

and

0.95 + 0.5   becoming   0.09
                               + 0.5
                                0.14

The correct process can be illustrated by using Dienes base–ten blocks or similar apparatus, but more effective help is usually achieved with the use of money. For example, children who begin by adding £1.23 + £5 with coins will rarely try to add the 5 and the 3, as in the written version above. Those children still tempted to do this usually respond to the suggestion that £5 may be written as £5.00, writing the .00 because it has no pennies, and so the written version becomes:

    £1.23
  + £5.00
    £6.23

If written examples are linked, with the child handling the equivalent money, generally it becomes clear that pounds are added to pounds, pennies are added to pennies, and so on. The child can be led to write them under each other, which automatically puts the decimal points (separating the pounds and pennies) under each other. This gives the child a focus so that the other example from above can be presented as £0.09 + £0.5(0) and written as:

      £   0.09
   + £   0.5(0)
      £   0.59

Money provides the concrete memory hook for the child.
    Another common error with decimal addition is shown below:

                                      1
3.97 + 1.04   becomes   3.97
                               + 1.04
                                4.101

A child who produces this error has been content to carry a 1 from the hundredths to the tenths column, but is unwilling to carry a 1 from the tenths to the units column, which requires him to cross over the decimal point. There is a lack of understanding here that the decimal columns are simply an extension of the whole number columns, that they are related in the same way (increasing and decreasing in powers of 10) and that they must follow the same rules. This problem was anticipated in Chapter 10, where the issue was clarified by the use of decimal number sequences. A demonstration with money can be used to provide further reinforcement. The example above can be viewed as £3.97 + £1.04 and written

$$\begin{array}{r} {\scriptstyle 1\ 1} \\ \text{£ } 3.97 \\ + \text{£ } \underline{1.04} \\ \text{£ } \underline{5.01} \end{array}$$

Thus 7 + 4 is 11 pence, which is changed (traded) for a single 10 pence, carried to the 10–pence column, and a one penny which is retained as the answer in the unit–pence column. Similarly, in the 10–pence column, the carried 1 is added to the 9 and 0 to give 10 lots of 10 pence. These can be traded for £1, which is carried into the pounds column.

Subtraction

Subtraction of decimal numbers presents children with virtually the same problems as addition. For example, 24.38 – 0.6 might generate the error

$$\begin{array}{r} 24.38 \\ -\ 0.6 \\ \hline 24.32 \end{array}$$

Here the tendency to line up numbers from the right regardless of place value is compounded by the fact that the 6 is easier to subtract from 8 than 3. The solution to this problem is, as for addition, to line up the decimal points. Again the best manipulative material to illustrate and develop this procedure is money.

Another common error pattern is illustrated by the example 48.5 – 2.36. This tends to generate two types of error:

• Lining up from the right

$$\begin{array}{r} {\scriptstyle 7\ 1} \\ 4\!\!\!/8.5 \\ -\ 2.36 \\ \hline 24.9 \end{array}$$ (or 2.49 and sometimes 2.4.9).

• Setting up correctly, but

$$\begin{array}{r} 48.5 \\ -\ 2.36 \\ \hline 6 \end{array}$$

The 6 is just transferred (effectively added) to the answer line, before the rest of the calculation is completed correctly.

$$48.5$$
$$-\ 2.36$$
$$\overline{46.26}$$

The use of an optional zero to 'square off' the calculation reminds the child that the 6 has to be subtracted, and gives him something to subtract from.

$$48.50 \qquad\qquad \overset{4}{4}\overset{1}{8}.\cancel{5}0$$
$$-\ 2.36 \quad \text{then} \quad -\ 2.36$$
$$\overline{} \qquad\qquad \overline{46.14}$$

This can be practised with coins and place–value columns.

Errors in the addition and subtraction of decimals can be reduced though the policy of instilling into children the universal need to preview and review a question—to absorb some meaning and value for the numbers and produce an estimate—then check their answers against the estimate. This is likely to reduce the incidence of misalign ment errors. Mention must also be made here of Ann Henderson's (1989) giant decimal point as another way of focusing attention on the all–important decimal point.

Multiplication and Division by Powers of 10

Multiplication by 10

As with so much work in mathematics, place value is important here, so a review of the topic may be an advisable precursor to the next work.

Confronted by the question 4.62×10, if the child can remember that $4 \times 10 = 40$ then this can help to lead him to see that 4.62×10 (4 and a bit times 10) should be forty–something. Alternatively, 4.62×10 can be interpreted as 10 lots of 4.62 and can be evaluated the 'long' way (as an addition):

$$4.62$$
$$4.62$$
$$4.62$$
$$4.62$$
$$4.62$$
$$4.62$$
$$4.62$$
$$4.62$$
$$4.62$$
$$+\ \ 4.62$$
$$\overline{46.20}$$

Many children will notice that the figures 4, 6 and 2 have not changed, as might be expected in a multiplication; nor has their order. (This observation is, of course, an extension of the 10 times–table pattern.) The numbers have moved along *one* place, so that each number is now 10 times bigger. Most children can appreciate this pattern when it is pointed out to them. Base–ten blocks or money can be used for manipulative work.

As always, a multiplication is more efficient, quicker and less prone to error than the repeated addition of 10 numbers.

The pattern can also be shown by considering each of the figures separately, using base–ten blocks, money or fractions to illustrate the procedure.

10	1 • $^1/_{10}$ $^1/_{100}$						10	1 • $^1/_{10}$
	• (0) 2	$\times 10 =$	$^2/_{100} \times 10 = {}^{20}/_{100} = {}^2/_{10} =$					• 2
	• 6	$\times 10 =$	$^6/_{10} \times 10 =$	$^{60}/_{10} =$				6 •
	4 •	$\times 10 =$					4	0 •
	4 • 6 2						4	6 • 2

£1 • 10p 1p					£10	£1 • 10p
• 0 2	$\times 10 =$	20p $= 2 \times$ 10p	$=$			• 2
• 6 (0)	$\times 10 =$	60p $\times 10 = $ £6	$=$		6 •	
4 •	$\times 10 =$	£40	$=$		4	0 •
4 • 6 2					4	6 • 2

When the pattern is written as $4.62 \times 10 = 46.2$, some children will imagine that the decimal point has moved rather than the figures. Whilst this is strictly incorrect, it is a simplification, whose value can out–weigh its disadvantages and it is often the only way some children can remember the rule. In reality, the figures and the decimal point both move, relative to each other.

Multiplication by 100

There are children who will be able to predict the effect of multiplying by 100 and they will conclude that the figures (or the decimal point) will move two places.

As with multiplying by 10, an example which relates to known facts can provide early understanding of the operation, as well as a valuable estimation procedure (useful also when calculators are used). For example, if it is known that $2 \times 100 = 200$, then 2.375×100 (which is 2 and a bit times 100) should be expected to be two hundred and a bit. Finally, if the digits are not to change, then the two hundred and a bit must be 237.5. This result can alternatively be justified by treating $\times 100$ as 10×10 in two stages (compare to $\times 4$ as $\times 2 \times 2$ in Chapter 6), and by using the same manipulative materials used for $\times 10$:

$$
\begin{aligned}
& 2.375 \times 100 \\
= \ & 2.375 \times 10 \times 10 \\
= \ & 23.75 \times 10 \\
= \ & 237.5
\end{aligned}
$$

Multiplication by 1000

At about this stage, children will usually see the pattern that the number of zeros in the multiplier dictates the number of places moved:

- Multiplying by 10   causes a movement of 1 place
- Multiplying by 100   causes a movement of 2 places,   so
- Multiplying by 1000   will cause a movement of 3 places.

For example, $27.1875 \times 1000 = 27187.5$. For justification, $\times\ 1000$ is equivalent to $\times\ 10 \times 10 \times 10$. The same manipulative materials may be used.

Multiplication by other powers of 10

The pattern can simply be extended, using similar arguments, illustrations and materials.

Division by 10

The initial goal is to show that division by 10 is the opposite of multiplication by 10. The answer becomes 10 times smaller rather than 10 times bigger. The topic could be introduced with money or base–ten blocks and the child being asked to show coins or blocks which are 10 times bigger or 10 times smaller. The answers are written on place–value paper. For example, $3p \times 10$ becomes 30p and conversely $30p \div 10$ becomes 3p. The movement of the numbers is demonstrated by their places on the paper. A good demonstration of the required rule depends on the argument that a division by 10 and a multiplication by 10 will cancel each other out, because they are opposites:

$$
\begin{aligned}
& 37.63 \times 10 \div 10 = 37.63 \quad \text{so} \\
& 376.3 \div 10 = 37.63
\end{aligned}
$$

The final line above shows that division by 10 causes a movement of one place. However, the movement is in the opposite direction to that caused by a multiplication by 10.

Direction of movement

A decision about convention is now needed, concerning how to describe the direction of a movement. Referring to the direction as left or right would be ambiguous, because if the figures move left, the decimal point moves right, and vice versa. Furthermore, terms such as left and right, forwards and backwards, in front and behind are all likely to confuse dyslexics, with their laterality problems (Miles, 1983). We suggest that a safer and more meaningful practice is to describe the direction of movement in accordance with whether the answer is bigger or smaller than the original number.

- Multiplication by powers of 10 produces answers which are bigger than the original number.
- Division by powers of 10 produces answers which are smaller than the original number.

This convention encourages overviews, estimates and reviews.

Division by 100, 1000 and other powers of 10

Divisions follow the same pattern as multiplications, in that the number of zeros in the divisor dictates the number of places moved (now in a direction which produces smaller answers).

- Dividing by 10 causes a movement of 1 place, so
- Dividing by 100 causes a movement of 2 places
- Dividing by 1000 causes a movement of 3 places, etc.

This work can be justified, if necessary, by arranging divisions as repeated divisions by 10, or as reverse multiplications.

Examples

$346.2 \div 100 = 3.462$
$1872.3 \div 1000 = 1.8732$
$23.721 \div 10000 = 0.0023721.$

The last example illustrates the need to insert leading zeros, and the need to explain this to a child. Again there is the importance of using and appreciating place value.

Rationalisation (1)

It is worth anticipating children's potential problems with trying to apply these procedures to whole numbers—only decimal numbers have been used so far in this chapter. Whole numbers do not display a decimal point, so three is written as 3 and not 3.0. Many calculators will change an entry of 3.0 to 3 as soon as an operation key is pressed. Children tend to simplify multiplication and division of whole numbers by powers of 10 into a process of gaining or losing zeros. For example,

$$2 \times 10 = 2\underline{0}$$
$$3000 \div 1000 = \cancel{3000} = 3$$

It is important that children do not see the treatment of whole numbers and decimals as two different processes. The two situations can be rationalised by treating whole number examples as decimal examples:

$$2 \times 10 = 2.(0) \times 10 = 20(.)$$

Here the digits and the decimal point have moved one place in a direction to make the answer bigger.

$$3000 \div 1000 = 3000.(0) \div 1000 = 3.(000)$$

Here there is a movement of three places to make the answer smaller.

Not only does this rationalise *all* multiplications and divisions by powers of 10, but these previously understood examples reinforce understanding of the new decimal work. Thus in $2 \times 10 = 20$ the digits and the decimal point *do* move one place.

Multiplication of decimals by decimals

There is an expectation, rightly encouraged previously in this chapter, that multiplying a number will produce an answer which is bigger than the original number. This has been true for powers of 10. However, for the example 0.6×0.8 this will not be the case (see Rationalisation (2)). Consequently, such examples are very difficult for children still in the earlier stages to answer correctly, unless they apply the proper rule, backed up by estimation skills based on good number concept.

Establishment of the rule can begin using the area model (Figure 12.1) for multiplication, as in other chapters of this book. Within the unit square shown in the figure, the required answer is shown by the area of the shaded rectangle. The small squares, each $^1/_{100}$, show the answer to be $^{48}/_{100}$ or 0.48, which is less than either of the original numbers, 0.6(0) and 0.8(0). Of course, this is because the answer represents part of a part.

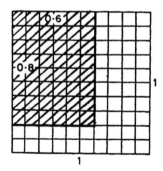

Figure 12.1

With or without the area model shown in Figure 12.1, the rule is best presented through fractions (Chapter 10 deliberately interrelated fractions, decimals and percentages), so 0.6×0.8 becomes:

$$\frac{6}{10} \times \frac{8}{10} = \frac{48}{100} = 0.48$$

In this example, the decimal places for 0.6 and 0.8 are treated as tenths. The tenths accumulate, by multiplication, into hundredths, so any rule for the decimal places must reflect this accumulation:

0.6	1 decimal place
×0.8	1 decimal place
0.48	2 decimal place

The decimal points do *not* line up under each other. The rule for positioning the decimal point can be stated as follows: The number of decimal places in the answer is equal to the total number of decimal places in the numbers of the question'. The digits in the answer (48) are the result of multiplying together the numbers in the question (6 and 8), and are obtained independently of the decimal places. Therefore, the numbers in the answer and the position of the decimal point are two separate considerations.

Examples

0.0003	4 decimal places
×0.02	2 decimal places
0.000006	6 decimal places

3.2	1 decimal place
×0.05	2 decimal places
0.160	3 decimal places

21.09	2 decimal places
×3	0 decimal places
63.27	2 decimal places

The final example shows that multiplication of a decimal by a whole number does not increase the number of decimal places. Quoting a special example such as this too early may lead to the impression that the decimal points do line up. Taken with other examples, this is seen to occur only in the exceptional case of a whole number multiplier.

Rationalisation (2)

In this chapter, it has been suggested that children are taught to expect a larger answer after multiplying by a power of 10, but a smaller answer after multiplying by a decimal. There is no ambiguity here, and the following explanation can be used to rationalise the situation, and also to encourage good estimation and checking strategy. Use is made of a sequence such as:

$$45 \times 100 \quad = \quad 4500$$
$$45 \times 10 \quad = \quad 450$$
$$45 \times 1 \quad = \quad 45$$
$$45 \times 0.1 \quad = \quad 4.5$$
$$45 \times 0.01 \quad = \quad 0.45$$

The pivotal value of the multiplier is 1, because any number times 1 remains unchanged. A multiplier bigger than 1 gives an answer bigger than the original number, whereas a multiplier less than 1 gives an answer less than the original number. This leads to the basic estimate/check procedure: 'If the multiplier is bigger than 1, expect the answer to be bigger, and if the multiplier is less than 1, expect the answer to be smaller'. The overview is, once again, an important ingredient of the procedure.

(An interesting side–track concerns children's gut estimation of questions such as 0.4×0.002. Given the choice of the answer being:

- bigger than 0.4
- a middle value between 0.4 and 0.002
- smaller than 0.002

most choose the middle value. A discussion as to the correct answer helps children understand the concept of multiplication by numbers less than 1 and acts as a useful reference/guide for similar problems.)

Division of Decimals

Division by a whole number

This work builds on the work of Chapter 9, with the added dimension of a decimal point, so a comparison with a whole–number example is a good lead in. The problem $81 \div 3$ is traditionally set out as

$$
\begin{array}{r}
27 \\
3\overline{)81} \\
60 \\
\overline{21} \\
21 \\
\overline{0}
\end{array}
$$

A pre–estimate of $81.6 \div 3$ might be 'a little more than 27, but less than 30'. The calculation could then be presented as

```
      27.2
  3)81.6
     60.0
     21.6
     21.0
       .6
       .6
        0
```

The result compares well with the pre–estimate. For division by a whole number, the decimal points line up with each other. This algorithm sets the model for other decimal divisions.

Division by a decimal

A question such as 8.64 ÷ 2 follows the procedure above, because it is a division by a whole number. The question 8.64 ÷ 0.2 will often be set out (erroneously) in the same way, as follows:

```
        4.32
  0.2)8.64
       8.
        .64
        .6
         4
         4
         0
```

Of course dividing by 0.2 should produce a different answer and thus will need a modification to the method of dividing by 2.

A rephrasing of the language of the question can help. Instead of 8.64 divided by 0.2, the question can be understood as 'How many 0.2s in 8.64?' or 'How many £0.20s in £8.64?' with the extra help of examining the value of 0.2(0) and of using money to set up the question. A pre–estimate is then unlikely to suggest anything like 4 for the answer.

For the written, exact version, a solution to the problem lies in modifying the question so that it becomes a division by a whole number. This can be explained using equivalent fractions: 8.64 ÷ 0.2 may be written as

$$\frac{8.64}{0.2} = \frac{8.64 \times 10}{0.2 \times 10} = \frac{86.4}{2} \quad \text{or} \quad 86.4 \div 2.$$

Multiplying the top and bottom of the fraction alters the division to 86.4 ÷ 2, without changing the final result. The process can also be seen as matching movements of the decimal places. The goal is to manoeuvre the decimal places of both numbers until the dividing number is a whole number (in this case 2).

The division can then proceed as in earlier examples:

```
      43.2
  2)86.4
    80.0
    ----
     6.4
     6.0
    ----
       4
       4
      ---
       0
```

Further examples

* 0.695 ÷ 0.05 becomes 69.5 ÷ 5 (moving both numbers two places)

```
     13.9
  5)69.5
    50.0
    ----
    19.5
    15.0
    ----
     4.5
     4.5
    ----
       0
```

* 13.2 ÷ 0.006 becomes 13200 ÷ 6 (moving both numbers three places), etc.
* 0.13 ÷ 0.8 becomes 1.3 ÷ 8 (moving both numbers one place)

```
    0.1625
  8)1.3000
    .8
    ----
    .50
    .48
    ----
     20
     16
    ----
     40
     40
    ----
      0
```

Note that in the final example 1.3 was written as 1.3000. The extra zeros are optional (see Chapter 10) and do not affect the value, but help with the setting out of the question.

Approximations/rounding

Sometimes it is desirable to give an approximate answer in round figures. For example, £8.29 might be described as 'nearly £8.30 (£8.3)', or 'about £8'.

- 8.29 is somewhere between 8.20 and 8.30. It is nearer to 8.30, because it is above the half–way position of 8.25. Therefore, rounded to 1 decimal place, 8.29 would be written as 8.3.
- 8.29 is somewhere between 8 and 9. It is nearer to 8, because it is below the half–way position of 8.50. Therefore, rounded to the nearest whole number, 8.29 would be written as 8.

Such separate judgements need not be made, when a general policy is agreed. Where practicable, a number line (Figure 12.2) shows quite clearly which approximation is nearer.

Figure 12.2

A numerical policy is more readily applicable, however. The accepted policy is demonstrated in Table 12.1 through rounding a complete set of numbers to 1 decimal place. The place to be retained is separated by a line from the place to be lost.

Table 12.1

				Nearer to	*Rounded to*
.60	=	.6	0	.60*	.6
.61	=	.6	1	.60	.6
.62	=	.6	2	.60	.6
.63	=	.6	3	.60	.6
.64	=	.6	4	.60	.6
.65	=	.6	5	.70*	.7
.66	=	.6	6	.70	.7
.67	=	.6	7	.70	.7
.68	=	.6	8	.70	.7
.69	=	.6	9	.70	.7

It can be seen that:

- When the place to be lost contains a 5 or more, the number retained is rounded up, by adding 1.
- When the place to be lost contains a 4 or less, the number retained is rounded down, by adding 0.

This is the policy normally applied, because it is even–handed—half of the numbers are rounded up, and half are rounded down. In fact it embodies the twin fallacies (see values with * in Table 12.1) that

- .60 needs rounding to .6, and
- .65 is nearer to .70 than .60.

Sometimes a division will produce an answer which is too long, and will have to be shortened, by rounding off excess places. Indeed, some divisions, such as 39.5 ÷ 7 would carry on for ever. The early part of this calculation is shown:

```
        5.64285, etc.
    7)39.50000
      35
      ̄ ̄ ̄ ̄
       4.5
       4.2
       ̄ ̄ ̄
        30
        28
        ̄ ̄ ̄
         20
         14
         ̄ ̄ ̄
          60
          56
          ̄ ̄ ̄
           40
           35
```

The answer to this division is now given in various approximations:

- 5.(64285 = 6 to the nearest whole number, because a 6 is rounded off;
- 5.6(4285 = 5.6 to 1 decimal place, because a 4 is rounded off;
- 5.642(85 = 5.643 to 3 decimal places, because an 8 is rounded off;
- 5.6428(5 = 5.6429 to 4 decimal places, because a 5 is rounded off.

Some decimals are particularly awkward to round. For example, approximating 9.999 to two decimal places. When rounding off the final 9, the 9 in the second decimal place must be rounded up, by adding 1. The likely problems here are avoided by actually carrying out an addition:

```
 9.99
+ 1
 ̄ ̄ ̄ ̄ ̄
10.00
```

The act of rounding up has a knock–on effect for all the other figures. The two zeros after the decimal point must be retained—normally regarded as optional, they are needed here to give the approximation to the required number of decimal places.

Rounding must be performed in a single step, for accuracy. Rounding in stages can produce errors. For example,

6.247 = 6.2 correct to 1 place.

However, rounding in stages gives

6.247 = 6.25 correct to 2 places, then
6.25 = 6.3 which is wrong.

Converting harder fractions to decimals

In this chapter, it is possible to cover the types of example, like $5/9$, which were beyond the scope of the methods used in Chapter 10. The diagrams in Figure 12.3 are intended to show that $5/9$ is the same as $5 \div 9$.

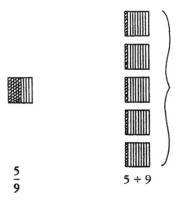

$$\frac{5}{9} \qquad 5 \div 9$$

Figure 12.3

The conversion of $5/9$ to a decimal can now be achieved by performing $5 \div 9$ as a decimal division, and rounding the answer to, say, three decimal places. It will be necessary to work out four decimal places, so that the size of the fourth decimal place, and its consequent effect on the third decimal place, can be determined.

```
        0.5555, etc.
    9)5.0000
       4.5
       ――
        50
        45
        ――
        50
        45
        ――
        50
        45
```

0.5555 = 0.556 correct to three decimal places.
$5/9$ = .556 correct to three decimal places.

This method of conversion works for any fraction, even the earlier easy examples. Furthermore, in Chapter 10, the conversion to a decimal of $7/8$ was seen to require some special knowledge. Now it can be carried out mechanically as $7 \div 8$.

```
       0.875
   8)7.000
       6.4
        60
        56
        40
        40
        00
```

$^7/_8$ is equivalent to the exact decimal .875.

Summary

As outlined at the beginning of this chapter, the methods used to justify the rules for decimals would seem far too complicated for most children. Instead, once the rules are understood, it is much simpler to stick to them. The working involved with deriving the rules may be worth showing to some children just once, or it may be held in reserve by the teacher, in case of awkward questions.

The rules concerning the positioning of the decimal point summarise as follows:

- For addition or subtraction, all the decimal points of the question and the answer line up vertically.
- The same is true for a division, once it has been modified into a division by a whole number. This is achieved by moving the figures (or the decimal point) in both numbers by the same number of places, as appropriate.
- The decimal points in a multiplication do not line up. The number of decimal places in the answer is given by the total number of decimal places in the question. The actual numbers can be multiplied together in the normal way.
- Multiplication and division of decimals by 10, 100, 1000, etc., never change the figures—they merely move them. The number of places moved is dictated by the number of zeros, whereas the direction of movement gives a bigger answer for multiplication,and a smaller answer for division.

Because addition, subtraction and division ultimately follow the same rule, some teachers prefer to teach them first, in the given order. Multiplication, the odd one out, is then dealt with last.

Finally, and leaving out much of the detail, the policy for approximating reduces to:

- 5 or more means round up
- 4 or less means round down.

Chapter 13
Percentages

Introduction

In Chapter 10 percentages were related to decimals and fractions, using a 10 by 10 square to show 100 equal parts in the form of a diagrammatic model. The key idea of this chapter is to provide a concrete image of percentages so that the formulae and algorithms have a memory base. The image should also instil an understanding of the concept of percentages. This is achieved by focusing on 100 and 1.

An Image of Percentage

Since percentage relates to 100, then the image presented to the pupil should involve a clear demonstration of 100. Further it should demonstrate dividing the quantity up into 100 parts (thereby identifying one part). A clear method for this uses empty 35 mm film tubes, 100 of them arranged in a 10–by–10 square (Figure 13.1).

There are five types of percentage problem, considered here.

- Finding a percentage of a quantity
- Increasing a quantity by a percentage
- Decreasing a quantity by a percentage
- One quantity as a percentage of another
- Finding the whole quantity

Each type is explained in turn.

Figure 13.1

Finding a percentage of a quantity

An example can be used to show the tubes in use. The question is, 'What is 12% of 300?' An 'easy' question is used to set up the illustration and lead into more 'difficult' numbers.

A total of 300 (plastic) pence are used. The pence are divided up into the 100 tubes (evenly). One tube is examined and will contain 3 pence. You can discuss and explain that the tube represents one out of 100 tubes and that its contents represent $\frac{1}{100}$ of the 300 pence or 1% of the 300. (The pupil is asked what two tubes represent and what is in the two tubes and then for three tubes, five tubes and 10 tubes, at which stage the pupil can be referred back to 10% as equivalent to $\frac{1}{10}$ as a check.) You can emphasise the process as dividing up into 100 (equal) parts to obtain 1 part (1%) and the use of this 1% to find 12% or any other percentage.

This demonstration relates directly to the written algorithm; 300 is divided by 100 and the result is multiplied by 12. This can be represented as a flow chart (Figure 13.2) or as an equation:

$$\frac{300}{100} \times 12 = 3 \times 12 = 36$$

$$300 \longrightarrow \boxed{\div 100} \overset{3}{\longrightarrow} \boxed{\times 12} \longrightarrow 36$$

Figure 13.2

The work can be extended, depending on the age and ability of the pupil, to lead to the general formula for 'What is n% of N?', i.e. $(N/100)\,n$.

Other examples can be demonstrated and/or discussed, such as 8% of 60, where 60 is less than 100 so each tube gets less than 1. This may require some revision on dividing by 100 and obtaining decimals or by using money and imagining £0.60 in each tube.

The algorithm is clearly related to the concrete image of first dividing up into 100 parts, followed by taking n lots of these parts, i.e. a division followed by a multiplication.

Increasing a quantity by a percentage

Using figures familiar from the previous section, a good example to consider would be 'Increase 300 by 12%'.

The first possible process would be to find 12% of 300 and **add** it onto the 300. The method of the previous section would again give 36, which would this time represent the increase. This would be added to the 300 to give 336.

An alternative process depends on recognising that the result of increasing a quantity by 12% is to finish with 112%. The answer can then be found in a single calculation:

$$\frac{300}{100} \quad \times \quad 112 \quad = \quad 3 \times 112 \quad = \quad 336$$

The latter process has the advantage of requiring a single step, but the disadvantage of always involving larger numbers. The first process seems more straightforward, but it is longer, and pupils often would give the answer as 36, forgetting to add on the increase.

Decreasing a quantity by a percentage

Consider the example 'Decrease £60 by 8%', again using figures from the previous section.

The first possible process would be to find 8% of £60 and **subtract** it from the £60.

$$\text{Decrease} = 8\% \text{ of } £60 = \frac{£60}{100} \times 8 = £0.60 \times 8 = £4.80$$

$$\text{Answer} = £60 - £4.80 = £55.20$$

The alternative process here depends on recognising that the result of decreasing a quantity by 8% is to finish with 92%. Again the answer can be found with a single calculation:

$$\frac{£60}{100} \times 92 = £0.60 \times 92 = £55.20$$

The advantages and disadvantages are the same as for increasing.

One quantity as a percentage of another

This type of percentage is often presented as an examination–score type of question: if a pupil gets 46 out of 85 in his maths examination, what is his percentage mark? It is asking the pupil to convert x/y into a percentage. The film tubes keep the image of 100 in the pupil's mind. The procedure then it to change x/y into a decimal and to know that the resulting decimal represents the amount in one tube.

So, in the example above, 46 out of 85 becomes $46/85 = 0.5412$ which is 54.12%. This last step can be done by knowing that 0.5412 is the number in one tube and multiplying the decimal 0.5412 by 100 to find the number in 100 tubes, i.e. 100%.

This method uses the same image as for each type of problem. The focus is on what is in one tube (1%) and then to multiply that value for 1% up to the required value, in this case 100%.

(If we refer back to Chapter 10, the procedure could also be used to change x/y to an equivalent fraction with denominator 100. The pupil has to appreciate that a percentage is a fraction with a denominator of 100, where only the value of the numerator is quoted.)

Finding the whole quantity (100%)

Again the focus is on 1%. So in an example such as '36 is 12% of which number?' the first operation is to calculate 1%, i.e. what goes into one tube? The child is asked, 'If there are 36 in 12 tubes, can you work out how many in one tube?' This should result in an answer of 3 in each tube. The 100% is then a matter of multiplying 3 by 100, answer 300.

Summary

The film tubes provide the image of 1% and 100% in a way that allows the algorithm to be related directly to the image/model. The child has to evaluate the data in each question and form a mental image of what goes into each tube in order to understand a difficult concept and procedure. A 10 by 10 square grid diagram may provide an alternative model, where film tubes are not to hand.

Chapter 14
Positive and Negative Numbers

When do Negative Numbers Make Sense?

The subtraction 2 – 5 is impossible to carry out if it refers to pieces of cake, since if you only have 2, you cannot physically take away 5. The same applies to fingers of course, despite their wide use to help out in difficult situations.

Circumstances in which negative numbers do make sense can involve amounts of money *owed* to the bank, temperatures below zero, and questions of direction. Up, North and right are generally measured as positive, while down, South and left are measured as negative. This convention provides the valuable aid of the 'Number Line', which can be extended below zero.

Money owed to the bank

In this situation, 2 – 5 can be taken to describe the position of a person with £2 in the bank, who withdraws £5. Children may need to have it explained that permission can be obtained to do this! The person withdraws his/her £2 plus £3 more, and so ends up owing the £3 to the bank, which can be represented mathematically as –3. Older readers will remember that bank statements used to highlight this in red ink (hence the expression 'in the red') and these days (I understand), statements would say £3.00 DR.

Temperatures below zero

In winter, if the temperature is 2 degrees, there is nothing to stop it from falling a further 5 degrees. This will take it down to zero and 3 degrees below. This situation can be represented as 2 – 5 = –3. This can be seen on a thermometer which is a kind of number line.

Some Necessary Clarifications

Up to a certain point, many mathematical conventions need not be questioned. The acceptance of negative answers requires the questioning of some conventions., so that thorough foundations are established to help when the going becomes difficult. To put it another way, when 2 – 5 was impossible, certain problems could not arise!

The meaning of 2 (without a sign)

Does 2 mean +2 or –2?

To many people it might seem obvious that 2 means +2, although it may not be so obvious to a dyslexic pupil. That 2 means +2 can be taught as a rule or convention to be learned by heart. However, it is possible to use the explanation that to reach 2 from nothing it is necessary to add 2. This is even clearer from the written form

2 = 0 + 2 = +2

Use of a Number Line

Shown below is part of a thermometer, showing the result if the temperature had risen from 0 to 2 degrees, then fallen by 5 degrees. This illustrates the calculation for 0 + 2 – 5 or +2 – 5 or just 2 – 5 from above.

The answer is quite clearly demonstrated to be –3. The thermometer is acting as a vertical number line. In mathematics, number lines are more generally drawn horizontally, possibly for no other reason than that they fit more conveniently on a page that way. The calculation 2 – 5 = –3 is shown below on a horizontal number line.

Hills and Holes

In the following diagram of a piece of ground, a hole has been dug and a hill has been formed with the earth that was removed. The hill is the same size as the hole:

It would now be possible to replace the earth and exactly fill the hole.

The ground now looks as though nothing has happened.

Although equal in size, the hill and hole are opposites, because the hill points upwards while the hole points downwards.

Positive and Negative Numbers

Positive and negative numbers behave in the same way as hills and holes in that +1 taken together with -1 produces 0. Furthermore, positive numbers usually represent upwards (or to the right) while negative numbers represent downwards (or to the left). It is possible to exploit the relationship between hills and holes to help bring about an understanding of how negative numbers operate. This can also lead to written methods.

Notation

First another idea has to be introduced. It would be convenient if positive numbers looked like hills and pointed upwards (or to the right) and negative numbers looked like holes and pointed downwards (or to the left). By chance (I think!) this can be achieved by borrowing from older forms of notation. Forms of some ancient Egyptian number symbols can be used as follows:

∧	for	1
⌒	for	10
)	for	100

All of these symbols point upwards or to the right, and so can be taken to represent positive numbers. The system can be extended by the 'invention' of equal but opposite negative versions, pointing downwards or to the left. Usable forms are given below:

∨	for	−1
⌣	for	−10
(	for	−100

Of course, like hills and holes, when put together they should produce nothing. These symbols *do* combine to look and behave like nothings, as follows:

to represent	∨ −1	with with	∧ +1	gives giving	∧∨ (combined) 0
to represent	⌣ −10	with with	⌒ +10	gives giving	◠◡ (combined) 0
to represent	(−100	with with	) +100	gives giving	( ) 0

Using this notation with simple examples

The notation can be used to help explain the calculation which began the chapter.

2 − 5
can be written as   ∨∨∨∨∨ (with ∧∧ above)   =   ∨∨∨00
                                                 =   ∨∨∨
                                                 =   −3

The −5 'negates' all of the 2, before going a further 3 into the negative, giving − 3. This can be related to having £2 in the bank, and withdrawing £5. The symbols actually show the first £2 withdrawn matched with real money before the further £3 leads to a debt.

Comparision of the two written forms

It is possible to establish that there is a close relationship between the symbols used in this way and the number line. There follow worked examples, where both written forms are used, and the setting out is designed to show the connection.

7 – 4
shown on a number line

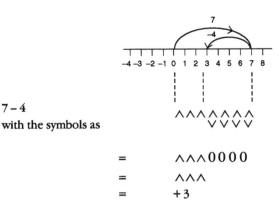

7 – 4
with the symbols as

$$= \qquad \wedge\wedge\wedge 0\,0\,0\,0$$
$$= \qquad \wedge\wedge\wedge$$
$$= \qquad +3$$

Careful examination shows that the arrangement of hills for +1 and holes for –1 lines up perfectly against the number line version, confirming that they are equivalent alternative illustrations. Both versions show that the –4 'negates' 4 of the 7, leaving 3.

5 – 9
shown on a number line

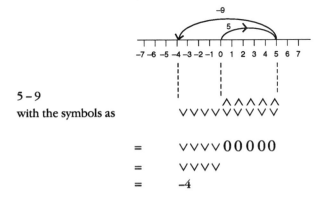

5 – 9
with the symbols as

$$= \qquad \vee\vee\vee\vee 0\,0\,0\,0\,0$$
$$= \qquad \vee\vee\vee\vee$$
$$= \qquad -4$$

Again the arrangement of hills and holes lines up with the number line version, showing the equivalence. Both versions show that the –9 'negates' all of the 5, going a further 4 into the negative to produce – 4.

Advantages of the 'hills and holes' notation

- The method provides another alternative. Many children will feel comfortable with calculations illustrated on a number line. Others might prefer to put together hills and holes, because this can also be done physically with cut-outs of the above symbols for $+1$, $+10$, $+100$, -1, -10, and -100, made from card or wood. These will form concrete manipulative materials and will suit the more kinaesthetic learners, while a visual version can be written down, as on these pages.
- The method readily extends to bigger numbers, which are impossible to represent on a number line limited to the width or length of the page. This all–too–real problem is dealt with later in this chapter.
- It can reinforce the conventional algorithms for subtraction such as $358 - 271$, where the process and need for 'borrowing' are often not well understood. In this, the method will be shown to extend one of the approaches of Chapter 4.
- While there is the relationship already shown, a number line takes time to draw and must be reasonably accurate. To draw a useful number line, it is necessary to guess successfully how far it must extend from zero in either direction to cover the calculation. The hill and hole symbols are more 'portable'. Zero takes care of itself, and the symbols are used only as they are needed. They can be used to demonstrate and explain important calculation types, examples of which are given below.

Important Types of Calculation

$6 + 2 + 3 = $ ∧∧∧∧∧∧ ∧∧ ∧∧∧ $ = $ ∧∧∧∧∧∧∧∧∧∧∧ $ = 11$

$-4 - 1 - 5 - 2 = $ ∨∨∨∨ ∨ ∨∨∨∨∨ ∨∨ $ = $ ∨∨∨∨∨∨∨∨∨∨∨∨ $ = -12$

These two examples show that, when all the signs are the same, the correct answer can be obtained by *adding* the numbers together and adopting their common sign for the answer. As in the rest of this book, there is no suggestion that children should learn this property as a rule, but most will quickly spot it as a short cut (referred to below as A). Those who do not will find that the symbols produce the answer very simply.

$-5 + 3 = $ ∨∨∧∧∧∨∨ $ = $ ∨∨ $ = -2$

$3 - 5 \ = \ $ ∨∨∧∧∧∨∨ $ = $ ∨∨ $ = -2$

The above two examples show that $3 - 5$ is the same as $-5 + 3$, not only because both give the same answer of -2, but because the symbols are identical throughout the working. This pair of examples also gives another illustration that 3 without a sign means +3.

$$5 - 3 = \quad \overset{\wedge\wedge\wedge\wedge\wedge}{\underset{\vee\vee\vee}{}} = \wedge\wedge = 2$$

Comparing this with the previous example shows that 5 – 3 and 3 – 5 are the reverse of one another. This is shown in the answers being 2 and –2, but more generally because the symbols are mirror images within the calculation. This is something else that many children will pick up as a short cut (referred to below as B). For example, they might well perform the harder calculation 236 – 592 as 592 – 236 and simply reverse the sign. Later, this is likely to be a temptation for them in the middle of some complex computations using a calculator, so it is important that they understand precisely what they are doing.

Clarification: A sign between numbers

In their earlier years, many children will have been told that the sign between two numbers describes what to do with the two numbers. Indeed, for a calculation like 7 – 3, it is common to hear even teachers say that the numbers are being subtracted. This is not only untrue, but is likely to be very confusing for a dyslexic, who takes literally what is said. In fact only the 3 is being subtracted (or taken away): it is being subtracted from the 7. The 7 is a +7, arguably the result of *adding* 7 to zero. In fact the – sign has nothing whatsoever to do with the 7, as can most easily be seen by re–writing 7 – 3 as – 3 + 7.

Confusion will arise in later calculations, such as in the following example where many pupils will become stuck trying to subtract both the 6 and the 15, then both the 9 and the 1. The apparent absence of a sign before the 6 makes it harder to explain why this is wrong.

$$6 - 15 + 4 + 5 + 9 - 1$$

In a question such as 4 – 2 +5 dyslexic children will often think they have to add the 2 and the 5.

The reality is that a number takes the sign immediately before it (and the sign behind it has no effect on it). In examples like these, there is some value to be gained from drawing short vertical guide lines, showing each number with its *own* sign, as illustrated below:

$$6 \big| - 15 \big| + 4 \big| + 5 \big| + 9 \big| - 1$$
$$4 \big| - 2 \big| + 5$$

Questions Containing Many Numbers

$$-3 + 6 - 1 - 5 + 2 - 7 + 4$$

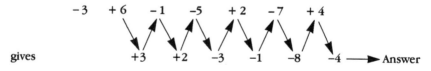

$$= \quad WW$$
$$= \quad -4$$

From the above layout of the symbols, another written interpretation suggests itself. All the positive numbers can be collected together to produce a positive total, and all the negative numbers can be collected together to produce a separate negative total. The two totals can then be combined. This is consistent with building on the short cuts referred to above: Short cut A to obtain the separate totals and short cut B to combine them.

i.e. $-3 + 6 - 1 - 5 + 2 - 7 + 4$

becomes $+6 + 2 + 4 - 3 - 1 - 5 - 7$

= $+ \quad 12 \; - \; 16$

= -4

As a further alternative, some children might choose to compute a running total as they move from one number to the next. The final total is the answer. Because only two numbers are combined at a time, this process keeps the totals small and it might be performed mentally, although each running total is written down here underneath the relevant numbers of the question.

$$\begin{array}{ccccccc} -3 & +6 & -1 & -5 & +2 & -7 & +4 \\ \end{array}$$

gives $+3 \quad +2 \quad -3 \quad -1 \quad -8 \quad -4 \longrightarrow$ Answer

This is already happening implicitly as the numbers are written out one by one in the symbol form above.

Distinguishing Two Meanings each for the + and − Signs

Sometimes a − sign will represent an operation known as 'take away', as in the calculation $9 - 4$ or 9 take away 4. At other times it will represent a direction or sense, as in −3 degrees or 'minus' 3 degrees. In this chapter, the *operation* will always be described with the expression 'take away', while the *direction* or sense signified in − 3 will be described with the word 'minus'.

Although subsequent confusion would be much less likely, a similar distinction should be drawn for the sign +. In this chapter, a sum such as 9 + 4 will be described as 9 'add' 4, while the direction of the number + 6 will be described as 'plus'.

Two interpretations of the subtraction process

The process of taking away will be shown by physically crossing out and then omitting symbols, while the minus direction will be evident from the symbols pointing downwards or to the left. The process of adding will be shown by counting together the additional symbols, while the plus direction will be evident from the symbols pointing upwards or to the right.

In the simple examples already covered in this chapter, such as 5 − 3, the sign can be interpreted to mean either the direction 'minus' or the operation 'take away'. So far the easier alternative has been chosen: that of adopting the 'minus' sense through the use of downwards pointing negative symbols. The other alternative can be adopted, but some calculations would then need to follow a slightly more complex process.

9 − 4		with the − sign considered as minus
=	∧∧∧∧∧∧∧∧∧ ∨∨∨∨	
=	∧∧∧∧∧	
=	5	

9 − 4		with the − sign considered as take away
=	∧∧∧∧∧⬈⬈⬈⬈⬈	
=	∧∧∧∧∧	
=	5	

The two alternatives above show more similarities than differences.

3 − 7		with the − sign considered as minus
=	∧∧∧ ∨∨∨∨∨∨∨	
=	∨∨∨∨	
=	− 4	

3 − 7		with the − sign considered as take away

To take away 7 by this method requires us to cross out and remove 7 of the ∧ symbols, when there are only 3. Solving this problem necessitates the more complex process anticipated above. The extra symbols can be 'manufactured' by introducing into the calculation sufficient zeros. In the reverse of previous practice, these zeros are split into hills and holes, then the 7 symbols can be taken away.

$3 - 7$

$=$ $0 + 0 + 0 + 0 + 3 - 7$

ᐱᐱᐱᐱᐱᐱᐱ
$=$ ᐯᐯᐯᐯ

$=$ ᐯ ᐯ ᐯ ᐯ

$=$ $- 4$

The latter process is clumsy for these easier calculations, but becomes invaluable for harder calculations. For example, in the following sections some numbers will have two signs in front of them, as in 4 – (–3) or 4 take away minus 3. Here two – signs are present and the use of both meanings helps to avoid confusion. Indeed a minority of text books would seek to emphasise the two different meanings by writing this calculation in the form 4 – ⁻3, where they give two slightly different variants of the sign. (Unfortunately this form of notation leads to some dangerous habits, so the bracket form is here much preferred.)

Substitution with negative numbers

By way of illustration, a number with two signs in front of it might arise in a question which required the sustitution of $y = -3$ in the formula $4 - y$. In questions of this kind, a good (if pedantic) discipline is to replace the letter with an empty bracket, substitute the number with its sign into the bracket, then carefully work out the bracket as shown in the next section.

          $4 - y$
$=$ $4 - (\ )$
$=$ $4 - (-3)$ and so on

Harder Questions

          $0 + (+5)$

$=$ $0 + $ ᐱᐱᐱᐱᐱ

$=$ ᐱᐱᐱᐱᐱ

$=$ $+5$

This example can be interpreted:

*   In money terms as 'Adding an increase results in having more' or
*   For temperatures as 'Adding heat produces a rise in temperature'.

$$0 + (-4)$$

$$= \quad 0 + \text{VVVV}$$

$$= \qquad \text{VVVV}$$

$$= \qquad -4$$

This example can be interpreted:

- In money terms as 'Adding a debt results in having less' or
- For temperatures as 'Adding cold produces a fall in temperature'.

$$0 - (+6)$$

The intention is to show the process of taking away by crossing out and then omitting the appropriate number of symbols. Here we should be crossing out six positive symbols, but there are none because the initial number is zero. As described above, the necessary procedure is to introduce sufficient zeros and separate each into a $+1$ symbol and a -1 symbol. The required number of symbols can then be taken away.

$$0 - (+6)$$

$$= \quad 0 + 0 + 0 + 0 + 0 + 0 - (+6)$$

$$= \quad \overset{\wedge}{\text{V}} \ \overset{\wedge}{\text{V}} \ \overset{\wedge}{\text{V}} \ \overset{\wedge}{\text{V}} \ \overset{\wedge}{\text{V}} \ \overset{\wedge}{\text{V}} - (+6)$$

$$= \quad \overset{\times}{\text{V}} \ \overset{\times}{\text{V}} \ \overset{\times}{\text{V}} \ \overset{\times}{\text{V}} \ \overset{\times}{\text{V}} \ \overset{\times}{\text{V}}$$

$$= \quad \text{V V V V V V}$$

$$= \qquad -6$$

This example can be interpreted:

- In money terms as 'Losing an increase results in having less' or
- For temperatures as 'Losing heat produces a fall in temperature'.

$$0 - (-3)$$

$$= \quad 0 + 0 + 0 - (-3)$$

$$= \quad \overset{\wedge}{\text{V}} \ \overset{\wedge}{\text{V}} \ \overset{\wedge}{\text{V}} - (-3)$$

$$= \quad \overset{\wedge}{\cancel{\text{V}}} \ \overset{\wedge}{\cancel{\text{V}}} \ \overset{\wedge}{\cancel{\text{V}}}$$

$$= \quad \wedge \ \wedge \ \wedge$$

$$= \qquad +3$$

This example can be interpreted:

- In money terms as 'Losing a debt results in having more' or
- For temperatures as 'Losing cold produces a rise in temperature'.

A Third Meaning for the − Sign: as a 'Reverser'

From the results of the last section can be extracted:

$$
\begin{array}{rcl}
+ \quad (+5) &=& +5 \\
+ \quad (-4) &=& -4 \\
- \quad (+6) &=& -6 \\
- \quad (-3) &=& +3
\end{array}
$$

These can all be explained by relating them to money transactions and temperature movements, as the last section demonstrated. For day–to–day use, however, it may well be quicker and more effective for pupils to be allowed to treat the results mechanically.

When removing a bracket and combining two signs into one, the extracts above show that a + sign outside the bracket leaves the sign inside unchanged. It might almost be ignored, and indeed as has already been seen, it is often omitted as with $2 = +2$. However, a − sign outside a bracket *reverses* the sign inside. This role as a reverser is universal throughout mathematics for the − sign. As a simpler example, the (hill) symbols for $+1$, $+10$ and $+100$ are reversed into the (hole) symbols for -1, -10 and -100.

This approach is greatly preferred to the use of a rule, such as

- Two negatives make a positive or
- Like signs give a +, unlike signs give a −, because
- There is a danger of misuse as in:

$-7 - 2 = +9$

- Such rules are far more appropriate for multiplying and dividing with negative numbers.

An earlier view of $3 - 5$ as the reverse of $5 - 3$ can now be seen, formally, as a result of the reversing role of the − sign. Since a − sign outside a bracket reverses the signs inside,

$$
\begin{array}{rl}
 & -(5-3) \\
= & -(+5-3) \\
= & -5+3 \\
= & +3-5 \\
= & 3-5
\end{array}
$$

i.e. $3 - 5 = -(5 - 3)$ which is the reverse of $5 - 3$. Therefore, the 'impossible' subtraction $3 - 5$ may be performed as $5 - 3$, as long as the sign is finally reversed to −.

Questions Containing Large Numbers

It has already been argued that the value of the number line breaks down for large numbers, because very large numbers mean very long or very inaccurate number lines. A number line has to be scaled in either ones *or* tens *or* hundreds, while the hill and hole symbols allow mixing of the collective units of 10, 100, –10 and –100. (In theory, symbols could be evolved for 1000 and –1000, but once understanding has been reached to 100, the generalisation upwards is not usually a problem.)

$$231 - 356$$

$$= \quad \begin{array}{l} (\,) \\ (\,) \\ (\quad \smile\smile\bigcirc\bigcirc\bigcirc \;\; \vee\,\vee\,\vee\,\vee\,\vee\, \overset{\wedge}{\vee} \end{array}$$

$$= \quad (\quad \smile\smile \qquad \vee\,\vee\,\vee\,\vee\,\vee$$

$$= \qquad\qquad -\,125$$

$$72 - 35$$

$$= \quad \wedge\wedge\wedge\wedge\wedge\bigcirc\bigcirc\bigcirc \;\; \vee\,\vee\,\vee\, \overset{\wedge}{\vee}\; \overset{\wedge}{\vee}$$

$$= \quad \wedge\wedge\wedge\wedge \qquad \vee\,\vee\,\vee$$

$$(= \quad +\,40 - 3)$$

The opposing directions of the symbols shows the calculation to have reached a point requiring some consideration. It is possible to proceed by evaluating $+40 - 3 = 37$, or to continue with the symbols as follows, by exchanging a $+10$ symbol for ten $+1$ symbols:

$$72 - 35$$

$$= \quad \wedge\wedge\wedge\wedge\wedge\bigcirc\bigcirc\bigcirc \;\; \vee\,\vee\,\vee\, \overset{\wedge}{\vee}\; \overset{\wedge}{\vee}$$

$$= \quad \wedge\wedge\wedge\wedge \qquad\qquad \vee\,\vee\,\vee$$

$$= \quad \wedge\wedge\wedge \qquad\qquad \begin{array}{l}\wedge\wedge\wedge\wedge\wedge\wedge\wedge\wedge\wedge \\ \vee\,\vee\,\vee\end{array}$$

$$= \quad \wedge\wedge\wedge \qquad\qquad \wedge\wedge\wedge\wedge\wedge\wedge\wedge$$

$$= \qquad\qquad +37$$

The symbols are here illustrating the decomposition that happens in the conventional column by column subtraction, which will itself then be better understood. It can be a rewarding exercise to examine closely the layouts above and below, to draw out the differences and similarities.

$$\begin{array}{r} 7^1 2 \\ -\,35 \\ \hline 37 \end{array}$$

254 – 637

In this example, the same problem will arise as in the last example, this time in the tens. Also, most of the residual symbols will be pointing in the negative direction to further confuse. For this reason, it is better to carry out this calculation as 637 – 254 and adopt a – sign at the end (using short cut B). The calculation will then proceed as in the previous example.

A Language Problem

For both subtraction (and division), dyslexic children can have a problem with performing calculations in the order intended by the question. For example, 'subtract 9 from 4' means 4 – 9 rather than 9 – 4. Many dyslexics would wrongly expect the order of the numbers in the calculation to follow the order of the numbers in the question, where the 9 precedes the 4.

Before they are made aware that negative answers are possible, children often use the notion that 'you always take the smaller number from the bigger number'. Unfortunately, this is of no help within algebra, where the question 'subtract p from y' offers no clue as to which is bigger or smaller. The notion becomes *untrue* when negative answers are possible, and children relying on it will totally lose their bearings in questions such as 'subtract –3 from +8'.

Being advised of the dangers and concentrating on the language used is the only safe way to master this kind of problem. In particular, it should be emphasised which number is to be subtracted (or taken away). For the latter question, setting the calculation out as $(-3) - (+8)$ would be wrong because it shows the +8 being subtracted, when the question clearly states: 'subtract –3 .....'. Only with the form $(+8) - (-3)$ are we subtracting the correct number: the –3.

Another approach, to make the order of the numbers match in the question and the calculation, can be achieved by either

- Pointing to the numbers of the calculation right to left as the question is read, or
- Reading the question 'in reverse' as 'from +8, subtract –3' to match the necessary order of the calculation.

Here again we are finding a way to emphasise which number is to be subtracted.

Parallel if slightly different problems occur with a division question such as 'divide 25 into 375' as opposed to 'divide 375 by 25'. The parallel solution is to emphasise by similar methods which number is being divided (the 375) and which number is dividing (the 25). The correct order in which to hit the calculator buttons is, of course, $375 \div 25$.

Multiplying with Negative Numbers

Everybody knows that if we have 4 rows of chairs with 5 chairs in each row, then the number of chairs is 4×5 or '4 times 5'. We do indeed have 5 chairs '4 times' or 20 chairs.

It is possible for dyslexic children to stretch to an understanding that 4×-5 could mean 4 debts of £5, making a total debt of £20 or -20.

What can be meant by -4×-5? Can we have something -4 times? Perhaps not, but there are other interpretations, and other reasons for needing to know the numerical answer. Even non–dyslexic grown–ups will struggle to remember why the answer here should be $+20$!

A set of illustrations

By way of justification, we can construct a set of simplistic illustrations. Imagine that future time is counted in positive years, then time in the past should be counted in negative years. Imagine that the cost of building a certain type of house increases by £2000 a year, and that the value of a car decreases by £500 a year.

In five years time, the house will cost £10000 more because

$(+5) \times (+2000) = +10000$

In two years time, the car will be worth £1000 less because

$(+2) \times (-500) = -1000$

Four years ago, the house would have cost £8000 less because

$(-4) \times (+2000) = -8000$

Three years ago, the car would have been worth £1500 more because

$(-3) \times (-500) = 1500$

Within this set of illustrations, we have justified answers for all possible combinations of the $+$ and $-$ signs. However, any further illustrations would have to be treated on their own merits and children could not really learn and build from this way of working.

The rule

This is one of those rare instances where the use of a simple-to–remember rule is the safest way for dyslexic children to proceed. Consider the combinations below with their correct answers.

$(+4) \times (+5) = +20$

$(+4) \times (-5) = -20$

$(-4) \times (+5) = -20$

$(-4) \times (-5) = +20$

For multiplying a *pair* of numbers, the rule which can be derived here is:

LIKE   signs give a +

UNLIKE   signs give a −

The proper place to employ this rule is for multiplication, and for division as we shall see later. As argued before, the value of this rule should not be diluted by using it for the removal of brackets, where any − sign should be treated as a 'reverser' to avoid confusion of various kinds.

Universal Multiplication Chart

Using this rule, it is possible to extend a normal multiplication table chart to cover negative numbers as well as positive. Such a chart is constructed in Table 14.1. The numbers to be multiplied are shown around the edges, while the answers are in the body of the chart. The chart is quartered, showing positive numbers upwards and to the right, with negative numbers downwards and to the left. Zeros take up their expected places between the positives and the negatives.

The chart can be used like any other multiplication chart. To multiply two numbers, one is located on a horizontal scale, while the other is located on a vertical scale. By following line across and down (or up) into the body of the chart, the answer will be found where the lines cross.

However, the chart is most useful in *explaining* how the signs behave. Thereafter a normal multiplication chart can be used in combination with the rule from above. For example, children can be encouraged to see that the 5 times table carries on downwards, beyond zero in a predictable sequence. A similar behaviour shows the same result for the 5 times table as it carries on to the left beyond zero. As authors, we have argued before (Chinn and Ashcroft, 1992) that sequences are very convincing for dyslexic children, in this and other situations. If the numbers to be multiplied are in a sequence, then the sequence in the answers can be expected to continue.

$$3 \times 4 = 12$$
$$3 \times 3 = 9$$
$$3 \times 2 = 6$$
$$3 \times 1 = 3$$
$$3 \times 0 = 0$$
so $$3 \times -1 = -3$$
and $$3 \times -2 = -6$$
etc.

This sequence carries us from normal positive multiplication into the region where unlike signs give a negative answer. From the last sequence, changing the directions gives:

$$3 \times -2 = -6$$
$$2 \times -2 = -4$$

Table 14.1

×	10	9	8	7	6	5	4	3	2	1	0	-1	-2	-3	-4	-5	-6	-7	-8	-9	-10
10	100	90	80	70	60	50	40	30	20	10	0	-10	-20	-30	-40	-50	-60	-70	-80	-90	-100
9	90	81	72	63	54	45	36	27	18	9	0	-9	-18	-27	-36	-45	-54	-63	-72	-81	-90
8	80	72	64	56	48	40	32	24	16	8	0	-8	-16	-24	-32	-40	-48	-56	-64	-72	-80
7	70	63	56	49	42	35	28	21	14	7	0	-7	-14	-21	-28	-35	-42	-49	-56	-63	-70
6	60	54	48	42	36	30	24	18	12	6	0	-6	-12	-18	-24	-30	-36	-42	-48	-54	-60
5	50	45	40	35	30	25	20	15	10	5	0	-5	-10	-15	-20	-25	-30	-35	-40	-45	-50
4	40	36	32	28	24	20	16	12	8	4	0	-4	-8	-12	-16	-20	-24	-28	-32	-36	-40
3	30	27	24	21	18	15	12	9	6	3	0	-3	-6	-9	-12	-15	-18	-21	-24	-27	-30
2	20	18	16	14	12	10	8	6	4	2	0	-2	-4	-6	-8	-10	-12	-14	-16	-18	-20
1	10	9	8	7	6	5	4	3	2	1	0	-1	-2	-3	-4	-5	-6	-7	-8	-9	-10
0	0	0	0	0	0	0	0	0	0	0	0	0	0	0	0	0	0	0	0	0	0
-1	-10	-9	-8	-7	-6	-5	-4	-3	-2	-1	0	1	2	3	4	5	6	7	8	9	10
-2	-20	-18	-16	-14	-12	-10	-8	-6	-4	-2	0	2	4	6	8	10	12	14	16	18	20
-3	-30	-27	-24	-21	-18	-15	-12	-9	-6	-3	0	3	6	9	12	15	18	21	24	27	30
-4	-40	-36	-32	-28	-24	-20	-16	-12	-8	-4	0	4	8	12	16	20	24	28	32	36	40
-5	-50	-45	-40	-35	-30	-25	-20	-15	-10	-5	0	5	10	15	20	25	30	35	40	45	50
-6	-60	-54	-48	-42	-36	-30	-24	-18	-12	-6	0	6	12	18	24	30	36	42	48	54	60
-7	-70	-63	-56	-49	-42	-35	-28	-21	-14	-7	0	7	14	21	28	35	42	49	56	63	70
-8	-80	-72	-64	-56	-48	-40	-32	-24	-16	-8	0	8	16	24	32	40	48	56	64	72	80
-9	-90	-81	-72	-63	-54	-45	-36	-27	-18	-9	0	9	18	27	36	45	54	63	72	81	90
-10	-100	-90	-80	-70	-60	-50	-40	-30	-20	-10	0	10	20	30	40	50	60	70	80	90	100

$$1 \times -2 = -2$$
$$0 \times -2 = 0$$
so $\quad -1 \times -2 = 2$
and $\quad -2 \times -2 = 4$
etc.

Again the sequence in the numbers being multiplied justifies the sequence in the answers continuing, this time into the region where like signs (two negatives) give a positive answer.

Table 14.2 is a copy of Table 14.1, but the answers to the above two linked sequences have been erased to confirm the regions they extend into. Table 14.2 also shows that these sequences form only a small sample of what could be obtained from such a chart. While at one time we might have been content to use only such a small sample of sequences, we now prefer to use the whole of Table 14.1, where there are dozens of sequences interlocking with one another. Incidentally, erasing larger areas of a chart such as that in Table 14.1 and asking children to replace the missing numbers provides a very good exercise.

Multiplying more than a pair of numbers

The rule that we have advocated using applies for multiplying only a pair of numbers. If it is required to multiply more than two numbers at a time, then they should be taken in pairs, as far as possible. The pairings can be chosen in any way, and the preferred pairings will vary from person to person.

$$
\begin{array}{cccccccc}
& (-3) & \times & (-1) & \times & (+3) & \times & (-2) & \times & (+5) \\
= & & (+3) & & \times & & (-6) & & \times & (+5) \\
= & & (+3) & & & \times & & (-30) \\
= & & & & (-90)
\end{array}
$$

Powers of negative numbers

$$
\begin{array}{llll}
(-2)^1 & & & = (-2) \\
(-2)^2 & = (-2) \times (-2) & & = (+4) \\
(-2)^3 & = (-2)^2 \times (-2) & = (+4) \times (-2) & = (-8) \\
(-2)^4 & = (-2)^3 \times (-2) & = (-8) \times (-2) & = (+16) \\
(-2)^5 & = (-2)^4 \times (-2) & = (+16) \times (-2) & = (-32)
\end{array}
$$

etc.

It can be seen that

- ODD powers produce a NEGATIVE answer, while
- EVEN powers produce a POSITIVE answer

Table 14.2

×	10	9	8	7	6	5	4	3	2	1	0	-1	-2	-3	-4	-5	-6	-7	-8	-9	-10
10	100	90	80	70	60	50	40	30	20	10	0	-10	-20	-30	-40	-50	-60	-70	-80	-90	-100
9	90	81	72	63	54	45	36	27	18	9	0	-9	-18	-27	-36	-45	-54	-63	-72	-81	-90
8	80	72	64	56	48	40	32	24	16	8	0	-8	-16	-24	-32	-40	-48	-56	-64	-72	-80
7	70	63	56	49	42	35	28	21	14	7	0	-7	-14	-21	-28	-35	-42	-49	-56	-63	-70
6	60	54	48	42	36	30	24	18	12	6	0	-6	-12	-18	-24	-30	-36	-42	-48	-54	-60
5	50	45	40	35	30	25	20	15	10	5	0	-5	-10	-15	-20	-25	-30	-35	-40	-45	-50
4	40	36	32	28	24	20	16	12	8	4	0	-4	-8	-12	-16	-20	-24	-28	-32	-36	-40
3	30	27	24	21	18	15	12	9	6	3	0	-3	-6	-9	-12	-15	-18	-21	-24	-27	-30
2	20	18	16	14	12	10	8	6	4	2	0	-2	-4	-6	-8	-10	-12	-14	-16	-18	-20
1	10	9	8	7	6	5	4	3	2	1	0	-1	-2	-3	-4	-5	-6	-7	-8	-9	-10
0	0	0	0	0	0	0	0	0	0	0	0	0	0	0	0	0	0	0	0	0	0
-1	-10	-9	-8	-7	-6	-5	-4	-3	-2	-1	0	1	2	3	4	5	6	7	8	9	10
-2	-20	-18	-16	-14	-12	-10	-8	-6	-4	-2	0	2	4	6	8	10	12	14	16	18	20
-3	-30	-27	-24	-21	-18	-15	-12	-9	-6	-3	0	3	6	9	12	15	18	21	24	27	30
-4	-40	-36	-32	-28	-24	-20	-16	-12	-8	-4	0	4	8	12	16	20	24	28	32	36	40
-5	-50	-45	-40	-35	-30	-25	-20	-15	-10	-5	0	5	10	15	20	25	30	35	40	45	50
-6	-60	-54	-48	-42	-36	-30	-24	-18	-12	-6	0	6	12	18	24	30	36	42	48	54	60
-7	-70	-63	-56	-49	-42	-35	-28	-21	-14	-7	0	7	14	21	28	35	42	49	56	63	70
-8	-80	-72	-64	-56	-48	-40	-32	-24	-16	-8	0	8	16	24	32	40	48	56	64	72	80
-9	-90	-81	-72	-63	-54	-45	-36	-27	-18	-9	0	9	18	27	36	45	54	63	72	81	90
-10	-100	-90	-80	-70	-60	-50	-40	-30	-20	-10	0	10	20	30	40	50	60	70	80	90	100

This is because even powers could all be taken in whole pairs to produce like signs and give a positive answer (although it was not done that way above). Odd powers would always have an extra minus number left at the end to produce unlike signs and a negative answer.

Dividing with Negative Numbers

Taking the examples used to illustrate the multiplication rule, and rearranging them to suit a different purpose, we see that

$$(+4) \times (+5) = (+20) \text{ therefore } \frac{(+20)}{(+5)} = (+4)$$

$$(-4) \times (-5) = (+20) \text{ therefore } \frac{(+20)}{(-5)} = (-4)$$

$$(-4) \times (+5) = (-20) \text{ therefore } \frac{(-20)}{(+5)} = (-4)$$

$$(+4) \times (-5) = (-20) \text{ therefore } \frac{(-20)}{(-5)} = (+4)$$

Only the four divisions on the right–hand side of the page concern us here. The four combinations of signs allow us to conclude that, for dividing a pair of numbers:

- LIKE signs give a +
- UNLIKE signs give a −

Just as a multiplication table chart can always be used in reverse for divisions, Table 14.1 may also be used for divisions which may contain negative numbers. Furthermore, the respective quarters of the chart will confirm that divisions follow the above rule like multiplications.

A harder substitution question

The following example is chosen to include virtually each type of calculation in this chapter. Consequently, it is not simple and its choice is also a reminder that many dyslexics will go on to be very successful mathematics students and need to cover difficult topics, even though they have initial problems.

For the quadratic equation $a x^2 + b x + c = 0$, one solution is given by the formula

$$x = \frac{-b - \sqrt{b^2 - 4ac}}{2a}$$

For the quadratic equation $-x^2 - 4x + 5 = 0$, we must substitute into the formula $a = -1$, $b = -4$ and $c = +5$

Replacing each letter with an empty bracket gives

$$x = \frac{-() - \sqrt{()^2 - 4\,()\,()}}{2\,()}$$

Substituting each number with its sign gives

$$x = \frac{1\,(-4) - \sqrt{(-4)^2 - 4\,(-1)\,(+5)}}{2\,(-1)}$$

$$x = \frac{+4 - \sqrt{(-4)\,(-4) - 4\,(-5)}}{(-2)}$$

$$x = \frac{+4 - \sqrt{+16 + 20}}{(-2)}$$

$$x = \frac{+4 - \sqrt{+36}}{(-2)}$$

$$x = \frac{+4 - 6}{(-2)}$$

$$x = \frac{-2}{(-2)}$$

Therefore $\underline{x = +1}$

The other solution to the quadratic equation can be found by substituting the same values into the very similar formula:

$$x = \frac{-b + \sqrt{b^2 - 4\,a\,c}}{2\,a}$$

As an exercise it would be worth using this formula to confirm that the other solution is $x = -5$.

Summary

Looking at an area of difficulty in another way is often invaluable to a child, or a teacher for that matter. The hills and holes or the tallying symbols, derived from ancient Egyptian forms, provide just such other ways of looking at problems with negative numbers, and more besides. The written forms of the symbols offer advantages over the number line, which is already a very powerful tool. Cut out versions of the symbols offer a way of introducing concrete materials for those who have not passed that stage. Above are possible designs for the symbols to be cut from wood or card as hills and holes. The symbols for 10 and 100 can be interchanged by simply turning them around, or they can be made deliberately different for those children who would be confused. A compromise is to make use of a black horizontal line, such as is used on cards to distinguish 6 from 9.

A similar successful idea was reported by Kitz and Nash (1995) working on what they call 'remedial algebra' in the USA. They used black gambling chips to represent +1 and white chips to represent −1, and argued that a white and a black 'neutralized' one another. However, with both chips circular, they did not look like a zero when placed together, an important advantage of the symbols we have chosen to use in this chapter, which could be made in different colours, of course. While Kitz and Nash extended their ideas into algebraic expressions, using additional symbols (like rods for x), they did not extend their numerical treatment to the collective units of 10 and 100, important in this chapter for taking us higher and lower than a number line could go.

The universal multiplication chart can look rather intimidating at first. Quartering the chart makes it more manageable, and also sections off the chart to align with the rule advocated. The top right section represents the multiplication of two positive numbers, while the bottom right section represents the multiplication of a positive number by a negative and so on. The chart is intended to be used to explain to children and convince them, at least as much as for reference in locating answers for specific multiplications. The same could be said of division, of course, since it is the reverse of multiplication and it follows the same rule and chart.

Chapter 15
Time

This chapter addresses two aspects of time: telling the time and simple problems with time. The timing of the topic's introduction should be considered carefully (see Chapter 17). Copeland (1984) observed that some children at age 10 are still not ready for a true understanding of time, so some of the work in this section may be too advanced for children who are slightly older than this, but whose learning difficulties have held them back.

Being unable to tell the time is a classic weakness for dyslexics. The advent of the digital watch has enabled more children to say the time, but has not necessarily enabled them to have a concept of time. Being able to read a timetable or work out journey times are life skills, and involve an understanding of the 24–hour clock. Concentrating on the two basic areas referred to in the previous paragraph covers the majority of needs without over–complicating the issue.

Time involves the child in some new ideas, particularly working in new number bases: 12, 24 and 60. 'Traditional' time–telling involves not only adding time (as minutes and quarters) after the hour, but also counting down time to the next hour. The topic also uses some fraction work and a number line, but these too are different, since both are based on a circle.

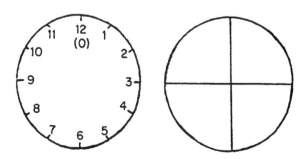

Figure 15.1

Thus the child has to adapt to these new demands and will probably cope more successfully if the work is built on his existing knowledge and adjusted to this new framework. The new framework will be stronger if it is based, not on the digital clock or watch (which has the tempting advantage of being easy to read), but on the traditional analogue clock. The clock face provides better visual memory hooks, a better understanding of the relative place of times, gives 12 a prominent place, and can be used to develop more strategies for the child. A digital clock does not have these advantages.

Setting the Scene

Obviously, the best visual aid is a clock. Although cardboard 'play' clocks are cheap, a better demonstration is achieved with a real clock. A real clock has hands which are synchronised, so that as the minute hand moves round, the hour hand moves towards the next hour. This gives the child the image of time: seconds, minutes and hours all moving constantly onwards, each at its own pace. The clock face has 12 at the top, and 12, like 100 for percentages is a critical number to remember.

As mentioned above, one of the teaching approaches advocated in this book is to start work from the child's interests and his existing knowledge base (a base that is usually bigger than he thinks, once some careful teasing out of facts and organisation is accomplished). The initial approach described below is an illustration of this technique.

Starting with the assumption that the child must have had some experience of time, such as the time school finishes, the time a favourite television programme starts and so forth, the teacher asks the child to say some times he knows, and the teacher writes them down to show the child on paper and also shows them on a clock. The teacher may need to prompt with questions such as, 'What time do you get up to go to school/on a weekend?' Work of this kind concentrates on showing the child the need to identify hours and minutes for telling the time, without asking the child actually to tell the time.

Looking at material such as the day's television programme times confirms this need and shows how times are presented. This is again linked to the clock, with exercises that include asking the child to identify the hands, show the number of minutes and the number of hours around the clock. The synchronised hour and minute hands can be used by the child to confirm that as the minute hand moves once around the clock, the hour hand moves steadily on to the next hour.

The combination of the material showing written times and observation of the clock can lead to a discussion of morning and a.m., and evening and p.m., and the importance of 12 o'clock. Thus it develops into a day being two circuits of the clock, and therefore 24 hours. (Another social skill problem involving time is the dyslexic's tendency to confuse the names of meals and to say 'Good afternoon' or 'Good morning' at the wrong time of day. It may be useful to introduce these items into appropriate examples.)

The clock and the movement of the hands round and round shows the continuous nature of time. It also shows that the minute hand can point to any number up to 60, and that 60 coincides with the 0 of the next circuit. Likewise it shows that the hour hand can point to any number up to 12, and that 12 coincides with the 0 of the next circuit. The child should be shown how the hour hand is half–way to the next hour, when the minute hand is on 30 (half past). The clock face needs to be seen as a number line, but instead of going on and on like a linear number line, it circles back to zero every 60 seconds for the second hand, every 60 minutes for the minute hand and every 12 hours for the hour hand. (At this stage the 24–hour clock is held in abeyance.)

Telling the Time

Digital time

The times for television programmes are likely to be published as digital times, quoting the hour and the number of minutes after the hour. The hours range from 1 to 12 and the minutes from 0 to 59 in examples such as 4.00, 6.55 and 8.15.

Although children must learn to read these, it is strongly advised that they are encouraged never to write their own times with a point between the hours and minutes, as in 6.55, since this is likely to suggest that time works in decimal (base 10). This will undermine much of what is contained elsewhere in this chapter and wrongly suggest that one can employ a calculator as for routine number calculations. The colon, much used in digital displays is a safe replacement, giving 6:55, the form used in the rest of this chapter.

Adults above a certain age may feel uncomfortable reading out times as 'eight fifteen' and 'six fifty five', and find themselves tempted to convert to 'quarter past eight' and 'five to seven'. Ways of explaining these more colloquial forms to children follow in the next sections.

Quarter past, half past and quarter to

(In the UK 'past' and 'to'; in the USA 'after' and 'before'.)

These reference times can be fairly easily mastered. The clock face can be divided in half (possibly using a cut out circle for the clock face) and the number of minutes in a half hour discussed. This leads on to quarters, again with paper folding.

The ideas of time past and time to form part of the understanding of times as opposed to just saying the time (from a digital watch). The child is introduced to half being a change over point. Up to the half the minutes are counted as time past, so the first quarter is 'quarter past'.

The half is 'half past', but after this, time starts to look forwards towards the next hour, so the last quarter is 'quarter to' the next hour. (There is some similarity here to the work the child did in 'making change'—counting on the money to take him up to the pound or whatever.)

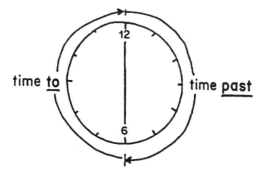

Figure 15.2

A rational explanation for the child is that you only refer to the nearest hour. After 30 minutes, the next hour is nearer. The position of the hour hand aids this explanation. Other examples abound, such as count down for rockets, the number of shopping-days to Christmas and so forth.

Figure 15.3

Minutes past

There are 30 minutes which can be 'past' the hour. These are not numbered on the clock, but are grouped in fives for each hour number. This acts as another reinforcement of the 5 times table. The quarter hour acts as a mid–way reference point of 15 minutes.

Minutes to

There are 29 minutes which can be 'to' the hour, starting straight after the half (30) and counting down to the hour (0). Again they are grouped in fives, working down through the mid–way reference point of 'quarter to' (15).

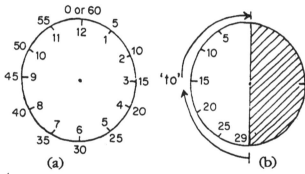

Figure 15.4

The child must remember that as the minute hand gets closer to the next hour, the number of minutes left 'to' the hour gets less.

Ante meridian (a.m.) and post meridian (p.m.)

The 12 hours between midnight and midday are referred to as a.m., while the 12 hours from midday to midnight are known as p.m. Each time appears twice throughout the day, and the suffix a.m. or p.m. must be written to distinguish between, say, 7:30 in the morning (a.m.) and 7:30 in the evening (p.m.).

For older children (say 12 or 13), the following exercise can provide an interesting lead in:

Here is an new form of addition. See if you can find how it works:

$$6 + 2 = 8$$
$$7 + 4 = 11$$
$$8 + 7 = 3$$
$$10 + 8 = 6 \qquad \text{(10 a.m. to 12 noon, 12 noon to 6 p.m.)}$$
$$11 + 5 = ?$$

This introduces the child to the concept of base 12 as a puzzle and focuses attention on the need to use a different base when adding hours. It also emphasises the importance of 12 as a finish/start point. The descriptive names of midday and midnight add to this image of 12 as special and help the child conceptualise a.m. and p.m.

The 24–hour clock

The advent of the digital watch, digital clock and video recorder has familiarised children with the 24–hour clock. It is, therefore, less likely to be a revelation to many children. The clock face, the length of the day ($2 \times 12 = 24$) and the base 12 work above all acted as introductory material to this topic. Consequently, it should not be difficult to show a child how the 24–hour clock replaces the need for a.m. and p.m. by allowing the hours to continue increasing after midday. A clock face with the 24 hour numbers helps to build an image for the child, showing the circle labelled both from 1 to 12 and from 13 to 24. It can be a useful aid to understanding, as well as a reference tool. He can see the equivalence of p.m. times and 24 hour times, as with 8 and 20 coinciding.

Table 15.1 shows times in the normal school day for Year 10 at Mark College, shown in the 24–hour clock and with a.m. and p.m. times. These are all very familiar times to our children. Some of the times are left blank for a child to fill in as an exercise.

Table 15.1 Times in a normal school day at Mark College

	a.m. or p.m.	24 hour clock
Get out of bed	7:30 a.m.	07 30
Breakfast	8:00 a.m.	08 00
Assembly	8:50 a.m.	
Lesson 1		09 00
Lesson 2		09 40
Morning break	10:20 a.m.	10 20
Lesson 3	10:40 a.m.	
Lesson 4		11 20
Lunch	12:00 Midday	12 00
Lesson 5	1:00 p.m.	13 00
Lesson 6	1:40 p.m.	13 40
Afternoon Break	2:20 p.m.	
Lesson 7		14 40
Lesson 8	3:20 p.m.	15 20
Free Time	4:00 p.m.	
First Prep.	5:00 p.m.	17 00
Dinner	6:00 p.m.	
Second Prep.		20 00
Bed Time	9:45 p.m.	21 45
Lights Out	10:00 p.m.	

Working from the known to the unknown, children gain an understanding of the conventions of the system, using the clues in Table 15.1. For example, it becomes clear that no separator appears between the hours and minutes in the 24–hour clock and that the hours have leading zeros where necessary to make them double figures. Children will then recall already having heard a time referred to as 'oh eight hundred hours'.

Conversion requires 12 hours to be added or subtracted depending on the problem. It helps the child to have a reference time for use as a model to check if he has to add or subtract. This could be the end of school, say '4 p.m. as 16 00 hours' or a favourite television programme, '7:30 p.m. as 19 30 hours'.

	$5 + 12 = 17$		
so	5 p.m.	would be	17 00
and	5:24 p.m.	would be	17 24

	$19 - 12 = 7$		
so	19 00	would be	7 p.m.
and 19 05		would be	7:05 p.m.

Time Problems

Finishing times

Questions can be posed such as:

- Problem A: If I start a journey at 9 a.m. and travel for 10 hours, when do I arrive? or, the more difficult,
- Problem B: If I start a journey at 8:45 p.m. and travel for 2 hours 37 minutes, when do I arrive?

Several alternative methods are available for these essentially addition problems:

Conversion to the 24–hour clock

With times all in the 24–hour clock, the (travelling) time is simply added on, to give a finishing time in the 24–hour clock which may be converted back if required.

Problem A

9 a.m. converts to 09 00

then   09 00

      + 10

      19 00

and 19 00 converts back to 7 p.m.

Problem B

8:45 p.m. converts to 20 45

$$\begin{array}{r} {}^{1}\ {}^{1} \\ 20\ 45 \\ + 2\ 37 \\ \hline 23\ 22 \end{array}$$

then

and 23 22 converts back to 11:22 p.m.

With additions of this kind, it must be remembered that there are 60 minutes in 1 hour, so we are working in base 60 at the boundary between hours and minutes. In the right hand column of this example, the single minutes add up to 12 and we can carry the 1. However, in the second–from–right column, the minutes add up to 8 tens (80), which must be recognised as 1 hour 20 minutes. We must not carry the 8, but instead we must carry the 1 hour into the hours column and retain the 2 tens (20) in the minutes. Had the problem taken the number of hours over 23, then (working in base 24 would show that) we would have exceeded one full day and gone into the next.

Via 12 o'clock on the number circle

Problem A

Figure 15.5

>   12 − 9 = 3 hours (travelled before 12)
> leaving   10 − 3 = 7 hours to travel after 12
> so finishing time will be 7 p.m.

Using a time line

Problem B This problem is easier to handle if the circular clock face is 'unrolled' to form a 'time line'.

The 2 whole hours carry us from 8:45 to 10:45, then we must add the 37 minutes:

$$\begin{array}{r} ^{1\ 1}\\ 10:45 \\ +\ 37 \\ \hline 11:22 \end{array}$$

Here we must show the same awareness of carrying an hour when exceeding 60 minutes.

Elapsed times

The methods used for finishing times can be modified to deal with subtraction problems such as

- Problem C: A woman works from 10 a.m. until 3 p.m. How long does she work?
- Problem D: A journey begins at 7:35 a.m. and ends at 1:27 p.m. How long does the journey take?

Conversion to the 24–hour clock

With times both in the 24–hour clock, they are merely subtracted.

Problem C

3 p.m. converts to 15 00
then   15 00
       − 11 00
       ───────
          4 00
so the woman works for 4 hours (and no minutes).

Problem D

7:35 a.m. converts to 07 35
1:27 p.m. converts to 13 27

$$\begin{array}{r} ^{2\,6}\\ \text{then}\quad 1\cancel{3}\ 27 \\ -\ 7\ 35 \\ \hline 5\ 52 \end{array}$$

so the journey takes 5 hours and 52 minutes.

Here again we are working in base 60 at the boundary between hours and minutes. That is, at the point where we 'borrow' an hour to help with the subtraction, we borrow 60 (= 6 × 10) minutes as shown.

Via 12 on the number circle

Problem C

Figure 15.6

After 12,	time worked = 3 – 0	= 3 hours
Before 12,	time worked = 12 – 10	= 2 hours
Total time worked		= 5 hours

Using a time line

Problem D

Time travelled before 8 a.m.	= 60 – 35	= 25 minutes
Time travelled after 1 p.m.		= 27 minutes
Total minutes		= 52 minutes

Whole hours travelled between 8 a.m. and 1 p.m. = 5 hours
Total time travelled = 5 hours and 52 minutes

Summary

The child can progress from reading hours (o'clock) to quarters and halves, to minutes past and minutes to, mastering one stage before he faces the next. The importance of 12 and 60 are stressed, especially the need to start counting again when 12 or 60 is reached. Visual images of clock faces are used to reinforce the calculation procedures.

Chapter 16
Teaching the Full
Curriculum

Introduction

Faced with a dyslexic child, who at a young age is experiencing great difficulty with mathematics, many teachers will feel it is best to persevere with the basics of numeracy until the child has mastered them. The teacher might regard these basics as so fundamentally important that to proceed to other topics would not seem to represent the best use of time or effort. As time passes, and the child continues to experience many of the same difficulties, there grows the temptation to concentrate even harder on a narrow range of activities. Such a situation can come to extend over a period of years, during which the dyslexic child is enduring constant failure, and losing all confidence in himself and the learning process. The loss of confidence is a serious additional problem, in a subject where confidence in performance is so important–mathematics is like walking a tight–rope, in the sense that if you think you are going to fall, then you will probably fall.

Varying the mathematical diet for such a child is a course of action which may have beneficial effects of three kinds.

- It may provide him with a small amount of success and bring back some confidence.
- Even more importantly, it may begin a process that gives him a alternative way of looking at the subject—a way around his problems, when there may be no way through them. If building a wall can be used as a metaphor for the learning of mathematics, then the wall of a dyslexic child will have many bricks missing, for parts of the subject he has not mastered. Of course a wall can remain standing around a few gaps, with the support of the bricks around the gaps, and the wider the wall, the more missing bricks it can bridge. Where the wall of a dyslexic child cannot be built directly upwards, it should be built across and then upwards, by widening his mathematical experience, especially at the foundation levels.

217

- It may give him abilities, such as telling the time, which can be regarded as social or 'survival' skills (Copeland, 1984), the lack of which can be embarrassing for the child (or his parents).

The introduction of mathematical topics other than number can be achieved in such a way that it reinforces the numerical work, rather than adding to the overall load. In a single chapter, it is impossible to cover very much curricular ground, but it is possible to describe some general principles and give a number of illustrative examples.

Some General Principles

Start early

Experience teaching pupils from 11 through to 16 seems to show that good early work pays huge dividends later. Very few special approaches need to be used for 14, 15 and 16–year–olds who have been given a very sound foundation. It seems that they respond to conventional teaching methods, and add their own motivation derived from increased confidence and being in sight of the achievable target of GCSE. The early work seems to align all their efforts in the right direction progressively, and begin a momentum in that right direction. The earlier this can start the better.

Plan for the long term

It is extremely important that long–term success should not be jeopardised for the sake of early gains, through the use of short cuts which are not soundly based. This can be taken to include reliance on special cases or too many rules which dyslexics are likely to forget, or remember wrongly.

For example:

- When faced with the mixed fraction $3\frac{1}{2}$, many secondary–aged dyslexics will feel they know how to convert it into a top–heavy fraction, because they remember the rule 'multiply that by that and add that'. When challenged which 'that' should be multiplied by which, and which 'that' should then be added, some will choose 3 times 1 add 2, some will choose 2 times 1 add 3, and some will choose 2 times 3 add 1 (the correct version). That most of them remember the rule wrongly is bad enough, but more dangerous still is their total conviction that they can rely on what they remember.
- In Chapter 11, the division of a fraction by another fraction was dealt with in two ways. One way was to make segment sizes the same then divide 'like with like'. The other way suggested, which initially seems

bizarre, was to invert the divisor fraction then multiply. Forethought should be given here to the fact that many dyslexics, despite their problems, will go on much further with their mathematics (even to degree level). Surprisingly, it is the latter method which will have more lasting value, in algebraic fractions such as

$$\frac{a^2 b^3 c}{w^2 y^2 z} \div \frac{a b c}{w y^2 z} = \frac{a^2 b^3 e^2}{w y^2 z} \times \frac{w^2 y z}{a b e} = \frac{a b^2}{w}$$

Use illustrations of wide applicability

Once children understand the concept of area, and can fluently calculate areas of rectangles (which is often thought to be the same thing), the area model can help in many ways. Towards the end of Chapter 8, the use of counting blocks for multiplications transforms into the use of scale drawings and then area sketches. For example, the single multiplication 38×14 performed as the four partial products 30×10, 30×4, 8×10 and 8×4 can be illustrated using the areas in Figure 16.1.

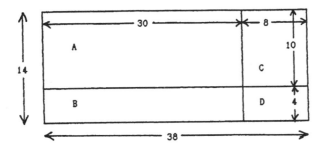

Figure 16.1

$$
\begin{aligned}
& 38 \times 14 \\
= \; & \text{area of whole diagram} \\
= \; & \text{area A} + \text{area B} + \text{area C} + \text{area D} \\
= \; & 30 \times 10 + 30 \times 4 + 8 \times 10 + 8 \times 4 \\
= \; & 300 + 120 + 80 + 32 \\
= \; & 532
\end{aligned}
$$

This idea can be exploited in a very similar way, to perhaps even greater benefit, in algebraic multiplication. Figures 16.2 and 16.3 show how to work out:

$(x + a)\,(y + b)$ and $(x - a)\,(y - b)$

Figure 16.2

$$(x + a)\ (y + b)$$
$=$ area of whole diagram
$=$ area 1 + area 2 + area 3 + area 4
$=$ $xy + xb + ay + ab$

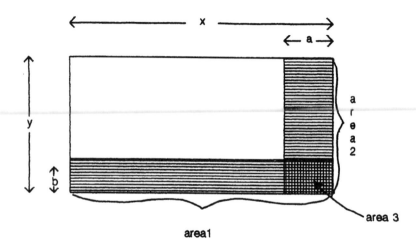

Figure 16.3

$$(x - a)\ (y - b)$$
$=$ area of whole diagram – area 1 – area 2 + area 3
$=$ $xy - xb - ay + ab$

There are many other instances where the area model can prove invaluable. It is used elsewhere in this book, for multiplying fractions, for example.

'Maths is easy—only writing it down is hard'

It is all too common to consider only the written form of maths, the most difficult form for most dyslexics. In fact the written form should be the last thing considered.

Example: long division

Consider 425 ÷ 17

$$
\begin{array}{r}
25 \\
17\overline{)425} \\
-34 \\
\hline
85 \\
-85 \\
\hline
00
\end{array}
$$

It might be taught as an algorithm or series of steps to be learned and performed in sequence. This would make things very difficult for a dyslexic, who has problems with short–term memory, tables and sequencing. A better approach would be to consider the real mathematics as happening when a physical division takes place. Then the written version constitutes only the record of a common event which is well understood. Rather than trying to follow a badly remembered and badly understood list of steps, a dyslexic is better encouraged to imagine dividing £4.25 between 17 people, or indeed to actually perform the division with coins. The written steps *will* match the physical steps.

Consider the £4.25 as 425p, in the form of 4 one pound coins, 2 ten pence coins and 5 one penny coins. First we would attempt to divide the 4 £1 coins between the 17 people:

$$
17\overline{)4}
$$

Clearly there are not enough even to have one each, so the 4 pounds would be changed into 40 ten pence pieces, which would join the existing 2 to give 42:

$$
17\overline{)42}
$$

Now we would attempt to divide the 42 ten pence coins between the 17 people (a separate problem in itself). They would receive 2 each, and this would use up 34 of the ten pence coins:

$$
\begin{array}{r}
2 \\
17\overline{)42} \\
34
\end{array}
$$

This would leave 8 ten pence coins that could not be divided between the 17 people:

$$
\begin{array}{r}
2 \\
17\overline{)42} \\
-34 \\
\hline
8
\end{array}
$$

These would be changed into 80 one penny coins, which would join the existing 5 to give 85:

$$\begin{array}{r} 25 \\ 17\overline{)425} \\ \underline{-34} \\ 85 \end{array}$$

Now we would attempt to divide the 85 one penny coins between 17 people. They would receive 5 each and this would use up all 85, with none remaining:

$$\begin{array}{r} 25 \\ 17\overline{)425} \\ \underline{-34} \\ 85 \\ \underline{-85} \\ 00 \end{array}$$

The written form, here obtained by recording the physical steps, is identical with the version achievable through performing a difficult algorithm. The difference is that a dyslexic child would understand what had happened, and how to repeat it.

Example: a rule for equations

Equations are a very important theme, which runs all the way through this subject. The very stylised procedures to be followed for solving them are highly likely to confuse many dyslexics. Therefore it is necessary for a teacher to be extremely alert and sensitive, as well as very careful about how this work is presented. Once again, the method which will be best understood is the method derived from physical experience.

In solving an equation like $x + 3 = 8$, there are various schools of thought. Pupils can be taught with flow charts. They can be taught that equations are like balance scales, pivoted about the = sign, and that any operation must be done to both sides to maintain the balance. For this example, it is possible to subtract 3 from both sides to leave $x = 5$. Although this method can be physically demonstrated with a special pair of balance scales, we have found it to seem 'artificial' and lead to some awkward subtractions at times. Our pupils tend to prefer another method, which they derive naturally for themselves. The teacher covers up an 'unknown' number of counters, adds 3 more and then shows the result to be 8. If the pupils are then asked to describe how to find the original number, none of them have any doubt that the extra 3 must be subtracted (revealing the original 5). In its written form this appears as:

$$x + 3 \quad = 8$$

then $x \qquad = 8 - 3$
and therefore $x \qquad = 5$

It looks as though the 3 has crossed over the $=$ and its sign has changed from $+$ to $-$. As the pupils described it, the number which was added must now be subtracted. The written form has reflected what the pupils found self evident.

For the equation

$$\frac{x}{2} = 5$$

the teacher again covers up the 'unknown' number of counters, this time explaining that they are being divided into two equal groups, and then showing one group to contain 5. Now if the pupils are asked to suggest how to find the original number, they will advise that the 5 should be doubled (multiplied by 2) giving 10 for the result. In its written form this appears as:

$$\frac{x}{2} = 5$$

then $x \quad = 5 \times 2$
and therefore $x \quad = 10$

It looks as though the 2 has crossed over the $=$ and its sign changed from division to multiplication, as the pupils suggested. Again the written form has reflected the pupils' way of thinking.

Almost incidentally, the pupils have derived for themselves a rule, which is easily remembered as

Change the SIDE
Change the SIGN

Although there is insufficient space here to demonstrate further examples, this is the rule pupils will carry with them throughout their mathematical careers, no matter how far their equations reach, and they will remember it and understand it all the better for having related it to physical experience. Further suggestions for teaching equations and another view deriving the rule are to be found later in the chapter.

Teaching the Other Parts of the Curriculum

Teaching dyslexic children mathematics since long before the National Curriculum, it always seemed that the structure of our pupils' learning was the first thing which should be tackled. Our curriculum was organised into five different parts: Using and applying mathematics, Number, Algebra, Space and shape, and Handling data.

The idea was not to separate the work in each part from the work in the other parts, because this would have conflicted with the policy to which experience had led us: that we should offer a wide mathematical 'wall', with the bricks cemented horizontally as well as vertically. Rather, the idea was to have all the separate pieces ready in advance, so that they could be assembled in the most efficient way. This is somewhat like having ready all the different tools and materials to build a wall, such as the trowels, shovels and spirit–levels, damp–proof membrane, air bricks and mortar etc.

Consequently, part of the rest of this chapter will offer hints about planning the curricular materials for the five parts: the rest of the chapter will suggest some methods of combining them.

Using and applying mathematics

Two uses for this kind of work are dealt with in this chapter. It naturally helps with combining different skills and knowledge from different mathematical areas, and this use will be discussed towards the end of the chapter. The other use for investigations involves children examining a new piece of curricular work and deriving the theory for themselves. This use is not as daunting for the children as it sounds.

A very simple instance concerns the angle–sum of a triangle. If a class full of children all draw a triangle, measure the angles and add them up, then the result will be about 180 degrees for all those who have not made a gross error. The gross errors might include mistakes in the addition, or using the wrong scale on the protractor. Once these have been corrected there should be enough answers just above 180 to balance those just below 180 and convince the children that 180 is the right answer. If the triangles are of many different shapes, then this will confirm the universal application of the result.

A later, more difficult, though related example concerns the angle–sum for any polygon. This used to be taught as 2n – 4 right angles, which is a difficult formula to remember that employs peculiar units. Asked to investigate this polygon problem, instead of being given the formula, children might need the hint that they should divide the polygon into triangles (preferably from one corner). If they all draw several polygons, they will usually be able to detect that they can always draw two triangles less than the number of the polygon's sides.

For the pentagon in Figure 16.4, this would be 5 – 2 = 3 triangles. From what they already know, children would be able to work this out as 3 × 180 = 540 degrees. Having worked the theory out for themselves, they are more likely to have understood it. They are also more likely to remember it, either via the easier formula (n − 2) × 180 degrees, or in a form of words like 'two triangles less than the size', or simply resolving always to divide their polygons into as many triangles as it takes.

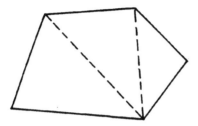

Figure 16.4

Number

Because the greater part of this book deals with numerical aspects of mathematics, this chapter will concentrate on the other parts of the curriculum.

Algebra

All the way up to GCSE level, a significant portion of the study of mathematics can be argued to involve not so much of an intellectual challenge, but more the acceptance and acquisition of conventions of syntax. Nowhere is this more true than in algebra. Of course the effective acquisition requires thorough explanation and practice of every possible type of problem.

Two areas of major importance within algebra concern formulae and equations.

Children will be expected to be able to derive formulae for simple situations. They will subsequently be expected to substitute values into given formulae.

When a problem quite correctly finishes with a formula, for example a + b + c as the perimeter of the triangle in Figure 16.5, there are children who will be dissatisfied with the lack of a numerical answer.

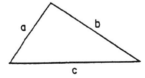

Figure 16.5

They can usually be convinced by the argument that a formula is an 'instruction' about what to do when the values of a, b and c become known. In this sense a formula is superior because it applies to every triangle, while a numerical answer is only correct for one specific triangle.

Errors in substitution questions can signal fundamental misconceptions.

Example

In this example 5n represents '5 times n', although the multiply sign is not usually visible. If it is required to substitute n = 4 into the formula 5n, then the multiply sign should make an appearance before the substitution takes place, if the common incorrect answer of 54 is to be avoided.

$$5n$$
$$= \quad 5 \times n$$
$$= \quad 5 \times 4$$
$$= \quad 20$$

Children often ask why the multiply sign is missed out, and a selection of reasons can be given, including the fact that it resembles the letter x too closely or that we say '5 pounds' rather than '5 times a pound' in everyday language or that it simply saves effort.

Example

Children substituting y = 2 into the formula $3y^2$ can produce the incorrect answer 36, especially with casual use of certain calculators. What they have computed is $(3 \times 2)^2$ rather than $3 \times (2)^2$. The 'squared' applies only to the y and not to the 3.

An earlier passage described how to arrive at the rule for solving equations. There are further problems implementing the rule. At the beginning, the numbers in an equation must be kept simple to avoid clouding the main issue However, children confronted with the equation x + 3 = 8 will often rush to guess the answer 5, and then be unhappy when their teacher insists (appearing pedantic) that they must set out all the steps properly. Ironically, the very simplicity of the numbers limits the children's acceptance of the need for a careful procedure. It is necessary to convince them that the need will soon increase, and one way is to show them an equation, such as 31.2x − x(2.5 − x) = 0.654, which they cannot solve in their heads but may have to solve in later years. This can be followed up by adopting the motto:

Look after your equations when they are young, and they will look after you, when you are older.

Shape and space

Application of the *Test of Cognitive Style in Mathematics* (Bath et al., 1985) has indicated that the mathematical style adopted in this branch of the subject, which covers topics such as angles, volume and symmetry is often different from the style for the subject as a whole.

Furthermore, the misconceptions experienced by dyslexics in this branch can produce some of the most confusing mistakes. For example, it has been known for a child to argue long and hard that in the diagram in Figure 16.6 'y = 40, because both angles are the same'.

Figure 16.6

Discussion showed that the misconception seemed to derive from observation that both angles were formed with the same pair of straight lines.

Handling data

The fifth part in our original curriculum split differed slightly from the National Curriculum version in being called 'graphs' rather than handling data. The calculation of means, medians and modes always seemed very *numerical* processes. Pie charts and histograms fit both titles, of course, but we felt that dealing graphically with a table full of co–ordinates (from a quadratic equation, for example) should also count as handling data. The graph in Figure 16.7 for squares and square roots is such an example.

When covering squares and square roots, a curved graph may be plotted for the easy square root values (x) and the easy square values (y) in Table 16.1.

Table 16.1

x	0	1	2	3	4	5	6	7	8	9	10
y	0	1	4	9	16	25	36	49	64	81	100

By reading from one scale to the curve, then from the curve to the other scale, the graph can provide much more data than the list of values. Broken lines on the graph show how this is done. Additional data is obtainable in at least two ways.

Figure 16.7

- Reading from the x scale to the y scale gives squares, while reading from the y scale to the x scale gives square roots. Through having this dual capability, the graph is providing one of the best ways to demonstrate that squaring and square rooting are opposite processes.

$$25 \quad = \quad 5^2$$
$$\text{so} \quad \sqrt{25} \quad = \quad 5$$

- Between the 11 plotted points, the curve contains an infinite number of other points, which may be used for values between those in Table 16.1. For instance, one of the broken lines shows that $6.7^2 = 44$ to the nearest whole number and another shows that $\sqrt{72} = 8.5$ correct to 1 decimal place.

Combining the Parts of the Curriculum

This final section contains a short series of examples which increase in complexity, to show how parts of the curriculum may be combined.

Example

Addition in two digits can be illustrated by covering concurrently the combination of angles, like those shown in Figure 16.8a.

$$\begin{array}{r} 25 \\ + \quad 50 \\ \hline 75 \end{array}$$

The idea of combining angles can be extended to the case where angles are represented by letters (Figure 16.8b).

Figure 16.8

It involves very little extra difficulty for children to add the above angles and obtain x + 35. It is also conceivable, at this stage, to form the equation x + 35 = 90, since the outer angle has been carefully chosen as a right angle.

Example

When children are practising subtraction of hundreds, tens and units, its application to an example such as that in Figure 16.8c can provide credibility and motivation.

$$\begin{array}{r} 360 \\ -\ \ 235 \\ \hline 125 \end{array}$$

Example

Sometimes a carefully chosen example from one part of the curriculum can help children to derive or confirm rules for another. At a time when perimeter has been studied, the diagram in Figure 16.9 could lead elsewhere.

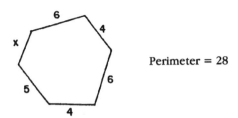

Perimeter = 28

Figure 16.9

Prompted by the question, 'How would you find x?', many children would have no difficulty in concluding that the given sides should be added, and the total subtracted from 28. A written version of the problem and its solution:

$$x + 6 + 4 + 6 + 5 + 4 = 28$$
$$x + 25 = 28$$
$$x = 28 - 25$$
$$x = 3$$

Indicates precisely how a quite difficult equation should be solved, and confirms the rule derived differently earlier in this chapter.

Change the SIDE
Change the SIGN

Example

Not to scale

Figure 16.10

The problem illustrated in Figure 16.10 can be regarded as a spatial problem. The calculation of the missing angle can be performed numerically, as 180 – 70, or interpreted algebraically in the form of the equation x + 70 = 180. Furthermore, if the problem was generalised to that shown in Figure 16.11 and the value of x was allowed to vary, between 0 and 180, then the corresponding values of y could be tabulated against it, as follows.

Figure 16.11

Table 16.2

x	0	20	40	60	80	100	120	140	160	180
y	180	160	140	120	100	80	60	40	20	0

Table 16.2 shows all possible pairs of values, for multiples of 20, and could be generalised into the relationship y = 180 – x. The graph in Figure 16.12 produces a backwards–sloping straight line (rare in itself at this level), which can be used to show every possible pair of values, and thereby demonstrate the problem–solving power of graphs.

Figure 16.12

Work on using and applying mathematics can have the other role, mentioned earlier, of forcing the combination of many parts of the curriculum.

Example

Investigating the question 'Can a person walk a million miles?', turns a child's thoughts to distances and times, and requires him to make various judgements and estimates. The thoughts on times will range from minutes to eat meals, through hours for sleep, days for rest, weeks, months and years, to decades and centuries. He may wonder how many times around the world is a million miles or if it is that far to the moon. He will have to make judgements about how long the person would live and their walking speed or how far they could reasonably be expected to walk in a day. Dyslexics' estimates in these areas can show wild misconceptions, which can be discussed very profitably.

Example

A briefly worded challenge for a child to draw a square and a circle with the same area provides another example. The sensible (or fortunate) child will choose a radius, draw a circle first and work out its area. To draw the square then only requires him to take the square root of this area to find the square's sides. This exercise involves choosing a radius and drawing a circle, remembering and evaluating the formula for the area of a circle, reversing the formula for the area of a square to obtain the length of its sides, then drawing the square. The less fortunate child will draw the square first and have a considerably more difficult job reversing the formula for the area of the circle!

Summary

This chapter's purpose has been to argue the importance to a dyslexic child of a structure which organises the widest possible range of mathematical experiences. While complete coverage of the matter would take several books, the chapter covers some general principles and includes illustrative examples. There are notes on the separate parts of the subject and some examples of when and how to combine these.

Chapter 17
The Teaching Programme at Mark College

Introduction

In this final chapter, it is our intention to show how we put our ideas into practice at Mark College in our roles as teachers and organisers. If in many instances we seem to repeat what has been written earlier it is because we regard it as sensible to continue taking our own advice. However, we have avoided the repetition of examples at every point to reduce the amount of text, whilst attempting to make this chapter a useful summary of the whole book.

Mark College and its Pupils

Mark College is a specialist secondary school for boys who have been diagnosed as dyslexic. Pupils usually join the college at age 11 and leave at age 16. Sixteen pupils of average or above average intelligence are usually admitted each year. Having been diagnosed as dyslexic, it is almost certain that their mathematical achievement does not match their potential. Each pupil must have his learning difficulties dealt with in the context of teaching groups of eight, a size dictated by the need for close individual attention, whilst retaining a sense of classroom community.

Our pupils come from a wide range of backgrounds: social, economic, emotional and educational. In many cases a child will present with considerable anxieties. The elimination of these anxieties is an important priority.

The curriculum is directed towards creating a relaxed, welcoming, empathetic and low–stress atmosphere. When this is achieved, the pupils start to feel confident that they can communicate their difficulties within an environment where their questions are answered empathetically and in alternative ways until an understanding is reached, rather than just more slowly and more loudly.

The early stages of the course provide work which is relatively easy, in order to restore a sense of success in pupils who may feel (or indeed may have been labelled) 'failures'. Equally, the work must not be perceived as too easy or patronising.

New pupils arrive with varying abilities and levels of achievement. In their previous six years of education many will have survived by adopting idiosyncratic methods (or an impressive range of avoidance strategies) and will only have a piecemeal understanding and knowledge of the subject. Our aim is to build on and around what the pupils do understand and know, trying to avoid imposing arbitrary changes which would only add to their confusions. We attempt to provide the structure and organisation which their learning difficulty denies them, while acknowledging that our teaching strategies must enable the full spectrum of learning styles to function (and broaden). Indeed, it is our experience that pupils often know more than they realise. They need help with organising and rationalising their information and ideas.

Against this background of intentions, it is critical that we maintain the rigour and integrity of the subject we are teaching. Mathematics is a precise means of communication across the curriculum and in everyday life. In addition, we must tailor our scheme to the National Curriculum through to the appropriate public examinations. However, it is possible to use our programme and work within its constraints to build a sound base for the further studies many of our pupils will pursue.

The Structure of the Course

The structure is based on a spiral with a small pitch, so that the child makes frequent returns to the same topics. This provides opportunities for the ever–essential over learning (and acknowledges the difficulty in achieving mastery of some topics). The spiral rotates around the axis of numeracy. Topics are changed frequently to promote and sustain interest. The topics return quickly and repeatedly so that a pupil's memory meets these important skills and concepts before the work is completely lost. At each return the topic is reviewed and then pushed to a slightly higher level, allowing for progress and giving time for 'digestion' by moving on before the topic is pushed too far.

Numeracy

The vertical axis of the course begins with the following topics.

- Sorting and classifying.
- Counting with whole numbers and using them to measure and draw.
- Adding in whole numbers.
- Subtracting in whole numbers.
- Multiplying in whole numbers.
- Dividing in whole numbers.

- Understanding about parts of whole numbers.
- The four operations for money.
- The four operations for decimals.
- The four operations for fractions.

The axis is regarded as a continuum rather than a collection of separate skills to be acquired independently. The pupils' own characteristic approaches are encouraged. For example, a pupil is liberated (and encouraged) to see a division such as $24 \div 4$ as:

- A reverse multiplication, giving 6, because $6 \times 4 = 24$.
- A repeated subtraction down to zero:

$24 - 4 = 20$	once,	1
$20 - 4 = 16$	twice,	2
$16 - 4 = 12$	three times,	3
$12 - 4 = 8$	four times,	4
$8 - 4 = 4$	five times,	5
$4 - 4 = 0$	six times,	6 = answer

- Repeated additions up to the right answer:

$0 + 4 = 4$	once,	1
$4 + 4 = 8$	twice,	2
etc. to		
$20 + 4 = 24$	six times,	6 = answer.

Note that special attention is given to the number facts for single–figure addition, subtraction, multiplication and division, since knowing these facts, or having quick and efficient strategies with which to work them out, reduces the load on working/short–term memory during calculations. This knowledge helps both computation and, subsequently, understanding of number.

General Mathematical Topics

These topics, such as perimeter, area, equations, angle–sums and graphs, are introduced only at the number facility level which the pupil has acquired. The levels of numeracy are carefully organised so that any difficulties are readily identified and easily diagnosed.

The mathematical variety needs to be as wide as possible, as early as possible, in order to maintain motivation and extend experience. In particular, algebra is introduced very early in the form of simple generalisations at the conclusion of a piece of fully understood work. For example, when perimeter has been mastered numerically it is not a large conceptual leap for a child to accept a + b + c as the formula for the perimeter of a triangle. This introduction of algebra also addresses the problem of generalising.

As well as maintaining interest, a wide variety of topics helps to build foundations which are wide, so that difficult areas can be spanned as missing bricks are spanned in a wall. Furthermore, relationships between mathematical topics are revealed and alternative paths explored and developed.

Using and applying mathematics

We are committed to the recommendations of the Cockcroft Report (Cockcroft, 1982) and the GCSE requirements for investigations, problem solving and practical work. Thus Attainment Target 1 of the National Curriculum was also welcomed as supporting this part of our programme. Of the nine or ten 40–minute lessons per week allocated to mathematics, two double lessons are set aside for investigations, problem solving and practical project work. One of these double lessons is likely to involve tasks related to current curriculum work, whilst the content of the other is from a wide range of topics. (Single lessons may used for shorter tasks.) The pupil's problems with organisation and his need to have experiences on which to build concepts are addressed by these activities. The pupils respond well to such practice and they gain valuable skills for applying their mathematics.

The use of patterns

We have long advocated the use of patterns in mathematics to act as the mortar which holds the bricks of the subject together (Ashcroft and Chinn, 1992). In our situation we consider patterns and their recognition can help in the following ways.

- Streamline the learning of facts.
- Add interest and motivation.
- Help with conceptual problems.
- Rationalise idiosyncrasies.
- Provide structure.
- Encourage generalisation skills.

Mental arithmetic

Throughout the course, pupils are encouraged and shown how to develop methods of calculating answers in their heads, something most of us do (or try to do) in everyday situations. Whether our expectation is for a correct answer or an estimate, the pupil is encouraged to use mental calculations as his first resort and then as his last resort when verifying or checking his answer.

Classroom Management: Making the Lesson Suit the Pupils

In general, the short attention span and memory deficits of our pupils dictate that a lesson should be divided into short subsections alternating exposition, demonstration, practical work, discussions, practice, etc. The perceptual and organisational difficulties of our pupils dictate the need for clarity of presentation and thorough preparation. Despite the latter requirement, there is a need for a teacher to be flexible enough to change direction in response to problems or opportunities he may perceive in the course of the lesson.

Board work must be clear and uncluttered, preferably without too much information on display at any one time. The teacher's presentation work should be both oral and visual. Memory overload must also be avoided.

Teachers should avoid talking (especially about important work) while the pupils are writing. A dyslexic pupil finds it hard enough to copy without this added distraction, which may be further compounded by worrying about what he is not hearing because he is trying to write.

Spread of ability

Even though the College only admits pupils of average and above average intelligence and groups its two mathematical groups according to attainment, the pupils' problems produce a significant spread of ability and attainment in a class group. So, if the teacher is devoting time to slower pupils, then his organisation and preparation should allow faster pupils to cover selected extra topics so that both faster and slower pupils can progress. There is always a need to see each pupil as an individual. Faster pupils can also be given the opportunity to develop their 'communication level of understanding' (Sharma, 1988b), by helping slower pupils.

Pupils' mathematical cognitive styles

Some pupils follow a rigid, step–by–step, formula/algorithm style when tacking mathematics. This is usually the way this type of learner is best taught. Conversely, other pupils work intuitively and are very answer–orientated; they may have been stifled and demotivated by being taught in a way which matches the first style and not, therefore, their own style. A good mathematician needs to be flexible and make appropriate use of either style.

Pupils can be helped to find their own best way of working if the teacher:

- Begins each lesson with an overall picture of its contents, using both oral and visual stimuli.
- Thoroughly explains the logic behind each method.
- Offers alternative methods from which to choose.
- Puts the work into a familiar context, or relates it to the pupils' own experiences and existing knowledge.

Evolving Expectations and Emphases

The nature of the pupil's difficulties and his previous experiences in class will often have produced poor levels of achievement and an antipathy for the subject. We begin by trying to restore confidence and build a positive attitude. Success achieved later as the pupil moves up through the College will lead him to recognise his real abilities and raise his expectations to higher levels. We try to equip pupils with enough knowledge and skills to attain their true potential.

The mathematics course must allow for development, over a period of five years, between these two extremes. By carefully managing the levels of pressure applied over the five years, the pupils' success can be kept at a steady optimum. Figure 17.1a shows the pattern of pressure applied and Figure 17.1b shows the expected rates of progress, compared to those of normal secondary pupils.

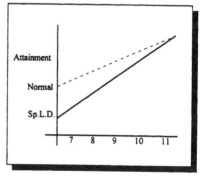

Figure 17.1 (a) Initially, the pressure of work will be low, to build confidence. Later strong motivation will allow the level of pressure to become even higher than normal. (b) On intake, levels of attainment will be lower than normal. Attainment levels will approach normal levels gradually, with the target of reaching (or overtaking) normal levels by the end of year 11, the time of GCSE examinations.

Although the progression will be gradual and continuous, the differences in emphasis require that specific changes are made at the end of year 8/beginning of year 9. The different objectives for years 7/8 and years 9/10/11 are now summarised.

Years 7 and 8

In these initial years the course is designed to begin to restore pupils' confidence in their ability to succeed in mathematics. We build on what pupils already know (and often they know more than they realise; their knowledge just needs organisation). Much of the work covers the basics in a manner which allows us to:

- Revise important work.
- Fill in as many gaps as possible.
- Rationalise pupils' established ideas which may, at this point, be right, wrong, confused or inefficient.

Lesson management

Pupils are taught together in groups of (usually) eight. In this situation they gain confidence in their teacher and are encouraged to lose their fear of making mistakes. The size of the group and its ethos enables the members of it to work together, share problems and accept mistakes without stress. The teaching follows a philosophy that is summarised, somewhat simplistically, as 'Mathematics is easy, only writing it down is hard'. The philosophy dictates the following sequence of steps:

- New topics are introduced via practical work, demonstrations, investigations, discussions and physical experiences. A variety of these is used to facilitate the development and understanding of each concept.
- An attempt is then made to translate the concept into a written form, linking the concrete experiences directly to the symbolic representation.
- This leads into worksheets or textbooks. The worksheets used at the College start with worked examples, which are related to the earlier experiences. The questions provide practice and revision. The worksheets are the third stage of the procedure and not, therefore, the sole resource from which pupils are expected to learn.

Teaching materials

Pupils in years 7 and 8 use worksheets, as mentioned above, developed by Ashcroft over the past 15 years of teaching dyslexics (available from Mark College). The sheets follow a structured course and are designed to:

- Present an advance overview of the section of work to be followed.
- Eliminate the need for notetaking, with its inherent risks of slow progress, mistakes, lack of clarity and readability.

- Start at the most appropriate point.
- Cover only a single topic, so that any point of difficulty can be readily isolated, identified and dealt with.
- Contain no more information than can be comfortably digested in one go.
- Present work clearly.
- Use the fewest possible and simplest words, yet introduce the necessary technical terms carefully.
- Incorporate exercises.
- Provide a practical revision aid (used as ready–made and organised notes).
- Be carefully related to other sheets.

Writing paper

If responses need more space than a worksheet provides, then pupils in years 7 and 8 write on 5 mm squared paper, either in loose–leaf form or in exercise books. The squares help with:

- Lining up calculations vertically and horizontally.
- Setting out tables and charts.
- Measurements and diagrams, especially those in centimetres and/or using right angles.
- Area problems.

Calculators

Since one of the aims of years 7 and 8 is to bring all pupils up to their optimum level of computational competence, the use of calculators is discouraged, except where the work is, for example, repetitive and they are an obvious time saver.

Mental arithmetic is necessary for everyday life and for estimations that check the answers later provided by a calculator. Early reliance on a calculator could well delay the acquisition of these mental arithmetic skills. Furthermore, many of the later mathematical processes, such as $(a + x)(b + y)$, are based on the early numerical processes, c.f. 35×24.

Years 9, 10 and 11

From year 9 onwards we see a more internalised, positive and motivated attitude.

Lesson management

Experience has shown that most pupils will have, by now, developed more belief in their ability to succeed in mathematics. Their expectations may also have become quite high. The self–determination to succeed is encouraged by the pupils beginning to work individually for some of their time.

A number of class lessons remain, of course, but individual routes can be provided in lessons, where pupils choose between:

- Help or further practice with current work.
- A revision of recent or incompletely mastered topics.
- Extension work.

It is possible to use published schemes to support this style of structure.

Teaching materials

From year 9, pupils are introduced to textbooks and they start to use mainstream material. An appropriate book, which becomes familiar and trusted, can provide help and reassurance, especially at examination times. Textbooks also provide different viewpoints and variety in language. The presentation of work in recently published textbooks has become more appealing, with good graphics, uncluttered pages and well–structured examples. We choose our textbooks carefully, so as not to risk the changes in attitude we have worked so hard to achieve. Some of the textbooks we have found to be successful are listed in Appendix 1.

Writing paper

During year 10, or earlier if they so choose, pupils graduate from 5 mm squared paper to 8 mm lined paper. Thus, we become aligned with practice in 'normal' schools and ready for examinations where lined paper is provided.

Calculators

In years 9, 10 and 11, the use of calculators becomes increasingly obligatory. Indeed, their use is expected at GCSE. We recommend the use of a simple solar–powered calculator with scientific functions, including fractions, percentage, degrees/minutes/seconds, and one which will not unnecessarily resort to scientific form for all answers. Good calculators can be bought cheaply. Calculators are an ideal aid for short–term memory and can help compensate for the pupils' remaining computational difficulties (which tend to be a matter of speed). We attempt to filter out logic and keying errors by encouraging methods of checking. The introduction and use of specific calculator functions are carried out mainly on the basis of need, as with the trigonometric functions, for example. Lessons can, however, be set aside for the exploration of other functions such as $n!$ (factorial n), which are of investigational rather than curricular interest.

The National Curriculum

We have always adapted our work towards the National Curriculum, although the frequent changes are sometimes not easy to keep up with. We anticipated the need to split the work into five Attainment Target areas and appreciate the structure inherent in the programme, which is so helpful to our pupils.

Our course for years 7 and 8 requires that pupils are taught at levels below those required at Key Stage 3 (which looks to teaching over levels 3 to 8) for part of the time. It would be very counterproductive to begin all our introductory work at level 3. The *Mathematics Non–Statutory Guidance* (National Curriculum Council, 1989) allows that 'certain pupils will benefit from work at a lower level in order to help them to consolidate a particular skill'.

In essence, then, we have parity at the end of Key Stage 4 as our ultimate goal, but the nature of our pupils and the programme we have designed to address their needs mean that we may not be on target (as defined by the National Curriculum) at earlier stages.

Assessment

Pupils are assessed regularly for the purpose of:

* Placement in appropriate teaching groups.
* Diagnosis of difficulties.
* Monitoring progress.
* Distinguishing mathematical cognitive style.

We make it clear to the pupils, most of whom have a long history of 'being tested', that our test results are for limited internal consumption only. This reduces their fear of the testing process to a level where it should only be distasteful!

Placement in teaching groups

Although our intake is of average or above–average intelligence, the pupils have a wide range of difficulties, which produce a full spectrum of mathematical achievements and abilities. We regard it as important to group pupils according to their current attainment level. In this arrangement, the diversity of their learning difficulties is not further compounded by great divides of performance. Pupils seem to feel safest and are more comfortable when asking questions or airing their problems if they are among those with similar levels of difficulty and achievement. There is flexibility of movement between groups as pupils move toward their full potential.

Monitoring progress

Standardised tests are given at the same or similar times each year for the purposes of comparison. We treat single test results with caution and always consider them in conjunction with progress in class, and with changes over a variety of situations, to obtain a real measure of progress.

Standardised test are so called because they have been given to a standard sample or population before publication. Any child's performance can then be compared with this standard population. The results can be expressed in various ways.

Some tests produce a 'mathematical age' which can be compared with a child's chronological age to give an idea of how far behind is his attainment. The results of subsequent tests will show how much improvement has been made. This can be related to the time which has elapsed to give a 'value–added' factor. For example, 18 months' progress in a year could be defined as a value–added factor of 1.5. Improvement in mathematical age can alternatively be graphed, as in Figure 17.1b.

Some tests produce a mathematical 'quotient', which resembles IQ and relates performance to an average figure of 100. For example, 96 is just below average, but within an average band.

Other tests produce a 'centile' or 'percentile' figure, which shows a child's position in the standard population as a percentage. For example, a percentile figure of 20 would indicate that 20% of the population would be expected to perform at or below the level of the child, while 80% would be expected to perform better.

Although we keep looking, we have not discovered a single standardised test which adequately covers the full age range of our pupils (from 11 to 16 years). Therefore, for many years we have used a combination of the Junior and Senior Levels of the Graded Arithmetic—Mathematics Test (Vernon and Miller, 1986). We have found that our pupils reach the 'threshold' age of the Senior Test (10 y 6 m) later than the normal population, so we must make use of the Junior Test for longer. The Junior Test itself has a 'ceiling' (12 y 3 m). Our pupils all reach these landmarks at different times. Therefore the time to change from the Junior Test to the Senior Test needs careful consideration, and a flexible period of overlap is necessary.

Recently, the Senior Test has been superseded by the Mathematics Competency Test (Vernon et al., 1995). This test contains some of the questions from the former test along with some new questions that give a wider spread across the National Curriculum attainment targets 2, 3, 4 and 5. This has allowed separate scores for each attainment target to produce a National Curriculum 'profile'. However, mathematical ages (and quotients) are no longer obtainable. This is a significant loss when parents and Local Education Authorities frequently require easily understandable progress figures. Percentile figures are the only standardised form of results. At Mark College, we will probably employ the tests alternately to gain the National Curriculum benefits of the new, while retaining the mathematical ages obtainable from the old. The old tests will be given each September and the new test each March.

Pupils' mathematical styles

To assess mathematical learning/cognitive style, we use the Test of Cognitive Style in Mathematics (Bath et al., 1986). It is used to distinguish between the step–by–step 'inchworm' and the intuitive, holistic 'grasshopper'. This American test is for use with individual pupils and provides a measure of the pupil's position on the continuum of styles from extreme inchworm to extreme grasshopper.

Diagnosis of difficulties

Some standardised tests are designed to test mathematical subskills separately so that particular problem areas can be identified. The results of these types of test can be used to direct subsequent teaching towards specific areas of weakness. An example of such a test is The Profile of Mathematical Skills (France, 1976).

For times–table and basic–addition facts testing we test twice, once at five–second intervals to test immediate recall and once at 15–second intervals to allow pupils to utilise strategies.

The Mark College test

The College has its own test designed for its dyslexic students. The test, written by Ashcroft, is based on a survey of the errors most commonly made by dyslexics (Joffe, 1980). It consists of items based on the areas where these errors occur. Consequently it helps with the diagnostic process and in measuring the effectiveness of remediation (see Appendix 3).

Schedule of assessment

To gain an overview of the levels of achievement and rates of progress of both groups and individuals, various standardised tests are applied at fixed points in the five–year College academic cycle. These are detailed in Table 17.1.

Table 17.1 Application of standardised tests.

| Year Group | 7 | | 8 | | 9 | | 10 | | 11 | |
Approx. age	11–12		12–13		13–14		14–15		15–16	
Month applied	Sep	Mar	Sep	Mar	Sep	Mar	Sep	Mar	Sep	Mar
Mark College Test (Ashcroft)	*		*		*					
Mathematics Competency Test (Vernon et al., 1996)		*		*		*		*		*
Graded Arithmetic–Mathematics Test (Vernon and Miller, 1986)										
Junior Level	*			*		*		*		
Senior Level				*		*		*		*

In–house examinations

The pupils take a College examination twice a year. This helps to prepare them for the rigours of public examinations and encourages revision and study skills. We give two papers each time.

- Paper 1 consists of short questions, and tests the width of pupils' knowledge and their accuracy.
- Paper 2 consists of longer questions, and tests the depth of pupils' understanding and their problem–solving abilities.

Public Examinations

Success in public examinations is in no way inconsistent with the objectives of our curriculum, although this is not our only objective. Success in these examinations is the yardstick against which pupils will be measured when they leave and a challenge they are ready to face. Results at GCSE are achievable for all our pupils according to their abilities and motivation (Chinn, 1996).

We regard it as our responsibility to use the examination system as efficiently and effectively as possible and to apply for whatever special provisions are available for each pupil on an individual basis. (Most usually this is 25% extra time and sometimes a reader or amanuensis.)

National Curriculum Testing for our age range is at Key Stage 3 and Key stage 4 (GCSE). Testing Key Stage 3 occurs in year 9. The graphs of Figures 17.1a and 17.1b show that our pupils are generally still below 'normal' at this point. Despite this, we prefer to maintain the integrity of our five–year programme, rather than pursue the counter–productive course of pushing our pupils too early for this stage. Our main examination target, therefore, is success at GCSE.

The system for GCSE mathematics examinations has always placed great responsibility on schools for entering pupils at the correct level. This responsibility seems unlikely to decrease and requires us to refine decisions about levels of entry continuously over years 9, 10 and 11. The unpredictable effects of emotional pressure on dyslexics at examination time could make these decisions difficult.

At Mark College we carefully monitor progress throughout the years and through the levels of the National Curriculum, measuring against the separate Attainment Targets. A pupil's progress, as monitored in class combined with results from tests and College examinations, is used to place him in the teaching group that is most suitable for his current learning needs and long–term potential. If this system remains effective then, when public examinations arrive, decisions about levels of entry virtually make themselves.

The College uses the SMP Graduated Assessment scheme for GCSE. This modular scheme places less emphasis on the terminal examination papers, which contribute 50% towards the final grade. Two three-week pieces of coursework, one practical and one investigational contribute 20%. The remaining 30% comes from three module tests which are undertaken during years 10 and 11. The module tests can be taken on up to six set occasions throughout the two–year period, and thus can be built into the structure of the curriculum. Past tests can be used for practice and reassurance, so that stress levels are reduced to bring correspondingly improved performances.

Summary

All the contributing factors which influenced the design of our programme have been covered. The advice should be given careful thought as other situations may require different responses to factors other than those we have chosen.

A version of this chapter appeared in *The Good Practice Guide to Special Educational Needs*, edited by Paul Widlake and published by Questions Publishing Company (1996).

Appendices

Appendix 1: Books, Journals, Tests and Games

Books

The following list collects together some useful titles for further reading. See also the references on p. 253 for books and journals cited in the text.

Background

Askew M, William D (1995) Recent Research in Mathematics Education 5–16. London: HMSO. ISBN 0–11–350049–1.

Copeland R W (1984) How children Learn Mathematics: Teaching Implications of Piaget's Research. New York: Macmillan. ISBN 0–02–324770–3

Cornelius M (Ed.) (1989) The Best of Mathematics in School. Harlow: Longman. ISBN 0–582–04088–4.

Crawley JF (1985) Cognitive Strategies and Mathematics for the Learning Disabled. Rockville, MD: Aspen Systems Corporation. ISBN 0–87189–120–4

Datta DK (1993) Math education at its best: The Potsdam model. Framingham, Mass: CT/LM. ISBN 0–9638605–1–8.

Ernest P (Ed.) (1989) Mathematics Teaching: The State of the Art. Lewes: Falmer Press. ISBN 1–85000–461–7 (pbk).

Krutetskii VA (1976) The Psychology of Mathematical Abilities in Schoolchildren. Chicago: University of Chicago Press. ISBN 0220–45492–4.

Llewellyn S, Greer A (1983) Mathematics: The Basic Skills. Cheltenham: Stanley Thornes. ISBN 0–85950–148–5.

McKeown S (1993) Dyslexia and Mathematics. Coventry: NCET. ISBN 1–85379–246–2.

Merlten R (Ed.) (1996) Teaching Numeracy. Leamington Spa: Scholastic. ISBN 0–590–53429–7.

Miles TR, Miles E (Eds.) (1992) Dyslexia and Mathematics. London: Routledge. ISBN 0–415–04987–3 (pbk).

Polzar G (1990) How To Solve It. London: Penguin. ISBN 0–14–012499–3.

Skemp RR (1986) The Psychology of Learning Mathematics, 2nd edn. Harmondsworth: Pelican. ISBN 0–14–022668–0.

Stoltz C, Brown M (1982) Low Attainers in Mathematics 5–16. School Council Publications. London: Methuen. ISBN 0–423–51020–7.

Walton M (1994) Maths Words. Obtainable from M. Walton, 17 Bryn Bras, Llanfairpwll, Gwynedd LL61 5PX.

Teaching

Ashlock RB(1982) Error Patterns in Computation. Columbus, OH: Charles E. Merrill. ISBN 0–675–09880–7.

Ashlock R, Johnson M, Wilson J, Jones W (1983) Guiding Each Child's Learning of Mathematics. Columbus, OH: Charles E. Merrill. ISBN 0–675–20023–7.

Bley N, Thomton C (1989) Teaching Mathematics to the Learning Disabled. Pro-Ed (8700 Shoal Creek Boulevard, Austin, TX 788758–9965). ISBN 0–89079–200–3.

Burge V (1986) Basic Numeracy. Farnham: Helen Arkell Centre. ISBN 0–9506070–6–1.

Chinn SJ (1996) What To Do When You Can't Learn the Times Tables. Baldock: Egon Publishers. ISBN 1–900754–00–2.

Chinn SJ (1998) What To Do When You Can't Do Addition and Subtraction. Baldock: Egon Publishers.

Clemson D, Clemson W (1994) Mathematics in the early years. London: Routledge. ISBN 0–415–09628–6.

Deboys M, Pitt E (1988) Lines of Development in Primary Mathematics, 3rd edn. Belfast: Blackstaff Press. ISBN 0-85640–194–3.

Eggleston SJ (1983) Learning Mathematics. How the Work of the Assessment of Performance Unit can Help Teachers. London: DES. ISBN 0–85522–152–6.

French D et al. (1992) Mental Methods in Mathematics: A First Resort. Leicester: The Mathematical Association. ISBN 0–906588–27–8.

Geere B (undated) Seven Ways to Help Your Child with Maths. Seven Ways Series, published by Barbara Geere.

Henderson A (1989) Maths and Dyslexics. Llandudno: St David's College. ISBN 0–9512529–1–7.

Pimm D (1987) Speaking mathematically. Communication in mathematics classrooms. London: Routledge. ISBN 0–415–03708–5.

Reisman F (1978) A Guide to the Diagnostic Teaching of Arithmetic, 2nd edn. Columbus, OH: Charles E. Merrill. ISBN 0–675–008297–4

Textbooks

For Years 7, 8, (9)
Various Authors (1992). Century Maths Series. Stanley Thornes.

For Years (7, 8,) 9
Llewellyn S, Greer A (1996) Mathematics: The Basic Skills, Fifth Edition. Stanley Thornes. ISBN 0–7487–2509–1.

For Years 10, 11
Rayner D (1994) Higher GCSE Mathematics: Revision and Practice. Oxford University Press. ISBN 0–19–914574–1.

Rayner D (1994) Intermediate GCSE Mathematics: Revision and Practice. Oxford University Press. ISBN 0–19–914575–X.

Ledsham A, Wardle ME (1996) Foundation GCSE Mathematics: Revision and Practice. Oxford University Press. ISBN 0–19–914576–8.

Journals

Focus on Learning Problems in Mathematics. Center for Teaching/Learning of Mathematics, P.O. Box 3149, Framingham, MA 01701, USA.

Math Notebook. Center for Teaching/Learning of Mathematics, P.O. Box 3149, Framingham, MA 01701, USA (available from P. Brazil, see below in section on videos).

Computer Programs

Maths Programmes. BDA Computer Booklet C5. (1996) Clayton, P. and Hutchins, J. Reading: British Dyslexia Association. ISBN 1–898862–05–2.

Steve Chinn will be producing a computer program (on CD) during 1998 for times tables. Available from Mark College, Mark, Somerset TA9 4NP.

Videos

The Teaching and Learning of Mathematics. Mahesh Sharma. Produced by Oxford Polytechnic (now Oxford Brookes University).

From Theory to Practice: Teaching Place Value. Mahesh Sharma.

Both available from Mrs P. Brazil, The Warren, Mapledurham, Reading RG4 7TQ.

Tests

Bath JB, Chinn SJ, Knox DE (1986) Test of Cognitive Style in Mathematics. East Aurora, NY: Slosson. (Out of print.)

Brighouse A, Godber D, Patilla P (1984) Mathematics 8–12. National Foundation for Educational Research. Windsor: NFER–Nelson.

Chinn SJ (1998) Diagnostic Inventory of Basic Skills and Learning Style in Mathematics. London: The Psychological Corporation.

France N (1979) Profile of Mathematics Skills.Windsor: NFER–Nelson.

Gillham W, Hesse K (1987) Basic Number Screening Test. Sevenoaks: Hodder and Stoughton.

Ginsburg HP, Baroody AJ (1990) Test of Early Mathematics Ability. Austin TX: Pro–Ed (8700 Shoal Creek Boulevard, Austin, TX 78758–9965).

Jastak SJ, Jastak GS (1984) Wide Range Achievement Test (Revised). Jastak Associates, Inc. (15 Ashley Place, Suite 1A, Wilmington, DE 19804). (Updated in 1996 as WRAT–3 and available from the Dyslexia Institute, 133 Gresham Rd., Staines, TW18 2AJ, England.)

Vernon P with the assistance of Miller K (1986) Graded Arithmetic—
Mathematics Test. London: Hodder and Stoughton Educational
(Senior version is now updated as the Mathematics Competency
Test).

Games and activities

Bolt B (1982) Mathematical Activities. A Resource Book
for Teachers. Cambridge: Cambridge University Press. ISBN
0–521–28518–6.

Bolt B (1982) More Mathematical Activities. Cambridge: Cambridge
University Press.

Bolt B (1983) Even More Mathematical Activities. Cambridge:
Cambridge University Press.

Bolt B (1984) The Amazing Mathematical Amusement Arcade.
Cambridge: Cambridge University Press.

Burns M (1987) The I Hate Mathematics Book. Cambridge: Cambridge
University Press. ISBN 0–521–33659–7.

Burton L (1984) Thinking Things Through. Problem Solving in
Mathematics. Oxford: Blackwell. ISBN 0–631–13813–7.

Fineberg E, Berkovi J (1997) Number Quest. Horsham: Dorling
Kindersley ISBN 0–7513–5659–X.

Kirby D (1989) Go Further with Games. London: Unwin Hyman. ISBN
0–0444–8099–7.

Kirby D (1992) Games in the Teaching of Mathematics. Cambridge:
Cambridge University Press. ISBN 0–521–42320–1.

Kirby D (1993) More Games. Glasgow: Collins Educational. ISBN
0–00312-5556.

Kirby D (1993) Starting Games. Glasgow: Collins Educational. ISBN
0–00312-5548.

Mottershead L (1978) Sources of Mathematical Discovery. Oxford:
Blackwell. ISBN 0–631–10221–3.

Games are also available from Crossbow Educational, see Appendix 2.

Appendix 2: Teaching Materials

Some materials can be made, others have to be bought. Unless a
supplier is specified, the material is widely available from educational
suppliers such as Hope, NES, Taskmaster, etc. (see addresses below).

Dominoes
Playing cards
Blank playing cards
Money (plastic or real)
Base ten blocks (from NES, Hope or Taskmaster)

Poker chips (import 'real' ones from America, or buy stackers from
    Crossbow Educational)
Large (2 cm+) counters
Cocktail sticks (in boxes of 100, bundles of 10 and singly)
Squared paper
Place value cards (make your own)
Abacus
Geo boards
Dice (various shapes and values; blank sided dice are obtainable)
Cuisenaire rods (from Cuisenaire Company and Taskmaster)
Film tubes from 35 mm film
Multi–link cubes
Unifix cubes
Metre rules: mm divisions, cm divisions and dm divisions
Pipe cleaners
Number square, 1 to 100, with counters
Clock faces (synchronised hands)
Calculators
Pie chart scales
10 dm cube (1 litre)
Tape measure
Trundle Wheel
Kitchen scales

Suppliers' addresses

Crossbow Educational, 8 Causeway Road, Cinderford, Glos. GL14 2BY.
Cuisenaire Company, 11 Crown Street, Reading, RG1 2TQ.
Galt Educational, Cheadle, Cheshire, SK8 2PN.
Hope Education Ltd, Orb Mill, Huddersfield Road, Waterhead, Oldham,
    Lancs, OL4 2ST.
NES, Ludlow Hill Road, West Bridgford, Notts, NG2 6HD.
Philip and Tacey, North Way, Andover, Hampshire, SP10 5BA.
Taskmaster Ltd, Morris Street. Leicester. LE2 6BR.

References

Ackerman PT, Anhalt JM, Dykman RA (1986) Arithmetic automatization failure in children with attention and reading disorders: associations and sequela. Journal of Learning Disabilities 19(4): 222–32.

Ackerman PT, Dykman RA (1996) The speed factor and learning disabilities: The toll of slowness in adolescents. Dyslexia 2(1): 1–22.

Ashlock RB (1982) Error Patterns in Computation. Columbus OH: Merrill.

Ashlock R, Johnson M, Wilson J, Jones W (1983) Guiding Each Child's Learning of Mathematics. Columbus, OH: Merrill.

Askew M, William D (1995) Recent Research in Mathematics Education 5–16. London: HMSO.

Austin JD (1982) Children with a Learning Disability in Mathematics. School Science and Mathematics, 201–8.

Bath JB, Chinn SJ, Knox DE (1986) The Test of Cognitive Style in Mathematics. East Aurora, NY: Slosson (out of print, see Chinn, 1998).

Bath JB, Knox DE (1984) Two styles of performing mathematics. In Bath JB, Chinn SJ, Knox DE (Eds.) Dyslexia: Research and its Application to the Adolescent. Bath: Better Books.

Bierhoff H (1996) Laying the Foundations of Numeracy: A Comparison of Primary School Textbooks in Britain, Germany and Switzerland. London: The National Institute of Economic and Social Research.

Bley N, Thornton C (1989) Teaching Mathematics to the Learning Disabled. Austin TX: Pro–Ed (8700 Shoal Creek Boulevard, Austin, TX 78758–9965).

Burge V (1986) Basic Numeracy. Farnham: Helen Arkell Centre.

Burton L (1984) Thinking Things Through. Problem Solving in Mathematics. Oxford: Blackwell.

Buswell GT, Judd CM (1925) Summary of Educational Investigations Relating to Arithmetic. Supplementary Educational Monographs. Chicago: University of Chicago Press.

Buxton L (1981) Do You Panic About Maths? London: Heinemann.

Chasty HT (1989) The challenge of specific learning difficulties. Proceedings of the First International Conference of the British Dyslexia Association. Reading: BDA.

Chinn SJ (1991) Factors to consider when designing a test protocol in mathematics for dyslexics. In Snowling M, Thomson M (Eds.) Dyslexia: Integrating Theory and

Practice. London: Whurr.

Chinn SJ (1992) Individual diagnosis and cognitive style. In Miles TR, Miles E (Eds.) Dyslexia and Mathematics. London: Routledge.

Chinn SJ (1994) A study of the basic number fact skills of children from specialist dyslexic and normal schools. Dyslexia Review 2: 4–6.

Chinn SJ (1995a) Learning difficulties in mathematics. Learn 17: 26–35.

Chinn SJ (1995b) A pilot study to compare aspects of arithmetic skill. Dyslexia Review 4: 4–7

Chinn SJ (1996) The relationship between the grades achieved in GCSE mathematics by 26 dyslexic male students and their scores on the WISC. Dyslexia Review 7: 8–9.

Chinn SJ (1998) Diagnostic Inventory of Basic Skills and Learning Style in Mathematics. London: The Psychological Corporation.

Chinn SJ, Ashcroft JR (1992) The use of patterns. In Miles TR, Miles E (Eds.) Dyslexia and Mathematics. London: Routledge.

Choat E (1982) Understanding in young children's mathematics. Mathematics in Schools 10 (2): 3–6.

Cobb P (1991) Reconstructing elementary school mathematics. Focus on Learning Problems in Mathematics 13 (2): 3–32.

Cockcroft WH (1982) Mathematics Counts. London: HMSO.

Cope CL (1988) Math anxiety and math avoidance in college freshmen. Focus on Learning Problems in Mathematics 10 (1): 1–13.

Copeland RV (1984) How Children Learn Mathematics. Teaching Implications of Piaget's Research. New York: Macmillan

Crawley JP (1985) Cognitive Strategies and Mathematics for the Learning Disabled. Rockville, MD: Aspen Systems Corporation.

Crisfield J (1996) The Dyslexia Handbook. Reading: British Dyslexia Association.

Critchley McD (1970) The neurological approach in assessment and teaching of dyslexic children. In White FA, Naidoo S (Eds.) Assessment and Teaching of Dyslexic Children. London: ICAA.

De Bono E (1970) Lateral Thinking: A Textbook of Creativity. London: Ward Lock Educational.

Deboys M, Pitt E (1988) Lines of Development in Primary Mathematics, 3rd edn. Belfast: Blackstaff Press.

Duffin J (1991) Oh yes you can. Times Educational Supplement 10 May: 49.

Ernest P (Ed.) (1989) Mathematics Teaching: The State of the Art. Lewes: Falmer Press.

Fawcett AJ, Nicholson RI (1992) Automatisation deficits in balance for dyslexic children. Perceptual and Motor Skills 75: 507–529.

Fleischner JE, Garnett K, Shepherd MJ (1982) Proficiency in arithmetic basic facts computation of learning disabled and non–disabled children. Focus on Learning Problems in Mathematics. 4(2): 47–56.

France N (1979) The Profile of Mathematical Skills. Windsor NFER–Nelson.

Geere B (undated) Seven Ways to Help Your Child with Maths. Seven Ways Series published by Barbara Geere.

Gillham W, Hesse K (1987) Basic Number Screening Test. Sevenoaks: Hodder and Stoughton.

Ginsburg HP (1997) Mathematical learning disabilities: A view from transdevelopmental psychology. Journal of Learning Disabilities 30(1): 20–33.

Ginsburg HP, Baroody AJ (1990) Test of Early Mathematics Ability. 2nd edn. Austin

TX: Pro–Ed (8700 Shoal Creek Boulevard, Austin, TX 78758–9965).

Hackett G (1996) Primary maths in trouble. Times Educational Supplement 4168: 1.

Hart K (1978) Children's Understanding of Mathematics. London: John Murray. pp. 11–16.

Hart K (1989) There is little connection. In Ernest P (Ed.) Mathematics Teaching: The State of the Art. Lewes: Falmer Press.

Harvey R (1982) 'I can keep going up if I want to': One way of looking at learning mathematics. In Harvey R, Kerslake D, Shuard H, Torbe M (Eds.) Language Teaching and Learning. 6. Mathematics. London: Ward Lock Educational.

Henderson A (1989) Maths and Dyslexics. Llandudno: St David's College.

Homan DR (1970) The child with a learning disability in arithmetic. The Arithmetic Teacher 18: 199–203.

Jastak SJ, Jastak GS (1984) Wide Range Achievement Test. Revised edn. Wilmington DE: Jastak Associates, Inc. (15 Ashley Place, Suite 1A, Wilmington, DE 19804).

Joffe L (1980) Dyslexia and attainment in school mathematics: Part 2, Error types and remediation. Dyslexia Review 3 (2): 12–18.

Joffe L (1983) School mathematics and dyslexia ... a matter of verbal labelling, generalisation, horses and carts. Cambridge Journal of Education 13 (3): 22–7.

Kane N, Kane M (1979) Comparison of right and left hemisphere functions. The Gifted Child Quarterly 23 (1): 157–67.

Kavanagh JK, Truss TJ (Eds.) (1988) Learning Disabilities: Proceedings of the National Conference. Parkton, MD: York Press.

Kennedy LM (1975) Guiding Children to Mathematical Discovery. Belmont, CA: Wadsworth.

Kibel M (1992) Linking language to action. In Miles TR, Miles E (Eds.) Dyslexia and Mathematics. London: Routledge.

Kirby D (1989) Go Further with Games. London: Unwin Hyman.

Kirby D (1992) Games in the teaching of Mathematics. Cambridge: Cambridge University Press.

Kirby D (1993a) Starting Games. Glasgow: Collins Educational.

Kirby D (1993b) More Games. Glasgow: Collins Educational.

Kitz WR, Nash RT (1995) Applying effective instructional strategies for teaching dyslexic students in a remedial college algebra course. Annals of Dyslexia 45: 143–60.

Krutetskii VA (1976) In Kilpatric J, Wirszup I (Eds.) The Psychology of Mathematical Abilities in School Children. Chicago: University of Chicago Press.

Kubrick S, Rudnick JA (1980) Problem Solving—A Handbook for Teachers. Needham Heights, NY: Allyn and Bacon.

Lane C (1992) Now listen hear. Special Children 54: 12–14.

Lane C, Chinn SJ (1986) Learning by self–voice echo. Academic Therapy 21: 477–81.

Light JG, Defries JC (1995) Comorbidity of reading and mathematics disabilities: Genetic and environmental etiologies. Journal of Learning Disabilities 28: 96–105.

Luchins AS (1942) Mechanisation in problem solving: the effect of Einstellung. Psychological Monographs 54 (6).

MacKay D (1994) Show your working—and fail. Times Educational Supplement 4072: 22.

Madsen AL, Smith P, Lanier P (1995) Does conceptually oriented instruction enhance computational competence? Focus on Learning Problems in Mathematics 17 (4): 42–64.

Magne O (1996) Bibliography of literature dysmathematics. Didakometry. Malmo,

Sweden: School of Education.

McDougal S (1990) Table Time. The Exciting New Way to Learn Multiplication Tables. Brornlcy: Harrap.

McLeish J (1991) Number. London: Bloomsbury.

Miles E (1983) Dyslexia: the Pattern of Difficulties, Oxford: Blackwell.

Miles E (1992) Reading and writing in mathematics. In Miles TR, Miles E (Eds.) Dyslexia and Mathematics. London: Routledge.

Miles TR (1993) Dyslexia: The Pattern of Difficulties, 2nd edn. London: Whurr.

Miles TR, Miles E (Eds.) (1992) Dyslexia and Mathematics. London: Routledge.

Mottershead L (1978) Sources of Mathematical Discovery. Oxford: Blackwell.

Mtetwa D, Garofalo J (1989) Beliefs about mathematics: an overlooked aspect of student difficulties. Academic Therapy 24 (5): 611–18.

National Curriculum Council (1989) The order of activities should be flexible. Mathematics Non–Statutory Guidance 5.3: B8.

National Foundation For Educational Research with Brighouse A, Godber D, Pantilla P (1984) Mathematics 8–12. Windsor: NFER–Nelson.

Peer L (1996) Winning with Dyslexia. Reading: British Dyslexia Association.

Polya G (1962) Mathematical Discovery, Vol. 1. New York: Wiley.

Pritchard RA, Miles TR, Chinn SJ, Taggart AT (1989) Dyslexia and knowledge of number facts. Links 14 (3): 17–20.

Pumfrey PD, Reason R (1991) Specific Learning Difficulties (Dyslexia): Challenges and Responses. Windsor: NFER–Nelson.

Rayner D (1987) Mathematics for GCSE, Books 1 and 2. Oxford: Oxford University Press.

Rayner D (1988) General Mathematics. Revision and Practice. Oxford: Oxford University Press.

Reisman P (1978) A Guide to the Diagnostic Teaching of Arithmetic. 2nd edn. Columbus, OH: Charles E Merrill.

Riding R, Cheema I (1991) Cognitive styles—an overview and integration. Educational Psychology 11 (3 & 4): 193–215.

Rothman RW, Cohen J (1989) The language of math needs to be taught. Academic Therapy 25 (2): 133–42.

School Mathematics Project (1985–1987) SMP (11–16). Green Series. Cambridge: Cambridge University Press.

Sharma MC (1985) Mathematics as a second language. Math Notebook 4: 1–4.

Sharma MC (1986) Dyscalculia and other learning problems in arithmetic: a historical perspective. Focus on Learning Problems in Mathematics 8 (3,4): 7–45.

Sharma MC (1987) Reversal problems in maths and their remediaton. Math Notebook 5: 6–7.

Sharma MC (1988a) Levels of knowing mathematics. Math Notebook 6: 1–20.

Sharma MC (1988b) Mathematics workshop at Mark College.

Sharma MC (1989) Mathematics learning personality. Math Notebook 7: 1–2.

Siegel M, Fonzi JM (1995) The practice of reading in an inquiry–oriented mathematics class. Reading Research Quarterly 30 (4): 632–73.

Siegler RS (1989) How domain–general and domain specific knowledge interact to produce strategy choices. In Light P, Sheldon S, Woodhead M (1991) Learning to Think. London: Routledge.

Skemp RR (1971) The Psychology of Learning Mathematics. Harmondsworth: Penguin.

Skemp RR (1986) The Psychology of Learning Mathematics. 2nd edn. Harmondsworth: Pelican.

Smith R (1996) An investigation into the effects that dyslexia has on children in mathematics. Professional development project for BSc(Ed), University of Exeter.

Springer SP, Deutsch G (1993) Left Brain, Right Brain. New York: Freeman & Co.

Steeves J (1979) Multisensory math: an instructional approach to help the LD child. Focus on Learning Problems in Mathematics 1 (2): 51–62.

Stoltz C, Brown M (1982) Low Attainers in Mathematics 5–16. School Council Publications. London: Methuen.

Sutherland P (1988) Dyscalculia. Sum cause for concern? Times Educational Supplement 18 March.

Turner Ellis SA, Miles TR, Wheeler TJ (1996) Speed of multiplication in dyslexics and non–dyslexics. Dyslexia 2: 121–39.

Vernon P with the assistance of Miller K (1986) Graded Arithmetic—Mathematics Test, Junior. London: Hodder and Stoughton Educational.

Vernon PE, Miller KM, Izard JF (1996) Mathematics Competency Test. London: Hodder and Stoughton Educational.

Wheatley GH (1977) The right hemisphere's role in problem solving. The Arithmetic Teacher 25: 36–9.

Wheatley GH, Frankland RL, Mitchell OR, Kraft R (1978) Hemispheric specialization and cognitive development: implications for mathematics education. Journal for Research in Mathematics Education. 9: 20–32.

Widlake P (Ed.) (1996) The Good Practice Guide to Special Educational Needs. Birmingham: Questions Publishing Company.

Wigley A. (1995) Minding one's Ps and Qs. Mathematics Teaching 153: 30–3.

Wilson J, Sadowski B (Eds.) (1976) The Maryland Diagnostic Test and Interview Protocols. University of Maryland: Arithmetic Center.

Index

259